WJEC/Eduqas

Religious Studies
for A Level Year 2 & A2

Philosophy
of Religion

Peter Cole and Karl Lawson
Edited by Richard Gray

Illuminate Publishing

Published in 2018 by Illuminate Publishing Ltd, P.O Box 1160, Cheltenham, Gloucestershire GL50 9RW

Orders: Please visit www.illuminatepublishing.com
or email sales@illuminatepublishing.com

© Peter Cole, Karl Lawson

British Library Cataloguing-in-Publication Data

A catalogue record for this book is available from the British Library

ISBN 978-1-911208-65-5

Printed by Standartu Spaustuve, Lithuania

07.18

The publisher's policy is to use papers that are natural, renewable and recyclable products made from wood grown in sustainable forests. The logging and manufacturing processes are expected to conform to the environmental regulations of the country of origin.

Every effort has been made to contact copyright holders of material reproduced in this book. If notified, the publishers will be pleased to rectify any errors or omissions at the earliest opportunity.

This material has been endorsed by WJEC/Eduqas and offers high quality support for the delivery of WJEC/Eduqas qualifications. While this material has been through a WJEC/Eduqas quality assurance process, all responsibility for the content remains with the publisher.

WJEC/Eduqas examination questions are reproduced by permission from WJEC/Eduqas

Series editor: Richard Gray
Editor: Geoff Tuttle
Design and Layout: EMC Design Ltd, Bedford

Acknowledgements

Cover Image: © Mellimage/Shutterstock

Image credits:

Illustrations: Daniel Limon / Beehive Il[lustration]

Photo acknowledgements: **p. 1** ©Mellimage / Shutterstock; **p. 6** (left) Public domain; **p. 7** Jasminko Ibrakovic; **p. 8** (top) Bjanka Kadic / Alamy Stock Photo; **p. 8** (bottom) Everett Historical; **p. 9** Public domain; **p. 11** Mike Peel – Creative Commons; **p. 13** Public domain; **p. 18** (top) bilha Golan; **p. 18** (bottom) Public domain; **p. 20** Public domain; **p. 21** (top) JustAnotherPhotographer; **p. 21** (bottom) lassedesignen; **p. 22** (middle) ArtOfPhotos; **p. 22** (bottom) Creative Commons; **p. 25** SUMITH NUNKHAM; **p. 28** Dmytro Zinkevych; **p. 33** (top) Nice_Media; **p. 33** (bottom) Creative Commons; **p. 34** (top) Creative Commons; **p. 34** (bottom) Dan Etherington – Creative Commons; **p. 35** Public domain; **p. 37** (top) Anthony Correla; **p. 37** (bottom left) Christopher Michel – Creative Commons; **p. 37** (bottom 2nd left) David Shankbone – Creative Commons; **p. 37** (bottom 3rd left) Dmitry Rozhkov – Creative Commons; **p. 37** (bottom right) Fri Tanke – Creative Commons; **p. 38** The Print Collector / Alamy Stock Photo; **p. 39** paintings; **p. 46** Photo by Terry Smith / The LIFE Images Collection / Getty Images; **p. 48** (top) Google Art Project / Creative Commons; **p. 48** (middle) Creative Commons; **p. 48** (bottom) Art Directors & TRIP / Alamy Stock Photo; **p. 49** Wold Religions Photo Library / Alamy Stock Photo; **p. 51** Creative Commons; **p. 53** (bottom) Tinxi / Shutterstock.com; **p. 61** Renata Sedmakova / Shutterstock.com; **p. 62** (left) David Hume by Allan Ramsay, 1766 Public domain; **p. 62** (right) Public domain; **p. 64** David Grossman / Alamy Stock Photo; **p. 65** Gino Santa Maria; **p. 66** incamerastock / Alamy Stock Photo; **p. 73** Heartland Arts; **p. 75** Elena_Titova; **p. 76** (top left) Public domain; **p. 76** (bottom left) Creative Commons; **p. 76** (right) Evening Standard; **p. 77** Creative commons; **p. 84** Ellagrin; **p. 85** IR Stone; **p. 86** pixelparticle; **p. 87** igor kisselev; **p. 88** (left) Skylines; **p. 88** (right) Jin Flogel; **p. 90** nasirkhan; **p. 91** Amplion; **p. 92** Crystal Eye Studio; **p. 94** Tupungato; **p. 93** ra2studio; **p. 95** (left) Iqconcept; **p. 95** (right) JUAWA; **p. 96** agsandrew; **p. 97** Jan Krcmar; **p. 98** Victorpr; **p. 99** Rasica; **p. 100** Komlev; **p. 102** Filipe Frazao; **p. 103** Emi; **p. 104** Jannarong; **p. 105** Pressmaster; **p. 106** David Acosta Allely; **p. 107** Roman Yanushevsky / Shutterstock.com; **p. 108** Ian Dagnall / Alamy Stock Photo; **p. 109** (left) Yurchyks; **p. 109** (middle) Adwo; **p. 109** (right) Niphon Subsri; **p. 109** (bottom) agsandrew; **p. 110** Mopic; **p. 110** (left) Angelal-ouwe; **p. 110** (right) agenturfotografin; **p. 111** margouillaat photo; **p. 112** (left) Yury Bobryk; **p. 112** (right) Keystone Pictures USA / Alamy Stock Photo; **p. 113** kraftwerk; **p. 114** Sasikumar3g; **p. 115** SimpleB; **p. 116** artmig; **p. 117** Dmitry Guzhanin; **p. 118** intueri; **p. 119** (left) PRABHAS ROY; **p. 119** (middle) david156; **p. 119** (right) Horizonman; **p. 120** Adrian Niederhaeuser; **p. 121** EtiAmmos; **p. 122** Digital Storm; **p. 123** Tnymand; **p. 124** MicroOne; **p. 125** (top) 1ZiMa; **p. 125** (bottom) DVARG; **p. 126** (top) Mikalai Steshyts; **p. 126** (bottom) Gougnaf; **p. 127** (top) B; **p. 127** (middle) James Steidl; **p. 127** (bottom) LittleElephant; **p. 128** LeshaBu; **p. 129** lukpedclub; **p. 130** Kheng Guan Toh; **p. 131** woaiss; **p. 132** Terri Butler Photography; **p. 135** (top) EtiAmmos; **p. 135** (bottom) bleakstar; **p. 136** Satina; **p. 137** (top) Brian Maudsley; **p. 137** (bottom) Stava Gerj; **p. 138** Elenarts; **p. 139** (top left) Deyan G. Georgiev / Shutterstock.com; **p. 139** (top middle) Callahan; **p. 139** (top right) Marcin Roszkowski; **p. 139** (bottom) Vladimir Zadvinskii; **p. 140** (top) stockillustration; **p. 140** (bottom) spectrumblue; **p. 143** latesmile; **p. 144** ibreakstock; **p. 145** iQoncept; **p. 146** Scanrail1; **p. 148** Granger Historical Picture Archive / Alamy Stock Photo; **p. 149** V_ctoria; **p. 150** kkuroksta; **p. 151** Hare Krishna; **p. 153** (bottom) FrameAngel; **p. 153** (top) Tyler McKay; **p. 154** eenevski; **p. 155** (top) Anna Grigorjeva; **p. 155** (bottom) samui; **p. 156** Axel Bueckert; **p. 157** Lance Bellers; **p. 158** Rashad Ashurov

Contents*

*   The contents listed correspond to the Eduqas Full A Level
    Specification which matches equivalent WJEC A2 Specification as follows:

Philosophy of Religion

About this book

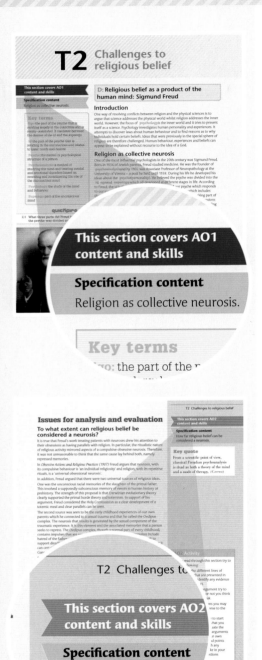

With the new A Level in Religious Studies, there is a lot to cover and a lot to do in preparation for the examinations at A Level. The aim of these books is to provide enough support for you to achieve success at A Level, whether as a teacher or a learner, and build upon the success of the Year 1 and AS series.

Once again, the Year 2 and A2 series of books is skills-based in its approach to learning, which means it aims to continue combining coverage of the Specification content with examination preparation. In other words, it aims to help you get through the second half of the course whilst at the same time developing some more advanced skills needed for the examinations.

To help you study, there are clearly defined sections for each of the AO1 and AO2 areas of the Specification. These are arranged according to the Specification Themes and use, as far as is possible, Specification headings to help you see that the content has been covered for A Level.

The AO1 content is detailed but precise, with the benefit of providing you with references to both religious/philosophical works and to the views of scholars. The AO2 responds to the issues raised in the Specification and provides you with ideas for further debate, to help you develop your own critical analysis and evaluation skills.

Ways to use this book

In considering the different ways in which you may teach or learn, it was decided that the books needed to have an inbuilt flexibility to adapt. As a result, they can be used for classroom learning, for independent work by individuals, as homework, and they are even suitable for the purposes of 'flipped learning' if your school or college does this.

You may be well aware that learning time is so valuable at A Level and so we have also taken this into consideration by creating flexible features and activities, again to save you the time of painstaking research and preparation, either as teacher or learner.

Features of the books

The books all contain the following features that appear in the margins, or are highlighted in the main body of the text, in order to support teaching and learning.

Key terms of technical, religious and philosophical words or phrases

> **Key terms**
> Psyche: the mental or psychological structure of a person

Quickfire questions simple, straightforward questions to help consolidate key facts about what is being digested in reading through the information

> **quickfire**
> **2.1** What three parts did Freud believe the psyche was divided into?

Key quotes either from religious and philosophical works and/or the works of scholars

> **Key quote**
> …the ceremony of the totem-feast still survives with but little distortion in the form of Communion. **(Freud)**

Study tips advice on how to study, prepare for the examination and answer questions

Study tip

As you work through the course do not forget that you can bring in other evidence from other areas to help with your evaluation skills. Jung is always a good source to use when evaluating Freud.

AO1 Activities that serve the purpose of focusing on identification, presentation and explanation, and developing the skills of knowledge and understanding required for the examination

AO1 Activity

Try to find some supporting evidence and/or examples from the religion that you have studied for the following:

- Religion as an illusion
- Religion as collective neurosis

AO2 Activities that serve the purpose of focusing on conclusions, as a basis for thinking about the issues, developing critical analysis and the evaluation skills required for the examination

AO2 Activity

As you read through this section try to do the following:

1. Pick out the different lines of argument that are presented in the text and identify any evidence given in support.

Glossary of all the key terms for quick reference.

Specific feature: Developing skills

This section is very much a focus on 'what to do' with the content and the issues that are raised. They occur at the end of each section, giving 12 AO1 and 12 AO2 activities that aim to develop particular skills that are required for more advanced study at Year 2 and A2 stage.

The Developing skills for Year 2 and A2 are grouped so that each Theme has a specific focus to develop and perfect gradually throughout that Theme.

AO1 and AO2 answers and commentaries

The final section has a selection of answers and commentaries as a framework for judging what an effective and ineffective response may be. The comments highlight some common mistakes and also examples of good practice so that all involved in teaching and learning can reflect upon how to approach examination answers.

Richard Gray
Series Editor
2018

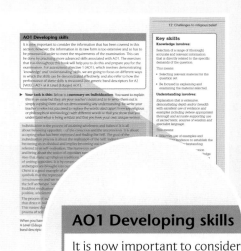

AO1 Developing skills

It is now important to consider section; however, the informati be processed in order to meet be done by practising more hat run throughout this ation. For ass

T2 Challenges to religious belief

Specification content

Religion as collective neurosis.

Key terms

Ego: the part of the psyche that is residing largely in the conscious and is reality-orientated. It mediates between the desires of the id and the superego

Id: the part of the psyche that is residing in the unconscious and relates to basic needs and desires

Psyche: the mental or psychological structure of a person

Psychoanalysis: a method of studying the mind and treating mental and emotional disorders based on revealing and investigating the role of the unconscious mind

Psychology: the study of the mind and behaviour

Superego: part of the unconscious mind

quickfire

2.1 What three parts did Freud believe the psyche was divided into?

D: Religious belief as a product of the human mind: Sigmund Freud

Introduction

One way of resolving conflicts between religion and the physical sciences is to argue that science addresses the physical world whilst religion addresses the inner world. However, the focus of **psychology** is the inner world and it tries to present itself as a science. Psychology investigates human personality and experiences. It attempts to discover laws about human behaviour and to find reasons as to why individuals hold certain beliefs. Ideas that were previously in the special sphere of religion are therefore challenged. Human behaviour, experiences and beliefs can appear to be explained without recourse to the idea of a God.

Religion as collective neurosis

One of the most influential psychologists in the 20th century was Sigmund Freud. Born in 1856 of Jewish parents, Freud studied medicine. He was the founder of **psychoanalysis** and by 1902 was Associate Professor of Neuropathology at the University of Vienna – a post he held until 1938. During his life he developed his ideas about the **psyche** (personality). He believed the psyche was divided into the **id**, **ego** and **superego**, which all developed at different stages in life. According to Freud, the id is the primitive and impulsive part of our psyche which responds to our instincts. The superego is the moral part of personality which includes the conscience and the ideal-ego. It is the ego that is the decision-making part of personality. The ego is the conscious self that is created by the dynamic tensions and interactions between the id and the superego and has the task of reconciling their conflicting demands with the requirements of external reality. The ego experiences moral conflicts that Freud thought were reflected in dreams and neurotic symptoms.

Freud

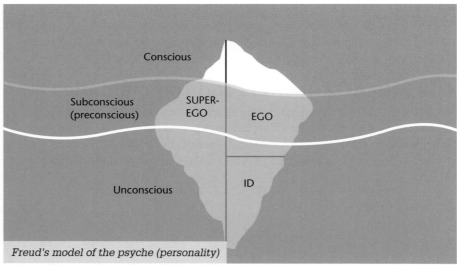

Freud's model of the psyche (personality)

Freud sought to understand religion and spirituality and in 1907 he presented a paper to the Vienna Psychoanalytical Society entitled 'Obsessive Actions and Religious Practices'. He noted that people who suffered from an **obsessional neurosis** involving compulsive repeated actions, exhibited similar patterns of behaviour to religious people who feel uneasy if they neglect repeated actions such as saying the rosary. Both are also meticulous about the detail of the way the actions must be carried out.

Freud also noticed that there was at least one significant difference. He thought that people suffering from obsessional neurosis did not understand the meaning of their actions whilst religious people understood the meaning of their practices. Freud argued that by means of psychoanalysis he had found that the obsessional neurosis did have meaning. It was caused by unconscious motives derived from past events in the intimate life of the patient, and these repressed **instinctual impulses** (such as the sexual urge) led to a sense of guilt. The repeated actions observed by Freud were interpreted as an unconscious protective measure against the temptation to give way to these instinctual impulses. In the same way he saw that religious rituals were similarly motivated. The instinctual impulses of the religious person included such impulses as self-seeking, which gave rise to a sense of guilt following continual temptation. Just as in the obsessional neurosis there is displacement from the actual important thing on to another object (e.g. from a husband, on to a chair), so in religion, there was a displacement (e.g. from doing something God disapproves of, on to the religious ritual of prayer/confession). The religious practices gradually become the essential thing. Hence Freud's description of 'religion as a universal obsessional neurosis'. The neurotic compulsions and religious rituals are found universally so it is called a **collective neurosis**.

Obsessional washing of hands and the religious ritual of washing

quickFire

2.2 What similarity did Freud see between a religious person and a person suffering from obsessional neurosis?

quickFire

2.3 What difference did Freud discern between a religious person and a person suffering from obsessional neurosis?

Key terms

Collective neurosis: a neurotic illness that afflicts all people

Instinctual impulses: an instinct that is in the unconscious but active in the psyche

Obsessional neurosis: sometimes called compulsive neurosis, uncontrollable obsessions that can create certain daily rituals

Key quote

One might venture to regard obsessional neurosis as a pathological formation of a religion, and to describe that neurosis as an individual religiosity and religion as a universal obsessional neurosis. (Freud)

Specification content

Religion as a neurosis: the primal horde.

Australian Aboriginal totem

quickfire

2.4 What is meant by 'a totem'?

Key quote

…the ceremony of the totem-feast still survives with but little distortion in the form of Communion. (Freud)

Key terms

Alpha-male: the dominant male in a community or group

Atonement: making up for wrongdoing; the reconciliation of human beings with God through life, suffering and the sacrificial death of Christ

Totem: something (such as an animal or plant) that is the symbol for the family or tribe

Totemism: a system of belief in which human beings are said to have some kinship or mystical relationship with a spirit-being, such as an animal or plant

Religion as a neurosis: the primal horde

Freud's conclusion was that religion itself was a form of neurosis, caused by traumas deep within the psyche. In 1913 Freud wrote *Totem and Taboo* in which he sought to explain the origins of these traumas. He based his theory on Charles Darwin's conjecture that human beings had originally lived in small 'hordes' or groups. Freud then speculated that over many generations the horde had been dominated by single dominant males who had seized the women for themselves and had driven off or killed all rivals, including their sons. He recognised that this single alpha-male surrounded by a harem of females was similar to the arrangement of gorilla groupings in their natural habitats where a single silverback is dominant. At some time a band of prehistoric brothers expelled from the alpha-male group returned to kill their father, whom they both feared and respected. This then enabled them to become dominant over the horde and gain women themselves.

However, after the event, the young males felt guilty for they had both loved and feared the father. Moreover, with their father's death they had become rivals among themselves for possession of the women. Burdened with guilt and faced with imminent collapse of their social order, the brothers formed a tribe and a totem took the place of the father, so uniting the tribe.

Freud had an interest in social anthropology and in his book he examines the system of totemism among the Australian Aborigines. He noticed that every clan had a totem (usually an animal) and people were not allowed to marry those with the same totem as themselves. Freud understood this as a way of preventing incest. The concept of the totem influenced the tribes to certain norms of behaviour and to go against them would be taboo. According to Freud, 'The totem members were forbidden to eat the flesh of the totem animal, or were allowed to do so only under specific conditions. A significant counter-phenomenon, not irreconcilable with this, is the fact that on certain occasions the eating of the totem flesh constituted a sort of ceremony …'

Freud saw a correlation between totemism and Darwin's primitive horde theory. His psychoanalysis of the totem ceremony revealed that the totem animal was in reality a substitute for the father who was both loved and feared. Over time the reputation of the slaughtered father grew to divine proportions. The totem became worshipped and became the god. There was a yearly commemoration by a ritual killing and eating of the totem animal. Eating and drinking are symbols of fellowship and mutual obligation. Freud argued that this insight through psychoanalysis explains the inherited sense of guilt that we all have. It results from a memory, perpetuated down thousands of years, of having killed the father or having entertained such thoughts.

Charles Darwin (1809–1882)

For Freud, this explained the Christian ritual of Holy Communion as Christ now replaced the father as the centre of religious devotion through his offering of atonement. The earlier totemic meal is now replaced by Holy Communion and identified with the son rather than a totem.

Religion as a neurosis: the Oedipus complex

Many people find Freud's explanation of the primal horde unconvincing as an account of the origin in human beings of the connection between the father complex and belief in God. The main reason is that the evidence base is questioned. However, his theory of the **Oedipus complex** has received more positive reactions as an account of the origins of this father complex and belief in God in the individual.

Freud thought that guilt played a fundamental role in the psyche and operates unconsciously. He believed that the sexual drive (libido) was the most basic instinct and most capable of causing major psychological problems. The libido is seen by Freud as not just the desire to have sex but represents the body's desire for satisfaction that originates in the id. In his account of the primal horde, Freud realised that the power of the sons' bitterness towards the father stemmed from the fact that the father was preventing their sexual desires from being fulfilled. Freud believed that this sexual frustration, conflict with the father and feelings of guilt are hidden deep in the unconscious but can be identified in a child's psychosexual development between the ages of three and six. He referred to this stage as the Oedipus complex. It is the stage during which a child begins to become sexual and recognise itself as a sexual being. A child develops a distinct sexual identity and begins to recognise the physical and social differences between men and women. This changes the dynamic between the child and their parent.

The term 'Oedipus complex' was named after the character in Sophocles' Greek tragedy *Oedipus Rex*. In the play Oedipus unwittingly kills his father and commits incest with his mother. When he realises this, he gouges out his own eyes in despair. Freud felt that the play's popularity through the ages derives from the existence of the underlying Oedipus complex in adults – an unconscious anxiety that most adults have experienced. This unconscious anxiety was illustrated by him from the testimony of his patients.

It was Freud's opinion that boys aged 3–6 years have a sort of love affair with their mothers. Thus at this stage in his childhood the son sees his father as a rival for his mother's love, her attentions and affection and would like to replace him but also fears the repercussions that might occur.

As a result, a child of this age can experience unconscious anxiety, even a castration complex, fearing the loss of his genitals. Freud suggested three reasons to explain this fear:

- With weaning, the boy has already been deprived of his mother's breast which he thought was part of him.

- When his parents had discovered him exploring his penis and appeared upset by this he had felt the threat of losing his penis.

- He would have discovered that some humans in fact do not have a penis and interprets this as the result of a punishment, not realising they are women.

If the Oedipus complex goes unresolved and is repressed then neurotic behaviour will result. Hence Freud linked the Oedipus complex with expressions of neurotic behaviour. He had already previously argued that the beliefs and practices of religion were merely expressions of neurotic behaviour.

As can be seen, both the primal horde theory and the Oedipus complex theory share the features of the desire to eliminate the father and the wish to possess the mother. Freud believed that both are possible explanations for the guilt and anguish which is often repressed and hidden and ultimately gives release to neurotic symptoms that are expressed through the belief and practices of religion.

Specification content

Religion as a neurosis: the Oedipus complex.

quickfire

2.5 Who was the 'Oedipus complex' named after?

Key term

Oedipus complex: the theory that young boys are sexually attracted to their mothers but resent their fathers. The feelings are repressed as they fear the father. Oedipus refers to a character in a Greek legend that unwittingly killed his father and married his own mother

Key quotes

It is the fate of all of us, perhaps, to direct our first sexual impulse towards our mother and our first hatred and our first murderous wish against our father. Our dreams convince us that this is so. **(Freud)**

We recognise that the roots for the need for religion are in the parental complex. **(Freud)**

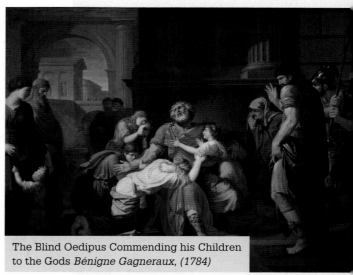

The Blind Oedipus Commending his Children to the Gods *Bénigne Gagneraux, (1784)*

Specification content

Religion as an illusion: wish
fulfilment.

Key quotes

Theology is anthropology.
(Feuerbach)

Religion is the dream of the human
mind ... (Feuerbach)

Specification content

Religion as an illusion: a reaction
against helplessness.

Key quotes

Religion was an attempt to get
control over the sensory world, in
which we are placed, by means
of the wish world, which we have
developed inside us as a result
of biological and psychological
necessities. (Freud)

Religion is a mere illusion derived
from human wishes. (Freud)

quickfire

2.6 What aspects of helplessness did
Freud identify that explained religious
ideas?

Religion as an illusion: wish fulfilment

In *The Future of an Illusion* (1927), Freud outlined his idea of religion as an 'illusion' based on wish fulfilment of the yearnings and longings of the ideal-ego aspect of the superego. Freud's ideas were heavily influenced by the philosopher Ludwig Feuerbach, who saw God as a 'projection' of the human mind based on human longings and desires.

Freud proposed that the origin of religion lies in our deepest wishes such as the desire for justice and the desire to escape death. Religion is seen to have emerged from such desires. For instance, each attribute of God can be interpreted to be an expression of an aspect of the hope human beings have to be free from their limitations (e.g. God's holiness – our desire to be free from sin).

Freud argued that the individuals who invented the religious doctrines did so because the doctrines fulfilled their wishes. Equally, the people who embrace religious views do so out of wish fulfilment. Such things as a desire for justice and a desire to escape death seem common across all cultures. Therefore, it is clear why such desires are met by the claim that an eternal, omnipotent, benevolent God will resurrect the dead, punish the unjust and reward the worthy with the promise of heaven.

Religion as an illusion: a reaction against helplessness

Freud connected religious ideas to a person's obvious helplessness in the face of the forces of nature. We are confronted by natural forces against which we feel defenceless and so need to invent a source of security. Religion creates this security with the belief that the natural forces are no longer impersonal. For example, the forces of nature might be turned into gods or goddesses who can be worshipped and controlled. Also, by means of religious devotion we are no longer powerless because we believe we can control them. Equally, we struggle with the internal forces of nature. For example our basic human instinct of aggression. Religious teaching seeks to limit war and violence, and introduces ideas of protecting the weak and loving one's enemies.

The sexual drive can be controlled through strict religious laws governing sexual behaviour and relationships. Those that obey will be rewarded. Just as the father protects the child, so religious belief provides a father figure to protect the adult. Therefore, Freud viewed religion as a childish delusion whilst atheism was a grown-up realism.

AO1 Activity

Try to find some supporting evidence and/or examples from the religion that you have studied for the following:

- Religion as an illusion
- Religion as collective neurosis
- The primal horde in religion
- The Oedipus complex
- Religion as wish fulfilment
- Religion as a reaction against helplessness.

Supporting evidence: redirection of guilt complexes

Freud became convinced that the workings of the mind could be rationally explained through the scientific method of observation and analysis. His reasoning was based on his continued psychoanalysis of patients who were suffering from neurosis, or physical symptoms that had no obvious physical cause. Freud let his patients speak freely in an attempt to unlock their previously repressed thoughts. From his many case studies Freud saw clear evidence for the Oedipus complex and concluded that repressed sexual feelings were at the root of these illnesses.

Case study exemplars

(i) Daniel Schreber

Daniel Schreber was a highly respected judge who, in his middle age, suffered from a religious neurosis where a mystical God occupied and penetrated his body, gradually transforming him into a woman. Although Freud did not actually meet with the judge, he studied the case and interpreted it as evidence that religious belief has its roots in the Oedipus complex, thereby showing that religion is inherently linked to neurosis.

Freud argued that in his infancy, Schreber's libido was directed towards his father rather than his mother. These homosexual desires were repressed but later re-emerged as a religious neurosis. The belief that God was turning him into a woman was interpreted as Schreber's desire for his father being transferred onto an acceptable object of desire, i.e. God. For Freud, the case study was indicative of the general neuroses he associated with religion where God forms a replacement for a person's relationship with their father.

(ii) Little Hans

Hans had a phobia of being bitten by a horse and so tried to avoid horses. Freud interpreted this as Hans's fear of castration. Hans also showed great anxiety when he once saw a horse collapse in the street. Again Freud saw these fears as symbols reflecting an inward conflict of the sexual drive. Hence, Freud interpreted this as an unconscious reminder to Hans of his death wish against his father, which made him feel guilty and afraid. In the successful treatment of Hans, Freud claimed that it was a direct and immediate proof of his theories.

(iii) The Wolf Man

Sergei Pankejeff was a patient of Freud's but to protect his identity, Freud referred to him as 'Wolf Man'. He suffered from depression and went to Freud for therapy. Freud focussed on a dream that Pankejeff had as a young child. The dream featured him lying in bed when the window suddenly opened and he saw six or seven white wolves. In terror of being eaten by the wolves he screamed and woke up.

Freud interpreted this as a repressed trauma of Pankejeff having witnessed his parents having sex. Again, Freud claimed that he was successful in treating the depression having identified the repressed trauma.

In support of Freud's theories, recent research in America at the University of Michigan focussing on brain activity suggests that unconscious conflicts cause or contribute to the anxiety symptoms the patient is experiencing.

Freud's view of the interpretation of dreams has caused **psychotherapy** to link obsessions, phobias and anxieties to repressed memories and guilt. Therapy using hypnosis has also been successful in delving into the unconscious mind. When repressed memories have been identified, the resultant anxiety/obsessional

Specification content
Supporting evidence: redirection of guilt complexes.

Freud's memorial statue in Hampstead

Key quote

To the strange superior powers of nature, the adult lends the features belonging to the figure of his father; he creates for himself the gods. **(Freud)**

quickfire

2.7 Name three of Freud's case studies.

Key term

Psychotherapy: treatment of mental or emotional illness by talking about problems rather than by using medicine or drugs

behaviour has often ceased. Indeed modern psychology recognises memory repression that can lead to denial (e.g. alcoholics) and displacement theories. More recently, research on brain activity has indicated that unconscious conflicts contribute to anxiety symptoms.

Supporting evidence: instinctive desires deriving from evolutionary basis (Charles Darwin)

Freud accepted Darwinian biology as his foundation. He made it clear that the study of evolution was an essential part of the training to be a psychoanalyst and Darwinian theory was essential to psychoanalysis. Such was Darwin's influence on Freud that Vitz comments: 'Darwin had such a profound influence on Freud's psychoanalytic theories that Freud wrote that Darwin's *Origin of Species* was one of the most significant books ever published.'

The theory developed by Freud was based on the Darwinian idea that all behaviour is the result of a few basic animal drives produced by natural selection to facilitate survival. The survival genes that were passed on included those for a high sexual drive. This is why the sex drive became central in Freud's theory of human behaviour.

Challenges: lack of anthropological evidence for primal horde

The whole theory of the horde was based on Darwin's theories that were just mere speculation by Darwin. It is now thought that there was a much greater variety in the way people were grouped. It is unlikely that they were exclusively in hordes. By Freud's own admission, the 'primal horde' had never been observed. Indeed, it is claimed that Darwin's words have been taken out of context and exaggerated. The primal horde is a concept that Darwin would not recognise and his writings have been misrepresented. It is Freud's construction rather than a theory by Darwin. Nor is there any evidence that all societies had totem objects that they worshipped. Even amongst those that did have totem objects, not all of them had totem meals. This lack of evidence casts serious doubt that the primal crime actually took place.

Even if the primal crime of the son killing the father actually happened, the idea that guilt can be transmitted in the way that Freud suggested appears to have no evidence for it. Freud's idea about transmitting guilt was influenced by the Lamarckian theory of 'inheritance of acquired characteristics'. Lamarck argued that learned characteristics could be passed on to an offspring through heredity. Despite experiments to test this theory, all have failed to prove positive. The major argument against such a theory is recent understanding of DNA and genetics. DNA is not involved in an organism's characteristics and an organism's characteristics do not control the composition of the DNA.

Challenges: no firm psychological evidence for universal Oedipus complex

Whilst Freud argued that the Oedipus complex accounted for people modelling God on their father, it is not the only image of God. It could be argued that it is more symptomatic of the male-centred nature of religious thinking.

Anthropologists have shown that beliefs, motives and emotional responses to situations vary remarkably from one culture to the next. For instance, Bronislaw Malinowski, a Polish anthropologist, studied the Trobriand race when he became stranded on the Trobriand Islands off the eastern coast of New Guinea. In his book *Sex and Repression in Savage Society* (1927) he found no evidence of the Oedipus complex, even though the Trobriand race had a religion. In Trobriand culture,

Specification content

Supporting evidence: instinctive desires deriving from evolutionary basis (Charles Darwin).

Key quote

Freud believed that Darwin's theory destroyed the belief in a spiritual force working within the organism. (Alexander and Selesnick)

Specification content

Challenges including lack of anthropological evidence for primal horde; no firm psychological evidence for universal Oedipus complex; evidence basis too narrow.

Key quote

Religion may be altogether disregarded. Its doctrines carry with them the stamp of the times in which they originated, the ignorant childhood days of this human race. (Freud)

quickfire

2.8 Name the anthropologist who studied the Trobriand race.

children were disciplined by their paternal uncles, so the role of sexual rival (the father) and the disciplinarian (the uncle) were separated. This suggests that sex has nothing to do with religion.

In some cultures the mother is dominant and the father's role in bringing up the child is very limited. In other cultures there is no male God figure or even no God figure at all. This seems to undermine the idea of the Oedipus complex as being universal.

A more likely explanation is that the complex does not cause the religion – rather the religion, with its strict rules on sexual behaviour and relationships, causes the Oedipus complex that then leads to the neurosis. Freud seems to have based his theory of the Oedipus complex on five main case studies and then generalised, assuming that the Oedipus complex detected in those cases was at work everywhere.

Malinowski with the natives of the Trobriand Islands

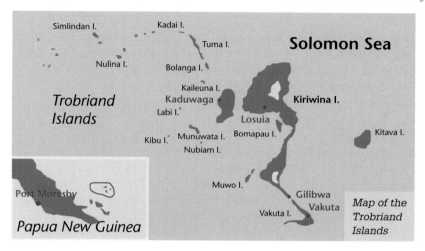

Map of the Trobriand Islands

Challenges: evidence basis too narrow

Freud constructed a theory to explain those religions with which he was familiar. Hence he focused on Judaism and Christianity arguing that the importance of the father figure developed into the male God. However, he failed to consider religions that are based upon female deities, such as the Egyptian Isis cult. Equally he did not consider religions such as Buddhism which did not have a god.

Freud regarded himself as a scientist and saw psychoanalysis as a new science. However, according to Karl Popper, every genuine scientific theory must be testable and therefore falsifiable, at least in principle. A theory which is compatible with all possible observations is unscientific. Freud's theory appears to be compatible with every possible state of affairs and so cannot be falsified. Hence, Freud's theory is not scientific.

A key critic of Freud's work is Adolf Grunbaum (*The Foundations of Psychoanalysis: A Philosophical Critique 1984*). He claimed that Freud's theories evaded any kind of empirical test but were adopted by many as they were shown to be successful as a treatment. One difficulty with the clinical evidence is that there is an element of suggestibility involved in the treatment process. Others have accused Freud of fabrication. Grunbaum challenged the view that only the psychoanalytic method can yield correct insight into the causes of neuroses and that correct insight was necessary for a cure of those neuroses. He pointed out that successful treatment had occurred without either of those two conditions being fulfilled.

More recent criticism has been levelled against Freud in relation to the occurrence of sexual abuse. He reported many instances of traumas suffered by his patients claiming they had been seduced in very early childhood by older male relatives. Freud doubted the truth of these allegations and replaced them with the certainty that it was the descriptions about childhood fantasies that were being offered. In the light of recent events, it may well be that the allegations were true.

Key quote

The teachings of psychoanalysis are based on an incalculable number of observations and experiences. (Freud)

AO1 Activity

Use the notes from your last activity to check and see whether or not they would stand up to the challenges above.

Key skills Theme 2 DEF

This theme has tasks that deal with the basics of AO1 in terms of prioritising and selecting the key relevant information, presenting this and then using evidence and examples to support and expand upon this.

Key skills

Knowledge involves:

Selection of a range of (thorough) accurate and relevant information that is directly related to the specific demands of the question.

This means:

- Selecting relevant material for the question set

- Being focused in explaining and examining the material selected.

Understanding involves:

Explanation that is extensive, demonstrating depth and/or breadth with excellent use of evidence and examples including (where appropriate) thorough and accurate supporting use of sacred texts, sources of wisdom and specialist language.

This means:

- Effective use of examples and supporting evidence to establish the quality of your understanding

- Ownership of your explanation that expresses personal knowledge and understanding and NOT just reproducing a chunk of text from a book that you have rehearsed and memorised.

As you work through each section of the book, the focus will be on a variety of different aspects associated with AO1 so that you can comprehensively perfect the overall skills associated with AO1.

AO1 Developing skills

It is now important to consider the information that has been covered in this section; however, the information in its raw form is too extensive and so has to be processed in order to meet the requirements of the examination. This can be done by practising more advanced skills associated with AO1. The exercises that run throughout this book will help you to do this and prepare you for the examination. For assessment objective 1 (AO1), which involves demonstrating 'knowledge' and 'understanding' skills, we are going to focus on different ways in which the skills can be demonstrated effectively, and also refer to how the performance of these skills is measured (see generic band descriptors for A2 [WJEC] AO1 or A Level [Eduqas] AO1).

▶ **Your task is this:** Below is **a summary of the Oedipus complex**. It is 200 words long. You need to use this for an answer but could not repeat all of this in an essay under examination conditions so you will have to condense the material. Discuss which points you think are the most important and then re-draft into your own summary of 100 words.

The Oedipus complex

The Oedipus complex was named after the character in the Greek tragedy Oedipus Rex by Sophocles. The play has remained popular and Freud felt that it was because it reflects an unconscious anxiety that most adults have experienced. In the play, Oedipus unwittingly kills his father and marries his own mother. When he realises this he gouges out his own eyes in guilt and despair. Freud felt that a similar guilt operates unconsciously in our psyche and is caused by our most basic instinct – our sexual drive. Freud identified a child's psychosexual development between the ages of 3 and 6 as the key phase when a child develops a sexual identity and this changes the dynamic between the child and their parent. Like Oedipus, we have a kind of love affair with our mother. Our father is thus seen as a rival but we fear our father. This conflict is the cause of our unconscious anxiety. The anxiety is so great that Freud felt it develops into a castration complex. The resulting Oedipus complex, if not resolved but instead repressed, led to neurotic behaviour. Freud thought that religion was merely an expression of this neurotic behaviour.

When you have completed the task, refer to the band descriptors for A2 (WJEC) or A Level (Eduqas) and, in particular, have a look at the demands described in the higher band descriptors towards which you should be aspiring. Ask yourself:

- Does my work demonstrate thorough, accurate and relevant knowledge and understanding of religion and belief?

- Is my work coherent (consistent or make logical sense), clear and well organised? *(WJEC band descriptor only but still important to consider for Eduqas)*

- Will my work, when developed, be an extensive and relevant response which is specific to the focus of the task?

- Does my work have extensive depth and/or suitable breadth and have excellent use of evidence and examples?

- If appropriate to the task, does my response have thorough and accurate reference to sacred texts and sources of wisdom?

- Are there any insightful connections to be made with other elements of my course?

- Will my answer, when developed and extended to match what is expected in an examination answer, have an extensive range of views of scholars/schools of thought?

- When used, is specialist language and vocabulary both thorough and accurate?

Issues for analysis and evaluation

To what extent can religious belief be considered a neurosis?

It is true that Freud's work treating patients with neuroses drew his attention to their obsessions as having parallels with religion. In particular, the ritualistic nature of religious activity mirrored aspects of a compulsive obsessive neurosis. Therefore, it was not unreasonable to think that the same cause lay behind both, namely repressed memories.

In *Obsessive Actions and Religious Practices (1907)* Freud argues that neurosis, with its compulsive behaviour is 'an individual religiosity' and religion, with its repetitive rituals, is a 'universal obsessional neurosis'.

In addition, Freud argued that there were two universal sources of religious ideas.

One was the unconscious racial memories of the slaughter of the primal father. This involved a supposedly subconscious memory of events in human history or prehistory. The strength of this proposal is that Darwinian evolutionary theory clearly supported the primal horde theory and totemism. In support of his argument, Freud considered the Holy Communion as a clear development of a totemic meal and clear parallels can be seen.

The second source was seen to be the early childhood experiences of our own parents which he connected to a sexual trauma and that he called the Oedipus complex. The neurosis that results is generated by the sexual component of the traumatic experience. It is this element and the associated memories that a person seeks to repress. The Oedipus complex, though a normal part of every childhood, contains impulses that are seen by the person as shameful. The impulses include hatred of the father and incest with the mother. This is a little more difficult to support directly as it tends to rely upon our interpretation of religious stories but it can certainly be seen in aspects of Hinduism such as myths surrounding Ganesh or Ganapati, for example.

Both sources suggest that there is an underlying neurosis to certain aspects of religious belief and practice.

Furthermore, Freud's case studies such as Little Hans reaffirmed Freud's view that religion was an outward expression of inner psychological conflict. The conflict is an imbalance in the personality that is reflected in certain neurotic behaviour akin to religious activity. The characteristic of a neurosis is a reawakening of repressed trauma which is accompanied by compulsive obsessional impulses. This can clearly be seen in the ritualistic and liturgical aspects of many religions.

It could be suggested, then, that this all fits exactly with Freud's understanding of the origin of religion. Therefore, religion is a neurotic illness that affected all people. Freud's position that it is a mental illness and therefore harmful is directly related to his understanding of neuroses.

Freud viewed monotheism as a belief that stimulated obsessive and compulsive neurosis. It embedded within it feelings of guilt. These guilt feelings originated from the individual's guilty relation with his own father and a memory from the primal horde crime of murdering the father. Monotheism therefore is an attempt to resolve this guilt. Therefore guilt is the major factor in the development of religion.

Freud also suggested that religion would eventually die out and be replaced by science. He sees a parallel between the development of the child and the development of humanity. The human race will develop into maturity and discard religion. The evidence from the rise of atheism and the argument that people are moving away from religion in the 21st century would appear to support this view.

This section covers AO2 content and skills

Specification content

How far religious belief can be considered a neurosis.

Key quote

From a scientific point of view, classical Freudian psychoanalysis is dead as both a theory of the mind and a mode of therapy. (Crews)

AO2 Activity

As you read through this section try to do the following:

1. Pick out the different lines of argument that are presented in the text and identify any evidence given in support.

2. For each line of argument try to evaluate whether or not you think this is strong or weak.

3. Think of any questions you may wish to raise in response to the arguments.

This Activity will help you to start thinking critically about what you read and help you to evaluate the effectiveness of different arguments and from this develop your own observations, opinions and points of view that will help with any conclusions that you make in your answers to the AO2 questions that arise.

Key quotes

Almost all the evidence that Freud presents has been discredited in one way or another. (Palmer)

Not all psychoanalysts agreed with Freud's view of God. (Armstrong)

AO2 Activity

List some conclusions that could be drawn from the AO2 reasoning from the above text; try to aim for at least three different possible conclusions. Consider each of the conclusions and collect brief evidence to support each conclusion from the AO1 and AO2 material for this topic. Select the conclusion that you think is most convincing and explain why it is so. Try to contrast this with the weakest conclusion in the list, justifying your argument with clear reasoning and evidence.

Specification content

The adequacy of Freud's explanation of religious belief.

However, the argument is not without challenges. Whilst it is appreciated that there is evidence to support Freud's views, the general feeling is that this evidence is not really 'scientific' in that it is not representative of the whole picture. Some see Freud as 'selective' in his evidence, some see his evidence as questionable and there are those who question the nature of the conclusions that he drew.

For instance, many challenge Freud's conclusions on the basis of a lack of real evidence. Although Darwin argued for the primal horde theory, there is little evidence to support it today in the field of biological and behavioural sciences and most think that there was a much greater variety of structure within the earliest groups and tribes.

Research also suggests that most people base their idea of God on their mother rather than their father. In particular, the work by Malinowski casts doubt on the Oedipus complex theory and the Hindu expressions of the feminine divine fully support this doubt. In reality, religious and theological ideas about God are much more complex than Freud's theories suggest. Some would go as far as to say that Freud's views about religion and God were very simplistic and theologically naïve at best and unsophisticated and ignorant at worst. Indeed, a more accurate explanation might be that it is religion that causes the Oedipus complex rather than vice versa.

Despite Freud's confidence in the powers of science his hypothesis was impossible to verify and so in that sense his work was unscientific. This is especially true as regards to the nature of psychology that interprets behaviour and draws conclusions that relate to how we perceive things in the first place. There appears to be no solid, physical evidence to support the conclusions.

Again, another line of argument would be that Freud was also inclined to ignore information unsuited to what he wanted to prove and preferred to select only those things that supported his views. This is not a scientific methodology. All variants and anomalies need to be accounted for through rigorous and repeated testing. All possible conclusions need to be considered and evaluated. Some would go as far to say that Freud simply discovered what he was looking for in the first place.

Another major criticism of Freud's views about religion as a neurosis is that he seems to misunderstand the essence of religion. He saw it merely in terms of sacred acts and rituals rather than a set of beliefs and doctrines that could be debated around evidence. Again, there could be argued to be a lack of respect and humility to Freud's approach in ignoring the maturity and complexity of religious traditions.

Overall, whilst there can be seen to be some correlation between religious behaviour and neurosis, the main issue to be resolved is how significant this is in the grand scheme of matters. In addition, it would be interesting to transpose Freud's interpretations of behaviour onto a military workplace, a school system or an office environment and see whether or not similar parallels of power, obsession and personal sense of duties can be explained through neuroses!

Study tip

As you work through the course do not forget that you can bring in other evidence from other areas to help with your evaluation skills. Jung is always a good source to use when evaluating Freud.

How adequate is Freud's explanation of religious belief?

Freud's explanations are a challenge to religious belief as it sees religion as a neurosis – a mental illness that is harmful. He sees religious belief as intellectually lacking since it cannot be rationally justified and it also devalues lives such that it makes people incapable of changing society for the better. However, is Freud right in his explanations of religious belief? Do his explanations stand up to scrutiny?

There do seem to be parallels between certain types of neurosis and religious ritual. People often display obsessional behaviour. This behaviour, for example, can centre on checking or contamination. The checking of things such as front doors, water taps and gas stove knobs can result in checking multiple times, sometimes hundreds of times and for hours on end, resulting in the person being late for work and other appointments. The checking can also cause damage to the objects that are constantly being checked. The need to clean and wash can also be a compulsion. It often involves repetitive hand washing until the person 'feels' they are clean. It is true that religion can also be seen to have aspects of obsessional behaviour. For example Muslims are required to wash five times per day before prayer. This washing is known as *Wudu* and is a form of ritual ablution. Parts of the body must be washed in a specific order and in a specific way. If a mistake is made, then the whole process must be begun again.

Freud's clinical work involving interpretation of dreams and psychoanalysis of patients was often successful in treating the obsession. This may be seen as validating his theories concerning the cause of the obsession as repressed trauma and guilt, therefore supporting the view that religion with its religious ritual stems from the same source, repressed memories and guilt. The repressed traumas Freud identified for religion included the subconscious memory from prehistory of the primal horde and the totemic meals that expressed sexual guilt.

In addition, Freud's theory of the Oedipus complex identified another form of repression involving a son's sexual attraction to his mother but resenting the father. Support for these views could be found in Darwin's theory of the primal horde, Robertson Smith's work on the totemic system, and the Oedipus complex supported by the work of Kline. Evidence from various anthropological studies supports Freud's argument for the totemism and the primal horde theory. There is evidence that the eating of the totem flesh constituted a sort of ceremony. It is not difficult to see in this evidence aspects of the Christian ritual of Holy Communion. The earlier totemic meal is now replaced by Holy Communion and identified with the son rather than a totem.

There can be no doubt that the 'father figure' features in religion and the ideal father in authority is exactly the idea of God who is able to answer human longings and desires. It can be seen that religious doctrines reflect our wish fulfilment. Across all cultures there is a desire for justice and escape from death. Therefore, it is clear why such desires appear in religions. Our sense of helplessness against the forces of nature drive us to invent some form of security. An eternal, omnipotent, benevolent God will answer our needs.

The sexual drive also needs controlling, so religions contain strict laws governing sexual behaviour and relationships.

Freud's focus on the role of the unconscious is now a popular topic in the fields of experimental and social psychology. The idea of unconscious, and the transference phenomenon, have been widely researched and, it is claimed, validated in the fields of cognitive psychology and social psychology (Westen and Gabbard 2002), though a Freudian interpretation of unconscious mental activity is not held by the majority of cognitive psychologists. Indeed modern psychology recognises memory repression that can lead to denial (e.g. alcoholics) and displacement theories. More recently, research on brain activity has indicated that unconscious conflicts contribute to anxiety symptoms.

However, many aspects of the evidence have been challenged including his fundamental approach. It is claimed that all Freud had were theories; there was no clear verifiable evidence or statistical data. In support of this line of argument many have questioned and rejected the validity of Freud's work both within modern psychology and beyond it.

Key quote

Freud's theories are archaic and obsolete. (Western)

AO2 Activity

As you read through this section try to do the following:

1. Pick out the different lines of argument that are presented in the text and identify any evidence given in support.

2. For each line of argument try to evaluate whether or not you think this is strong or weak.

3. Think of any questions you may wish to raise in response to the arguments.

This Activity will help you to start thinking critically about what you read and help you to evaluate the effectiveness of different arguments and from this develop your own observations, opinions and points of view that will help with any conclusions that you make in your answers to the AO2 questions that arise.

Key quote

It seems that the verdict must be 'not proven'; ... the Freudian theory of religion may be true but it has not been shown to be so. (Hick)

Freud's famous couch

AO2 Activity

List some conclusions that could be drawn from the AO2 reasoning from the above text; try to aim for at least three different possible conclusions. Consider each of the conclusions and collect brief evidence to support each conclusion from the AO1 and AO2 material for this topic. Select the conclusion that you think is most convincing and explain why it is so. Try to contrast this with the weakest conclusion in the list, justifying your argument with clear reasoning and evidence.

Whilst Freud's work was claimed to be scientific, his selective methodologies and the validity of his conclusions have been questioned and challenged. Indeed, the theories themselves have come under attack, and been rejected, replaced or simply ridiculed.

In particular, Darwin's primal horde theory has been rejected and the idea of a suppressed memory of guilt that is universal has been ridiculed. These are crucial to Freud's overall system of thought and so without these there seems to be little of value left in his theories. Even the Oedipus complex has been found not to be universal as has been shown by the work of Malinowski.

Perhaps the most damning criticism of Freud's work is the fact that Freud was no academic in the field of theology and religious studies. Indeed, as has been echoed many times, his approach displays naivety and ignorance and his theories could be argued to be disrespectful to the advanced and complex nature of religious traditions.

For example, in a letter about the reading of books on religion, Freud wrote 'I am reading books without being really interested in them, since I already know the results, my instinct tells me that'. This view appears to border on arrogance and certainly appears to be unscientific.

In addition, Freud's prediction that religion would die out as science took over does not seem to have been fulfilled. Although there may be a rise in atheism, there is also a resurgence of religious traditions in a great variety of forms throughout the world today. There are also aspects of religion that Freud's theories are not able to explain. For instance, how do the theories account for Buddhism?

Many might argue that Freud does not understand the essence of religion. To see it merely as sacred acts and rituals is to ignore that religions have a set of beliefs and doctrines that can be debated around evidence. He seems to ignore the maturity and complexity of religious traditions.

Freud's explanation of religious belief also seems based on questionable evidence. There have been various challenges to his theory. For instance, our recent understanding of DNA seems to rule out the idea that learned characteristics could be passed on to an offspring through heredity. The two basic foundations to Freud's explanation of religion involves the primal horde theory and the Oedipus complex. Both have been strongly disputed. By Freud's own admission, the 'primal horde' had never been observed. Indeed, it is claimed that Darwin's words have been taken out of context and exaggerated. Anthropologists have also shown that beliefs, motives and emotional responses to situations vary remarkably from one culture to the next. In some cultures the mother is dominant and the father's role in bringing up the child is very limited. In other cultures there is no male God figure or even no God figure at all. This seems to undermine the idea of the Oedipus complex as being universal.

However it is true that psychoanalysis and hypnosis have been shown to be successful in treating neurosis, but other approaches have also been successful that do not accept Freudian theories. The difficulty remains that Freud's explanation for religion involves theories that cannot be empirically tested.

Overall, there could be argued to be alternative explanations that are far more successful in challenging religion than those of Freud. Jung was much more respectful about religion but at the same times challenged aspects of it in his theories. The proposal of the idea of a 'God of gaps' is a better explanation of religious traditions for many or simply the explanation that religion serves a simple human need as a source of comfort and hope in light of the unknown.

Study tip

It is vital for AO2 that you actually discuss arguments and not just explain what someone may have stated. Try to ask yourself, 'was this a fair point to make?', 'is the evidence sound enough?', 'is there anything to challenge this argument?', 'is this a strong or weak argument?' Such critical analysis will help you develop your evaluation skills.

AO2 Developing skills

It is now important to consider the information that has been covered in this section; however, the information in its raw form is too extensive and so has to be processed in order to meet the requirements of the examination. This can be done by practising more advanced skills associated with AO2. The exercises that run throughout this book will help you to do this and prepare you for the examination.

For assessment objective 2 (AO2), which involves 'critical analysis' and 'evaluation' skills, we are going to focus on different ways in which the skills can be demonstrated effectively, and also refer to how the performance of these skills is measured (see generic band descriptors for A2 [WJEC] AO2 or A Level [Eduqas] AO2).

▶ **Your task is this:** Below is a **summary of two different points of view concerning whether religion is wishful thinking.** It is 300 words long. You want to use these two views and lines of argument for an evaluation; however, to just list them is not really evaluating them. Present these two views in a more evaluative style by firstly condensing each argument and then, secondly, commenting on how effective each one is (weak or strong are good terms to start with). Allow about 350 words in total.

Religion disregards rational justification. It is a cultural phenomenon. Religious beliefs continue because the human psyche desires them and so ignores the fact they cannot be justified. These basic human desires/wishes includes overcoming threats to humanity from external forces (nature such as earthquakes and death itself) and internal forces (human instincts) and a universal longing for a father-figure. Freud saw that by personalising these forces and turning them into gods, they could be controlled. The gods can then be placated. The object of worship becomes an exalted father who watches over us and compensates us for our suffering on earth with a future life after death. Freud sees in religion an infant's helplessness and a father's protection. Such illusions Freud saw as an insult to intelligence and a contradiction to reality. They caused people to devalue their lives and unable to change society for the better.

Freud's account of religion is a caricature. He assumes that theologians, biblical scholars and apologists have no interest in evidence and rational argument. They give rational justifications and appeal to historical evidence such as the accounts of Jesus in the Gospels. Freud's faith in science as opposed to religion seems itself an illusion. What is the evidence for Freud's theories of the id, ego and super-ego? Freud's own theories are unverifiable. To accuse religion as being a flight from reality is to assume that science is the only way that reality can be explained and understood. Religion is a different view of reality. Religion is no more an illusion than science. Freud ignores religions based on female deities or religions that do not have any single dominant object of worship. He ignores evidence from the Trobiand race, where the father played an insignificant role yet they had a religion. Is the God of the Bible for instance, the kind of God one would want to project given he is holy and just? If Religion is explained by the need for a father figure, then is atheism explained by no experience of a father figure? Freud therefore is selective about his evidence and ignores anything that doesn't fit.

When you have completed the task, refer to the band descriptors for A2 (WJEC) or A Level (Eduqas) and in particular have a look at the demands described in the higher band descriptors towards which you should be aspiring.

Key skills Theme 2 DEF

This theme has tasks that deal with the basics of AO2 in terms of developing an evaluative style, building arguments and raising critical questions.

Key skills

Analysis involves identifying issues raised by the materials in the AO1, together with those identified in the AO2 section, and presents sustained and clear views, either of scholars or from a personal perspective ready for evaluation.

This means:

- That your answers are able to identify key areas of debate in relation to a particular issue

- That you can identify, and comment upon, the different lines of argument presented by others

- That your response comments on the overall effectiveness of each of these areas or arguments.

Evaluation involves considering the various implications of the issues raised based upon the evidence gleaned from analysis and provides an extensive detailed argument with a clear conclusion.

This means:

- That your answer weighs up the consequences of accepting or rejecting the various and different lines of argument analysed

- That your answer arrives at a conclusion through a clear process of reasoning.

As you work through each section of the book, the focus will be on a variety of different aspects associated with AO2 so that you can comprehensively perfect the overall skills associated with AO2.

Specification content

Religion necessary for personal growth with reference to collective unconscious; individuation; archetypes; the God within.

Specification content

Religion necessary for personal growth: collective unconscious.

quickfire

2.9 According to Jung, what did the collective unconscious consist of?

Key terms

Archetypes: literally meaning 'original pattern' – they refer to symbolic forms which all people share in their collective unconscious. The archetypes give rise to images in the conscious mind and account for the reoccurring themes. These mould and influence human behaviour

Collective unconscious: elements of unconsciousness that are shared with all other people

Personal unconscious: memories that have been forgotten or repressed

Primordial: existing from the beginning

quickfire

2.10 According to Jung what did the psyche consist of?

The Psyche according to Jung

E: Religious belief as a product of the human mind: Carl Jung

Introduction

Carl Gustav Jung was born in 1875 in Switzerland. Like Freud, he worked with psychiatric patients after gaining his doctorate. Initially, Jung shared a similar understanding of the way the mind works but he soon came to realise that Freud's view of the subconscious was too narrow. So, he set out to demonstrate a wholly distinctive understanding of the mind, an understanding which would see religion in a much more positive light. Unlike Freud, who saw religion as a neurosis, Jung saw it as something necessary for personal growth.

Religion necessary for personal growth: collective unconscious

Jung agreed with Freud that the **personal unconscious** consisted of lost or repressed memories some of which take the form of complexes. It includes things we have forgotten because they had become irrelevant or had seemed unimportant at the time. In this way, Jung's personal unconscious is similar to Freud's pre-conscious. However, Jung regarded repressed material as only one kind of unconscious content. Below the personal unconscious Jung claimed lies the **collective unconscious**. It is this idea that sets him apart from Freud.

Freud (front left) and Jung (front right) at Clark University, Massachusetts, USA, in 1909

Key quotes

Until you make the unconscious conscious, it will direct your life and you will call it fate. **(Jung)**

This deeper layer I call the 'collective unconscious' … this part of the unconscious is not individual but universal … it has contents and modes of behaviour that are more or less the same everywhere and in all individuals. **(Jung)**

So, for Jung, the psyche consisted of the ego (consciousness), the personal unconscious and the collective unconsciousness. Just as evolution and heredity are seen as providing a blueprint for the body, so Jung saw evolution and heredity providing a blueprint for the psyche. According to Jung, the collective unconscious consists of **primordial** images, derived from early human history. These images stem from our ancestral past, and include both human and pre-human experiences. Jung claimed that these images or ideas could not be traced to the individual's own past experiences.

Though referred to as images, they are not literally pictures but more like predispositions to act like our ancestors in our response to the world. The resemblance of these contents to mythical and religious themes that have appeared throughout the centuries across the world led Jung to refer to them as **archetypes**.

Religion necessary for personal growth: archetypes

The word 'archetype' comes from the Greek meaning 'original pattern'. Archetypes are unlearned. They function to organise how we experience certain things, often evoking deep emotions. Jung viewed our primitive past as forming the basis of the human psyche, directing and influencing present behaviour. He noted that the symbols and images from different cultures are often very similar because they have emerged from archetypes shared by the whole human race. However, the archetypes are mysterious and not directly accessible to conscious thought. A person only becomes individually conscious of them when they are projected outwards, usually in the form of myths and symbols. Religious stories, symbolism and rituals, as well as dreams and day dreams are all ways to identify the archetypes.

However, the archetypes are not a set of definite mythological images or motifs that have been inherited. Archetypes are dynamic unconscious entities which generate images in the conscious mind, but they cannot be known directly. Archetypal figures such as the wise man, are not archetypes as such but rather archetypal images which have crystallised out of the archetypes. According to Jung, the archetypal figure 'is a tendency to form such representations of a motif'. Therefore, the number of archetypal images are limitless, although a number frequently reoccur. This meant that Jung was able to identify regular patterns of meaning within the world of archetypes. The representations of the archetypes may vary a great deal in detail but they do not lose their core meaning.

The four key archetypes

There were four key archetypes that Jung identified which are:

The persona

This is the mask we wear to make a particular impression on others and it may conceal our own true nature. The persona represents all of the different social masks we wear among different groups and in different situations. For example, a father may consider a trait such as disciplining as typical of a father and so adopt that trait rather than a trait which reflects their own actual personality. Because the persona is an idealised image and not a true reflection of our personal consciousness, it can lead to inner conflicts and a repression of our own individuality.

The shadow

The shadow refers to the suppressed, unconscious portion of the personality. It designates that side of an individual that he or she prefers not to reveal. Often it is symbolised as original sin, the devil or as a snake. It is considered to be the source of not only our creative but also our destructive energies. The shadow is in contrast with the persona, the public self. This darker side of our personality can be a source of shame and anxiety. So we tend to deny it. The shadow if unrecognised is projected on others who are thought to embody those repressed tendencies that are actually resident in that person's own pysche. The most known shadow image is the villain archetype.

Specification content

Religion necessary for personal growth: archetypes.

Key quote

The form of the world into which a person is born is already inborn in him, as a virtual image. **(Jung)**

quickfire

2.11 What is the meaning of the Greek word from which comes the word 'archetype'?

The persona archetype – the mask we wear.

The shadow archetype – the suppressed unconscious.

The anima and animus archetypes – taking on characteristics of the opposite sex.

The Self archetype – the balance between the conscious and the unconscious.

Key term

Mandala: geometric designs symbolic of the universe, often used in Buddhism as an aid to meditation; they are usually circular in form with one identifiable centre point

quickfire

2.12 List the four major archetypes.

A typical Buddhist mandala

The anima and animus

These are inner attitudes that take on the characteristics of the opposite sex. Each sex manifests attitudes and behaviour of the other by virtue of centuries of living together. As a person develops a gender identity they repress the aspects of their personality which might be considered to be reflective of the opposite sex. For instance, a male may repress empathy in social situations because it is considered in society as being feminine.

The anima is the archetypal image of woman present in the unconscious of every man. It is responsible for moods and is a complication in all emotional relationships. The most known anima image is the mother archetype and is represented in stories by characters such as Eve in Judaism, the Virgin Mary in Christianity and Shakti in Hinduism. The anima is often shown as a cave or a ship.

The comparable archetype in the female psyche is the animus, the woman's image of man. In the woman's unconscious, it is responsible for unreasoned opinion. It is often represented by an eagle or a bull and by phallic symbols such as towers. Both anima and animus need to be in balance.

The Self

The most important archetype is the Self and is the mid-point of the personality – balancing (midway between) the conscious and the unconscious. The Self represents the harmony and balance between the various opposing qualities that make up the psyche. The Self provides a sense of unity in experience. Jung considered that the aim of every individual was to achieve a state of 'self-hood'. Because it is almost impossible for any person to embody its own Self fully, this archetype is often given expression in geometrical or abstract form, such as a mandala. Very well-known figures which express the Self are Christ and Buddha. The Self archetypes comes closest to what many religions refer to as the 'soul'.

AO1 Activity

Jung identified four major archetypes but believed that there was no limit to the number that may exist. Indeed, when analysing film or literature there are different sorts of archetypes that a personality can exhibit such as hero, villain and maiden. Try to complete the following table with characters from the films Harry Potter, Star Wars and Lord of the Rings.

Archetype	Harry Potter	Lord of the Rings	Star Wars
Hero			
Villain			
Maiden			
Sidekick			
Wise old man			

Religion necessary for personal growth: individuation

Jung argued that as we acquire the qualities of an archetype from the collective unconscious, we repress those attributes of our true self because they do not conform to the archetype. However, those repressed traits that are our true self must be integrated into our consciousness if we are to realise our true self. This process by which a person moves toward the achievement of the Self is called individuation.

The integration results in the wholeness and balance of an individual's personality. The Self archetype works collectively with all other aspects of a person's psyche to integrate them and become whole. It is a form of 'self-development' or 'self-realisation' – a discovery of the true self.

Therefore, individuation aims to divest the Self of the false wrappings of the persona and the suggestive power of the primordial images. In doing so, it will balance the contradictory nature of the archetypes and unite opposites.

An example would be the need to unite good and evil so that we see ourselves as capable of both. The lotus symbol in Asian religions reflects this uniting of opposites, where the roots of the lotus are in the dirty mud below and its flower in the clean air above. In a similar way, Jung argued that we must get in touch with the shadow and anima/animus if we want to get in touch with the Self.

The way that the archetypes are brought into our consciousness from the collective unconscious is by means of the symbols of the archetypes. These archetypal symbols mediate the process of individuation as they express and bring about the union of opposites. Jung saw that these symbols are the images, dogmas and rites that form the religious traditions.

There are also some clear examples of archetypal symbols that can be found in Christian religious tradition:

Christ

Jung did not mean that Jesus Christ necessarily existed in history. Christ was not a figure 'out there' but a psychic reality inside the deepest level of the human psyche. He is seen as perfect, but incomplete, since he lacks a 'shadow'. The separation of Christ from God at his birth, symbolises our human separation from our parents. Christ's death symbolises the necessary sacrifice of the ego in order to become more complete.

The Eucharist

Holy Communion is also known as the Eucharist – this recalls how God sent his own son, who is also himself, to be sacrificed; however, the son rises again. For Jung, this symbolised those who sacrifice the selfish part of the ego, resulting in the self being transformed.

The Trinity

The Trinity – the Christian doctrine of the Father, Son and Holy Spirit who are three persons and yet one. Jung saw the symbol as one sided in that it lacked opposites (it was perfectly good). Therefore, Jung argued that a fourth element had been rejected and so needs adding to provide the energising opposition essential for the process of actualisation. This opposing fourth element could be Satan. Jung also argued that the trinity was exclusively masculine so an alternative opposing fourth element could be the Virgin Mary.

Specification content
Religion necessary for personal growth: individuation.

Key terms

Eucharist: the Christian ceremony based on Jesus Christ's last meal with his disciples and is also known as Mass or Holy Communion

Individuation: the process of attaining wholeness and balance

quickfire

2.13 What is the name given to the process by which a person moves towards the achievement of the Self?

quickfire

2.14 Name three examples of archetypal symbols identified in the Christian tradition.

Specification content

Religion necessary for personal
growth: the God within.

quickfire

2.15 Why is individuation seen as a
religious quest?

quickfire

2.16 How does Jung differ from Freud in
his view of religion?

Specification content

Supportive evidence including
recognition of religion as a source of
comfort.

Religion necessary for personal growth: the God within

Individuation is the journey towards becoming a full individual. It is the quest to find the 'God within' and the symbol of 'the Self'. In its widest sense, it is a religious quest, because it is through religious images that the personality achieves its goal of integration. The religious images are simply images of the deeper self.

Jung considers that God is a deep 'inner' reality rather than an external object or person. God is an expression of the collective unconscious. A 'religious experience' with God is really an encounter with the 'Self' and the experience is called 'spiritual' or 'numinous'. Rudolf Otto, the German theologian, described a 'numinous' experience as mysterious and awe-inspiring. During the experience the person feels in communion with a 'wholly other'.

Jung considered that the Self archetype creates the same symbolism that has always expressed deity. For Jung, the Self is the 'God within us'. He claimed that it was impossible to distinguish between a symbol of the Self and a God image.

As can be seen, Jung's understanding of the idea of God is very different from that of Freud. For Freud, God is a creation by the individual human mind and its neurotic desires. He sees it more as a mental illness and thought that religion would eventually die out and be replaced by science. In contrast, Jung sees religion as being helpful to balance mental health, a key to the process of integration and individuation.

Supportive evidence including recognition of religion as a source of comfort

It is generally agreed that Jung's theories were experience driven. His concepts were constructed from evidence derived from his personal experience and clinical observations. He concluded that the archetypes occur universally in all cultures and historical periods. Myths and religions contained similar themes that were also found in the dreams of his patients. Jung believed that the archetypes provided a way of interpreting dreams and myths and features of traditional religions.

Indeed, Jung viewed religion as a positive factor of psychological value. Although religion was seen as error, nevertheless it was a positive error in that it provided humankind with assurance and strength. He viewed the idea of God and religious phenomena as symbols that express and draw human beings towards psychic wholeness.

Jung became aware that the horrors of the First World War posed a spiritual problem for the modern person as the religious, social and political certainties had been torn down. As a result, people had become disconnected with humanity and spirituality. Uncertainty and disillusionment followed and civilisation became dominated by materialism, science and technology. The religious symbols that projected the archetypes were often absent and Jung maintained that this led to psychoneurosis. This was because neurosis and depression result from a disharmony between consciousness and unconsciousness. Healing and wholeness must come from restoring harmony within oneself and between oneself and the external world.

In 1932 he reported that:

'Among all my patients ... over thirty-five – there has not been one whose problem in the last resort was not that of finding a religious outlook on life. ... every one of them fell ill because he had lost what the living religions of every age have given to their followers, and none of them has been really healed who did not regain his religious outlook.' (*Psychotherapists or the Clergy*)

He saw the psychologist's task as one of regaining the inner vision for each of his patients and he argued that this was achievable by establishing a connection between the psyche and the sacred images.

There was a need to pay attention to messages from the unconscious and the spiritual realms through dream analysis, word associations, and interpretation of symbols, metaphors and creative activities. For Jung, understanding the symbolic meaning of the unconscious archetypes was a major step towards attainment of meaningful living.

Supportive evidence including recognition of religion as promotion of personal and social mindsets arising from religious belief

Jung saw support for his theories from his observation that human beings have collective ideas and common ethics that could be found in all religions. Indeed, religious belief was seen as aiding individuation and leading to wholeness of the individual.

Jung appreciated that there was a significant difference between Western and Asian minds. The Western mind he saw as extroverted and in search of an outer reality. In contrast, he saw the Asian mind as introverted and in search of the source of all existence, the psyche itself. Hence he saw particular value in the Asian techniques of meditation.

In Buddhist meditation, for example, removal of ignorance is vital: this involves removal of hindrances such as sensuous desires, ill-will and restlessness. The meditation seeks to uncover misconceptions about who and what we are. For example, the Brahma Viharas (Buddhist virtues) are meditative states, thoughts and actions to be cultivated in Buddhist meditation. These four Buddhist Virtues are loving kindness, compassion, altruistic joy and composure. This meditative practice is similar to the God archetype that involves the development of positive, wholesome images for reflection. Therefore, the idea of the Self archetype organising and harmonising the 'fuller picture' of reality is similar to the idea of meditation leading to enlightenment (nibbana/nirvana).

Jung felt that the way inward for people in the West was more difficult. There was nothing in the West really comparable to the Asian meditation tradition except psychotherapy. This involved such things as dream analysis and the aim was to guide the patient to a personal confrontation with the collective unconscious and its archetypes. For Jung, symbols only worked if they were dynamic. He believed that many symbols in organised religion had just become objects and had therefore lost their meaning and their power to actualise the God archetype. Jung concluded that organised religion was a failure.

Surveys on mental health, happiness and social benefits show a positive rating for those who are religious. This suggests that religion aids wholeness and helps to integrate conscious and unconscious contents into a coherent psychic totality.

Surveys suggest that social cohesion and social support is found among church members. It is a source of social integration of those often rejected by wider society. Religion is also seen as a source of comfort as it offers meaning to life and freedom of fear of death.

Specification content

Supportive evidence including recognition of religion as promotion of personal and social mindsets arising from religious belief.

quickfire

2.17 What difference did Jung see between the Western and the Asian religious mind?

Key quote

The religious images/symbols are (according to Jung) 'the means by which human beings discover both what they are and what they are capable of becoming'. (Palmer)

Buddhist meditation

Specification content

Challenges including lack of empirical evidence for Jungian concepts and reductionist views regarding religious belief arising from acceptance of Jung's ideas.

Key quotes

The hypothesis of the collective unconscious is ... a quite unnecessary elaboration to explain certain observations which can be more simply explained in another way. (**Brown**)

A subjective feeling of the truth of an idea is no support for its being accepted as a hypothesis. (**Popper**)

... if religion is a relation to psychic events ... to events of one's own soul ... then it is not a relation to a Being or Reality ... More precisely, it is not the relation of an I to a Thou. This is, however, the way in which the unmistakable religious of all ages have understood their religion ... (**Buber**)

Key terms

Empirical evidence: knowledge received by means of the senses, particularly by observation and experimentation

Theravada Buddhism: a school of Buddhism that draws its scriptural inspiration from the Pali canon

AO1 Activity

Find out some more archetypal symbols that can be found in religions you have studied and for each one:

a. Explain what it is an archetype of.

b. Whether or not there is supportive enough evidence for this.

c. Whether or not it would stand up to the challenges above.

Challenges – lack of empirical evidence for Jungian concepts

Jung's central claims concerning archetypes do have some support in that they appear in myths and religions of some cultures and also in dreams of people. However, it has not been possible to devise any method of research that could fully verify Jung's claims. It cannot be demonstrated by empirical evidence that there is a collective unconscious which contains the archetypes. A resemblance between effects does not establish a similarity in causes. Therefore, there may be other theories to account for the fact of parallel imagery.

The psychologist, Gordon Allport, pointed out that a far better explanation is that the images result from a conformity to culture. However, Jung assumes that similar images and motifs are evidence of archetypes, and because he claims that an archetype is a collective concept, these various images can be grouped such that a unity of meaning can be attached to all those in that group. As Michael Palmer comments: 'Thus, from the contingent appearance of such images Jung infers a necessary proposition about human beings in general, which will therefore be applicable no matter what images they may construct.' Jung does not provide us with any criterion by which we can distinguish one archetypal image from another.

It means that any image a person has must, by definition, relate to an archetypal group and so have a particular meaning. Another assumption that Jung makes is that human beings have an *a priori* disposition to construct God-images. In other words, God-images and therefore religious beliefs are innate. Jung avoided making predictions based on his theories and that freed him from ever being proved wrong.

Hall and Lindzey accused Jung of relying on clinical and armchair techniques of research rather than on experimentation and quantification.

Challenges – reductionist views regarding religious belief

Many would argue that an experience which stems from the mind and as such is in no way external to the subject, cannot be termed religious. Christ, for example, is more than just a symbol for something else. He is an historical person who many regard as the Son of God. Fromm said that Jung was 'seemingly indifferent to the striving for truth that lies at the heart of religious aspirations'.

Therefore, it seems that Jung did not believe in the existence of God in the traditional sense of an external being. He did not dismiss the possibility but thought we can never know whether God exists. Jung follows Kant in his views about theistic proofs. Both agree that no argument from experience can prove the existence of anything that lies beyond the boundaries of human experience. However, Jung argues that human beings possess the property of formulating God-images and so infers our collective unconscious contains the archetypal God-form.

The term 'religion' then becomes so broad in scope that it seems an applicable term to use for any system of ideas. This makes it virtually impossible for anyone to be referred to as a non-believer. Jung seems to ignore the existence of atheists and non-theistic faiths such as Theravada Buddhism.

What is important to Jung is not the historical Jesus and whether there was an actual person Jesus, but the psychic experience witnessed to by the title 'Christ'. For Jung, Jesus is the exemplification of an archetype. For Christians, such an understanding of Jesus and Christianity would be unacceptable.

Equally controversial was Jung's book *Answer to Job* (1951) in which he argues that both good and evil are aspects of God.

AO1 Developing skills

It is now important to consider the information that has been covered in this section; however, the information in its raw form is too extensive and so has to be processed in order to meet the requirements of the examination. This can be done by practising more advanced skills associated with AO1. The exercises that run throughout this book will help you to do this and prepare you for the examination. For assessment objective 1 (AO1), which involves demonstrating 'knowledge' and 'understanding' skills, we are going to focus on different ways in which the skills can be demonstrated effectively, and also refer to how the performance of these skills is measured (see generic band descriptors for A2 [WJEC] AO1 or A Level [Eduqas] AO1).

▶ **Your task is this:** Below is a **summary on Individuation**. You want to explain this in an essay but they are your teacher's notes and so to write them out is simply copying them and not demonstrating any understanding. Re-write your teacher's notes but you need to replace the words used (apart from key religious or philosophical terminology) with different words so that you show that you understand what is being written and that you have your own unique version.

Individuation is the process of attaining wholeness and balance. It is all about balancing opposites – of the conscious and the unconscious. It is about accepting what has been repressed and finding the Self. The goal of the individuation process is about the realisation of the Self. Individuation means becoming an in-dividual and implies becoming one's own self. Hence it is often referred to as self-realisation. The numerous archetypal symbols that express and bring about the union of opposites turn out to be the images, dogmas and rites that make up religious traditions. The Lotus symbol is a good example of uniting opposites. It is by means of the symbols of the archetypes that the archetypes are brought into our consciousness from the collective unconscious. Christ is a good example of an archetypal symbol. It is through the help of these symbols that the repressed traits that are our true self are integrated into our consciousness and we realise our true self. The mandala is often a symbol of the Self archetype. Some people see the process of individuation at work within Buddhist meditation. The Brahma Viharas is a good example of developing positive, wholesome images for reflection.

The process of individuation is therapeutically necessary and it is the archetypes that direct it. Individuation is innate to individuals, a natural law of the psyche. This means that to a greater or lesser extent all human beings engage in the process of self-realisation.

When you have completed the task, refer to the band descriptors for A2 (WJEC) or A Level (Eduqas) and in particular have a look at the demands described in the higher band descriptors towards which you should be aspiring.

Key skills

Knowledge involves:

Selection of a range of (thorough) accurate and relevant information that is directly related to the specific demands of the question.

This means:

- Selecting relevant material for the question set
- Be focused in explaining and examining the material selected.

Understanding involves:

Explanation that is extensive, demonstrating depth and/or breadth with excellent use of evidence and examples including (where appropriate) thorough and accurate supporting use of sacred texts, sources of wisdom and specialist language.

This means:

- Effective use of examples and supporting evidence to establish the quality of your understanding
- Ownership of your explanation that expresses personal knowledge and understanding and NOT just a chunk of text from a book that you have rehearsed and memorised.

Specification content

The extent to which Jung was more positive than Freud about the idea of God.

Key quote

Difficult to answer, I know. I don't need to believe. I know. (Jung at age 85 – when asked whether he believed in God)

Psychotherapy

AO2 **Activity**

As you read through this section try to do the following:

1. Pick out the different lines of argument that are presented in the text and identify any evidence given in support.

2. For each line of argument try to evaluate whether or not you think this is strong or weak.

3. Think of any questions you may wish to raise in response to the arguments.

This Activity will help you to start thinking critically about what you read and help you to evaluate the effectiveness of different arguments and from this develop your own observations, opinions and points of view that will help with any conclusions that you make in your answers to the AO2 questions that arise.

Issues for analysis and evaluation

The extent to which Jung was more positive than Freud about the idea of God

Freud is usually portrayed as being negative about the idea of God whilst Jung is seen as more positive. However, this is far from agreed as many see both Freud and Jung as equally negative.

Freud likened religion to mental illness. It was just another form of neurosis (in particular a sexual neurosis) where both the religious worshipper and the obsessional neurotic spend hours carrying out certain rituals. If the rituals are omitted or not performed in the correct way then the person becomes anxious and apprehensive. Therefore, just as the obsessional neurotic needs therapy and treatment to rid themselves of this neurosis, so also the religious worshipper needs therapy to free them from their neurosis. Seen in this light, religion is harmful and limiting.

Although Freud considers different causes of the neurosis (primal horde theory, totemism, Oedipus complex, father-figure), they all share the same theme – the neurosis is the result of repression.

Religion is not something that heals and makes whole but rather something that needs healing and curing. Religion is infantile and can lead to people not taking action to better society. They turn to pray to an omnipotent benevolent father-figure rather than act themselves. Freud sees the idea of God as a creation of the individual human mind and its neurotic desires. The neurosis of religion is seen to stem from the conflict between the conscious and unconscious mind, whereby the individual represses impulses and past associations.

In contrast, Jung appears to present a much more positive view of religion. He rejects the idea of religion as a sexual neurosis. The unconscious is not seen as some sort of storage room that stores uncomfortable material from a person's childhood, with those memories and impulses repressed. Instead, by unlocking the deepest level of the unconscious, it leads to the focus on the primordial and archetypal images of humanity, namely the collective unconscious. It is from the collective unconscious that we acquire the qualities of an archetype which, in turn, mould and influence our behaviour. For Jung, God is an expression of the collective unconscious.

Hence, religion is positive. It is about the evolving process in the development of the psychic personality – integrating the conscious and unconscious aspects of the psyche. Freud saw religion as a mixture of guilt-ridden repressions and obsessions expressed through ritual. Jung, however, saw religion as a natural and legitimate dimension of psychic activity. Religious images are simply images of the deeper self and through these religious images the personality achieves its goal of integration. Therefore, for Jung, God was a reality from the deepest part of the human collective unconscious.

Religion is therefore both positive and beneficial since it is necessary for human psychic development. It is an essential activity of human beings. A lack of religious feelings or belief implied a failure by the person to integrate the unconscious and the conscious mind. Whereas Freud saw symbols as a way an individual sought to avoid reality, Jung saw symbols as the way to gain knowledge of realities which in themselves were unknowable. Symbols transformed rather than led to neurosis. In suggesting the presence of this universal archetypal image of God, it can be seen that Jung confirms religion as a fundamental activity of the human psyche.

Rudolf Otto introduced the term 'numinous' in relation to religious experience. Jung 'extended its meaning ... by conferring a numinous quality upon the experience of the archetype' (Ellenberger: *The Discovery of the Unconscious*).

Hence, by bringing an experience of the archetype into consciousness, the individual can realise an authentic religious experience. The world's religions were founded by individuals who had intense religious experiences. For instance, Buddha attaining enlightenment under the Bodhi tree and Mohammed hearing God's voice in a cave in the desert. Whilst Freud regarded the essence of the religious experience as a neurotic symptom and therefore negative, Jung saw it as something positive – as either evidence of the divine or a psychological component within all of us, the Self, capable of insight and wisdom.

Some make out a case for both Freud and Jung being equally negative about the idea of God. Like Freud, Jung recognised a relation between religion and neurosis. Jung asserted that 'among all his patients in the second half of life there is not one whose main problem is not related to his attitude towards religion'.

Neither Freud nor Jung understood religion in its traditional sense. Freud viewed it in terms of rituals whilst Jung understood it in terms of religious symbols and religious experiences. Although Jung did not call religion a 'universal obsessional neurosis', he did view all religions to be collective mythologies. In essence they were not real but did have an effect on the human personality. Dr Szasz (*The Myth of Psychotherapy*) commented that 'in Jung's view religions are indispensable spiritual supports, whereas in Freud's they are illusory crutches'. Freud saw religions as delusionary and evil whilst Jung saw them as imaginary but good. Both can therefore be seen as negative. Jung saw religion only as a tool to tap into the self.

It could be argued that neither Freud nor Jung actually claimed that God did not exist. However, neither of them seemed interested in objective truth or thought of the idea of God in the traditional sense of an external being. Some regard Jung as a founder of the New Age Movement. When Jung, at the age of 85, was asked whether he believed in God he replied 'Difficult to answer, I know. I don't need to believe.' In letters he wrote after the interview, he tried to explain what he meant – 'The God-image is the expression of an underlying experience of something which I cannot attain to by intellectual means.' (Jung 1959).

Many see Jung as undermining the doctrines of Christianity. Jung's essay on Job was seen as very controversial in that it argued God sent his son to humankind to be sacrificed in repentance for God's sins, especially for his treatment of Job. Jung sees this as a sign of God's ongoing psychological development.

Some see truths of religion in Freud's claim that the present is a direct and unavoidable consequence of the past and the experience of repression is repeated in every individual. This could be seen to bear some links with Christianity in terms of the Fall and original sin. Therefore, there are some areas of Freud's theories that, although they could be suggested to be negative, would more accurately be described as being realistic.

Freud also highlighted the struggle between the superego and the id, which has parallels in religions with the struggle between the spiritual and the unspiritual. This is not necessarily a negative thing but could be seen as a learning experience and one that helps a person to grow emotionally and spiritually.

In comparison, Jung argued that each of us has a Self-archetype and the Self most closely approximates to the divine. Individuation is innate to individuals and this could be seen to have parallels with the idea of human beings created in the image of God and having a spiritual aspect or imprint as part of their being.

Indeed, a Jesuit theologian, Raymond Hostie, wrote that Jung had 'rediscovered the religious and the sacred and got rid of an overwhelming rationalism'. (*Religion and the Psychology of Jung*, 1957)

Overall, it would be unwise perhaps to suggest that Freud was positive about religion; however, although it is clear that Jung could be argued to be more positive, there are areas of Freud's theories that are not overtly negative.

Key quotes

For what I want to do I do not do, but what I hate I do… For I have the desire to do what is good, but I cannot carry it out. (**Romans 7**)

…my work has proved empirically that the pattern of God exists in every man … (**Jung**)

Study tip

Once again, think about your evaluation skills and try to develop your critical analysis by ranking the arguments put forward in order of effectiveness. Choose a strong argument and a weaker argument and explain the reasons why this is the case in your view.

AO2 Activity

List some conclusions that could be drawn from the AO2 reasoning from the above text; try to aim for at least three different possible conclusions. Consider each of the conclusions and collect brief evidence to support each conclusion from the AO1 and AO2 material for this topic. Select the conclusion that you think is most convincing and explain why it is so. Try to contrast this with the weakest conclusion in the list, justifying your argument with clear reasoning and evidence.

Specification content

The effectiveness of empirical approaches as critiques of Jungian views of religion.

To what extent are critiques of empirical approaches effective critiques of Jungian views of religion?

Empirical evidence includes the record of one's direct observations or experiences, and these can be analysed both quantitatively and qualitatively. Jung's methodology involved the inclusion of descriptions of certain observable psychic 'facts' such as dreams and visions. They are 'facts' in that they provide knowledge of our own psychic world.

Jung maintained that using subjective personal experiences was valid as an empirical method, since the imaging of reality by the psyche was the only reality for the individual who creates it.

In *Psychology and Religion* (1938) Jung claimed that 'although I have often been called a philosopher, I am an empiricist and adhere as such to the phenomenological standpoint'. For Jung, facts denote psychic phenomena since they provide knowledge of our own psychic world. Indeed, Jung argued that only psychic existence is immediately verifiable and so when empiricists investigate the world they discover facts which by necessity are psychic.

The problem appears to be that whilst empirical approaches can in themselves be criticised for being selective, unrepresentative, not entirely proof and subject to interpretation, there also appears to be another layer of similar criticism when applied to the Jungian view of religion because there is no empirical proof in the sense of physical proof. However, it should always be remembered that just as any physical experiment has an element of observation and interpretation, so too, Jung's methodology is also based on the two same principles of observation and interpretation.

It could be argued that Jung did use empirical evidence provided by his research into ancient myths and legends. The images he referred to clearly exerted a hold on the human mind. Further support came from his observation that human beings have collective ideas and common ethics that could be found in all religions. The constant recurrence of symbols from mythology in personal therapy supports the idea of an innate collective cultural residue.

Another line of argument that could be followed might focus on the success of his theories in leading to wholeness of the individual. His psychotherapy practices achieved positive results so it might be argued that the successful outcomes in his patients proved his theories correct.

In recent times, the Myers-Briggs Type Indicator (MBTI), has become a popular psychometric instrument, and was developed from Jung's theory of psychological types.

However, his methodology was questioned, not just because of the areas he included as valid evidence such as dreams and beliefs, but because he derived from them metaphysical explanations, such as the collective unconscious and archetypes.

Jung's approach was, and continues to be, challenged and accused of being unscientific. Michael Palmer notes that in 1968, the co-founder of the Jung Institute in Zurich, called for a 'more scientific approach in Jungian psychology'. Similarly, Mary Mattoon argued that these psychic 'facts' were 'useful in the context of discovery, but not in the context of justification'.

Alternatively, one could argue that a basic test of a scientific statement is whether it is falsifiable. Since Jung's evidence is derived from inner psychological states then the 'observation' of this is not really the same as observing at which temperature water boils.

Key quote

Although I have often been called a philosopher, I am an empiricist and adhere as such to the phenomenological standpoint. (Jung)

AO2 Activity

As you read through this section try to do the following:

1. Pick out the different lines of argument that are presented in the text and identify any evidence given in support.

2. For each line of argument try to evaluate whether or not you think this is strong or weak.

3. Think of any questions you may wish to raise in response to the arguments.

This Activity will help you to start thinking critically about what you read and help you to evaluate the effectiveness of different arguments and from this develop your own observations, opinions and points of view that will help with any conclusions that you make in your answers to the AO2 questions that arise.

In reality, Jung is concerned about what the state of mind is that is actually being experienced by the subject; he is not concerned whether the subjective experience has any grounding in a reality that is separate from the subject. This is where, for many, the second layer of investigation is removed from scientific method. Whatever is derived from the experience is subjective.

This would mean that truth in these circumstances is not about whether the experience corresponds to reality but about whether the subjective experience was a genuine experience.

For example, it is not the historical Jesus that is important for many Christians when considering the Christ of faith. Christian experience and the experience of the early Christian church is the interpretation of events that for many belong to the realm of faith and not science. It is this experience that, although real, is not necessarily 'real' in the empirical understanding of what reality consists of and is therefore not verifiable through scientific/historical methods. For thinkers like Jung and Rudolph Bultmann, a Christian theologian, the issues of what is 'real' and what is 'historical' are entirely different.

Jung argued that the truth of a psychic experience does not depend on whether it corresponds to reality but solely on whether it is 'felt' to be true. He rarely, if ever, made predictions and so this freed him from being proved wrong. His theories were shaped by his own dreams, thoughts and introspection in addition to that of his patients. Many would therefore claim that observations are not adequate scientific observation for the basis of a major theory on human personality.

Jung's approach towards empirical evidence means that it is not clear whether God is to be seen merely as part of the human psyche or as something distinct from it. The nature of religious experience is unclear. Is it something generated by the psyche and therefore merely psychological, or is it a response to an objective deity?

Another line of argument might be to challenge the value of empirical evidence on the grounds that we should be sceptical about our senses. As Hilary Putman noted, we could all be a brain in a vat, stimulated electrically in such a way as to give us the delusive experience of living the life with which we are familiar. Indeed we could also doubt our reasoning abilities. Such an approach to empirical evidence would mean that any critique of Jung's use of empirical approaches would be of no importance in weighing up Jung's view of religion.

Some would argue that these criticisms are sufficient to reject Jung's views about religion. His methodology is flawed and so his conclusions are invalid. However, they appear to be no more invalid than those of religious believers.

Others are more reluctant to dismiss Jung's explanations. They draw attention to Jung's study of comparative mythology, the findings of which give support for his theories. Indeed, many see his theories as a bridge between the scientific and the religious that is both respectful and non-judgemental by avoiding issues of empirical verification.

Overall, one could coherently argue that even if the evidence is not verifiable, Jung's theories still give an explanation for religious beliefs that is consistent with the evidence.

Study tip

When evaluating and critically analysing evidence and arguments it is good practice to challenge these by thinking of questions you could ask in response to what is argued or presented.

AO2 Activity

List some conclusions that could be drawn from the AO2 reasoning from the above text; try to aim for at least three different possible conclusions. Consider each of the conclusions and collect brief evidence to support each conclusion from the AO1 and AO2 material for this topic. Select the conclusion that you think is most convincing and explain why it is so. Try to contrast this with the weakest conclusion in the list, justifying your argument with clear reasoning and evidence.

Key skills

Analysis involves identifying issues raised by the materials in the AO1, together with those identified in the AO2 section, and presents sustained and clear views, either of scholars or from a personal perspective ready for evaluation.

This means:

- That your answers are able to identify key areas of debate in relation to a particular issue

- That you can identify, and comment upon, the different lines of argument presented by others

- That your response comments on the overall effectiveness of each of these areas or arguments.

Evaluation involves considering the various implications of the issues raised based upon the evidence gleaned from analysis and provides an extensive detailed argument with a clear conclusion.

This means:

- That your answer weighs up the consequences of accepting or rejecting the various and different lines of argument analysed

- That your answer arrives at a conclusion through a clear process of reasoning.

AO2 Developing skills

It is now important to consider the information that has been covered in this section; however, the information in its raw form is too extensive and so has to be processed in order to meet the requirements of the examination. This can be done by practising more advanced skills associated with AO2. The exercises that run throughout this book will help you to do this and prepare you for the examination.

For assessment objective 2 (AO2), which involves 'critical analysis' and 'evaluation' skills, we are going to focus on different ways in which the skills can be demonstrated effectively, and also refer to how the performance of these skills is measured (see generic band descriptors for A2 [WJEC] AO2 or A Level [Eduqas] AO2).

▶ **Your task is this:** Below is a **brief summary of two different points of view concerning the degree of success of Jung's explanation of religion**. You want to use these two views and lines of argument for an evaluation; however, they need further reasons and evidence for support to fully develop the argument. Re-write these two views in a fully evaluative style by adding further reasons and evidence that link to their arguments.

Jung has shown through his study of world religions the similarity between the different religions, particularly in their images and symbols. It seems reasonable to assume that those similarities are not just coincidental, but they originate from similar sources. Jung concluded that these symbols are symbols of archetypes that are in the collective unconscious. His psychoanalysis of patients was evidence that our repressed traits are brought into our consciousness by the archetypal symbols. They need to be integrated into our consciousness so we can realise our true self. This is a religious quest since religious images are simply images of the deeper self. A religious experience is an encounter with the Self. This understanding of religion is closer to Asian rather than Western religions. It explains religion for the 21st century.

Jung's explanation of religion is firstly without evidence and secondly not about religion. He claims to be scientific but he offers theories that cannot be verified. His whole evidence rests on subjective personal experiences but he seems unconcerned whether the content of these experiences accurately relate to reality. Equally, it describes religion but that is not what is meant traditionally by religion. Jung talks about Christ but not in the way Christians understand Christ. It fails on a third area and that is that Jung fails to explain atheism. There are better explanations of religion than Jung offers.

When you have completed the task, refer to the band descriptors for A2 (WJEC) or A Level (Eduqas) and in particular have a look at the demands described in the higher band descriptors towards which you should be aspiring. Ask yourself:

- Is my answer a confident critical analysis and perceptive evaluation of the issue?

- Is my answer a response that successfully identifies and thoroughly addresses the issues raised by the question set?

- Does my work show an excellent standard of coherence, clarity and organisation?

- Will my work, when developed, contain thorough, sustained and clear views that are supported by extensive, detailed reasoning and/or evidence?

- Are the views of scholars/schools of thought used extensively, appropriately and in context?

- Does my answer convey a confident and perceptive analysis of the nature of any possible connections with other elements of my course?

- When used, is specialist language and vocabulary both thorough and accurate?

F: Issues relating to rejection of religion: Atheism

Rejection of belief in deities

It is usually stated that Diagoras of Melos was the first atheist. He lived in the 5th century BCE and was a Greek poet and **sophist**. Only anecdotes remain about his views concerning the worship of national gods but his views seemed sufficiently offensive at the time to force him to flee Athens for fear of his life. Possibly an even earlier example of atheism can be found in the Asian religions of Jainism, Buddhism and Taoism, since they do not include a deity as such and can be dated as far back as the 6th century BCE. However, many would argue that this is a simplistic view of those religions and stems from their rejection of the idea of a creator god.

The word 'atheistic' appears in ancient Greek and has the meaning of 'godless' or 'disrespecting the local gods' even though they may have believed in other gods. A good example is Socrates who was accused of corrupting Athenian youth by encouraging them not to believe in the city's gods. Socrates regarded Homer's gods as corrupt, vain and self-serving – basically childish and embarrassing. He described them as human beings writ large, complete with vices and virtues.

The Greek word atheoi can be found in the New Testament in Ephesians 2:12. Here it means 'without God'. In other words, the people had no real knowledge of God rather than they refused to believe in God.

Justyn Martyr the Christian apologist in the second century, pointed out that Christians such as himself 'were even called "atheists" – which we are in relation to what you consider gods, but are most certainly not in relation to the Most True God'.

However, it was the great European movements of the **Renaissance** and the **Reformation** that coined the term 'atheist'. The term was used exclusively as an insult, according to the author Karen Armstrong, as nobody wanted to be regarded as an atheist since it implied the person lacked moral restraint.

Key quotes

If atheism were generally accepted, every form of religion would be destroyed, and cut off at its roots. There would be no more theological wars, no more soldiers of religion – such terrible soldiers. Deaf to all other voices, tranquil mortals would follow only the spontaneous dictates of their own being, the only commands which ... can lead to happiness. **(La Mettrie)**

Abandoning faith is the first step to enjoying life. There is no life to come, only a life in the present, which we ought to enjoy as much as possible. Obedience to natural desires is what really matters and belief in God is just a repressive superstition. **(Marquis de Sade)**

Papyrus 46 showing the word atheoi from Ephesians 2:12

This section covers AO1 content and skills

Specification content
Rejection of belief in deities.

Socrates (470–399 BCE)

quickfire

2.18 What forced Socrates to flee for his life from Athens?

quickfire

2.19 Which two great movements in Europe coined the term 'atheist'?

Key terms

Reformation: the religious movement in Europe in 16th century which led to the creation and rise of Protestantism

Renaissance: period of European history between 14th and 17th century which was a time of great revival of art, literature and learning

Sophists: Greek teachers and writers particularly skilled in reasoning

Key quotes

It is a short step from the thought that the different religions cannot all be true, although they all claim to be, to the thought that in all probability none of them is true. (Hick)

God is the sum of our values, representing to us their ideal unity, their claims upon us and their creative power. (Cupitt)

The Sea of Faith
Was once, too, at the full, and round earth's shore
Lay like the folds of a bright girdle furl'd.
But now I only hear
Its melancholy, long, withdrawing roar,
Retreating, to the breath
Of the night-wind, down the vast edges drear
And naked shingles of the world.

A stanza from the poem 'Dover Beach' by Matthew Arnold

Key term

The Age of Enlightenment:
an intellectual and philosophical movement in Europe in the 18th century

quickfire

2.20 Who first described God as 'the ground of our being'?

quickfire

2.21 What is the name given to the militant form of atheism associated with people like Christopher Hitchens and Richard Dawkins?

THERE'S PROBABLY NO GOD.
NOW STOP WORRYING AND ENJOY YOUR LIFE.

The atheist bus campaign

Two further movements in the 18th century made an impact on challenging belief in God. The first was **the Age of Enlightenment** which encouraged individuals to think for themselves and appealed to both human reason and the scientific method as the means of finding truth. Secondly, the French Revolution of 1789 mobilised intellectuals who saw the Church as an outmoded institution that propped up the monarchy.

By the 1770s, atheism was ceasing to be a dangerous accusation such that it was evolving into a position that some felt they could openly avow. The word atheism had now taken on the meaning of a denial of the existence of God or, at the very least, that one should live one's life with disregard towards a god.

The last person who was jailed for being an atheist in Britain was George Holyoake in 1842. He was sentenced to 6 months' imprisonment. In 1880, Charles Bradlaugh was elected as the Liberal MP for Northampton. His refusal to take a parliamentary Oath of Allegiance on the Bible, rather than just to affirm his Oath of Allegiance without religious basis, resulted in him not being allowed to take his seat. He was re-elected several times over five years, but did not take his seat until 1886. When he eventually took his seat he became Britain's first openly atheist Member of Parliament.

During the 20th century, atheists in Western societies had become more active and even state atheism emerged in Asian Europe and Asia, particularly in the Soviet Union and in Communist China.

Through increased travel and communication people became aware of other religions. As a result, it seemed that there were contradictions between the religions. They appeared to say different and incompatible things about the nature of ultimate reality, divine activity and the destiny of the human race. It was argued that which religion you follow depends on where you are born and has little to do with truth.

Don Cupitt (b. 1934)

The 1960s saw a movement from within the Christian Church that many viewed as closer to atheism than theism. This theological movement claimed it was no longer tenable to hold the traditional view of God being 'out there'. God is just a very powerful symbol, but has no 'real' objective or empirical existence.

The Anglican bishop John Robinson popularised these views in Britain. His book *Honest to God* (1963) described God as 'the ground of our being' instead of the traditional view that God was an objective personal force. Traditional theistic thinking placed God outside and above the world. However, Robinson placed God deep in the human person. So he argued that everyone needs to look inside themselves to find God.

Later Don Cupitt (1980s) who was both an Anglican priest and Dean of Emmanuel College Cambridge, presented a TV series entitled 'Sea of Faith'. The title was taken from the poem 'Dover Beach' by Matthew Arnold in which the poet expresses regret that belief in a supernatural world is slowly slipping away. In his TV series, Cupitt charted the transition from some form of traditional belief in God to a rejection of the supernatural world. God existed as an idea in the minds of believers rather than an external, objective being. This new understanding of religious faith gave rise to the 'Sea of Faith' Movement.

A feature of the 21st century has been the high profile promotion of a more militant form of atheism, whose term 'New Atheism' was associated with people like Christopher Hitchens and Richard Dawkins. It sees religion as a threat to the survival of the human race. The concept of God is seen as a totalitarian belief that destroys individual freedom.

The differences between agnosticism and atheism

As we have seen above, the definition of atheism has changed through the centuries. Alister McGrath defines atheism as 'the religion of the autonomous and rational human being, who believes that reason is able to uncover and express the deepest truths of the universe'.

There are various shades of atheism. Antony Flew in his book *The Presumption of Atheism* (1972) first introduced the terms 'weak' and 'strong' atheism. He argued that atheism should be the default position.

'**Negative (weak) atheism**' – where the atheist does not make the positive claim that God does not exist. It is the theist who makes the assertion and therefore it is the theist that bears the burden of proof. The atheist merely says that that she does not believe any deities exist but does not assert as true that no deities exist.

Hence, a negative atheist would say:

'*I don't believe that God exists, but tell me why you do believe in God?*'

'**Positive (strong) atheism**' – in this case both the atheist and the theist have to give reasons to defend their belief. A positive atheist asserts that she knows that God or gods do not exist. In a similar way the theist asserts that God exists.

Hence, a positive atheist would say:

'*I know God does not exist, and here are my reasons, so why do you believe in God?*'

Further types of atheism include:

'**Protest atheism**' – which is a revolt against God on moral grounds. In Dostoyevsky's novel *The Brothers Karamazov*, the atheist Ivan recounts a story about a young boy who was torn apart by hunting dogs in front of the boy's mother. Ivan comments that even if God did exist (which he did not believe anyway) he would want nothing to do with him.

Hence, a Protest atheist would say:

'*Even if God did exist I could not morally accept God.*'

'**New Atheism**' (antitheism) – the belief that religion is a threat to the survival of the human race. This view of atheism is a hostile reaction to theism and is expounded by Richard Dawkins in his book *The God Delusion*.

A New Atheist would say:

'*I don't believe God exists, and neither must you.*'

In contrast, agnosticism is commonly used to indicate a suspension of the decision to accept or reject belief in God. The term 'agnostic' was first used by the English biologist Thomas Huxley in a speech at a meeting of the Metaphysical Society in 1869. The word is derived from the Greek, meaning 'without knowledge'.

Therefore, agnosticism embraces the idea that the existence of God or any other ultimate reality is, in principle, unknowable. Our knowledge is limited and we cannot know ultimate reasons for things. It is not that the evidence is lacking, it is that the evidence is never possible.

Many people are convinced that agnosticism is some sort of 'middle way' or 'third way' between atheism and theism. But agnosticism is not about belief in God but about knowledge. It is not a creed but a methodology. Huxley argued that people

Specification content

The differences between agnosticism and atheism.

Key quotes

In this interpretation, an atheist becomes: not someone who positively asserts the non-existence of God; but someone who is simply not a theist. Let us, for future ready reference, introduce the labels 'positive atheist' for the former and 'negative atheist' for the latter. (**Flew**)

Others were quite sure they had attained a certain 'gnosis' – had more or less successfully, solved the problem of existence, while I was quite sure I had not, and had a pretty strong conviction that the problem was insoluble … So I took thought, and invented what I conceived to be the appropriate title of 'agnostic'. (**Huxley**)

Key terms

Negative (weak) atheism: where the atheist does not make the positive claim that God does not exist

New Atheism: also known as antitheism, it is the belief that religion is a threat to the survival of the human race

Positive (strong) atheism: believes that both the atheist and the theist have to give reasons to defend their belief

Protest atheism: a revolt against God on moral grounds

Thomas Huxley (1825–1895)

Key quote

As a philosopher, if I were speaking to a purely philosophic audience I should say that I ought to describe myself as an Agnostic, because I do not think that there is a conclusive argument by which one can prove that there is not a God. On the other hand, if I am to convey the right impression to the ordinary man in the street I think I ought to say that I am an Atheist, because when I say that I cannot prove that there is not a God, I ought to add equally that I cannot prove that there are not the Homeric gods. (Russell)

I have never been an atheist in the sense of denying the existence of a God. I think that generally ... an agnostic would be the most correct description of my state of mind. (Darwin)

I am agnostic only to the extent that I am agnostic about fairies at the bottom of the garden. (Dawkins)

Specification content

The rise of New Atheism (antitheism); its main criticisms of religion; non-thinking; infantile world-view; impedes scientific progress.

Key terms

Strong agnosticism: the assertion that it is impossible to know whether or not God exists

Weak agnosticism: the belief that the existence of God is currently unknown, but it is not necessarily unknowable

quickfire

2.22 Who first used the term 'agnostic'?

should not pretend that conclusions are certain which are not demonstrated or demonstrable.

Just as with atheism, there are various shades of agnosticism:

'**Strong agnosticism**' – the assertion that it is impossible to know whether or not God exists. It is unknowable because our knowledge is limited, and we cannot know ultimate reasons for things. It is not that the evidence is lacking, it is that the evidence is never possible.

A strong agnostic would say:

'*I don't know whether God exists or not, and neither do you.*'

'**Weak agnosticism**' – the belief that the existence of God is currently unknown, but it is not necessarily unknowable. God may exist or may not exist but judgement has to be withheld until evidence becomes available. This is the common usage of agnosticism where it indicates a suspension of a decision.

A weak agnostic would say:

'*I don't know whether God exists or not, but maybe you do.*'

In recent years the meaning of agnosticism has shifted again. The philosopher Nicholas Everitt, in *The Non-existence of God* (2004), uses it to apply to someone who thinks God's existence and his non-existence are equally probable. This usage reflects the postmodern idea of rejecting absolute certainties about knowledge.

AO1 Activity

Look at the different definitions of atheists and agnostics and if one suits your position explain why this is the case and justify this to your group. If you are a believer use the definition style used by Flew to explain your own position and justify this to the group.

The rise of New Atheism (antitheism)

On 11 September 2001 there was a series of four coordinated terrorist attacks by Islamic terrorists on the United States. In the aftermath, there began a powerful attack on religion, as religion was seen as the main cause of the catastrophe. It triggered a movement that saw not just religious extremists but religion in general as dangerous and deluded.

The first person to express this view was Sam Harris who published his views in his bestselling book *The End of Faith* (2004). By 2006 two other voices had joined the debate, publishing popular books of their own. Richard Dawkins wrote *The God Delusion* and Daniel Dennett wrote *Breaking the Spell*. In that same year, the term 'New Atheism' came into being. Its originator was Gary Wolf who wrote an article about the three authors for the British magazine *Wired*. A year later Christopher Hitchens wrote a best seller called *God Is Not Great* expressing similar views and the phrase 'the Four Horsemen (of the Non-Apocalypse)' soon began to be used to refer to the four of them.

Atheists in the past have argued that those who believe in God are wrong but have shown little or no hostility towards religious belief or practice. However, New Atheism is antitheism. It displays an intense anger against religion and sees it as harmful. Alister McGrath comments that New Atheism defines itself by what it is against rather than by what it is for.

Its main criticisms – non-thinking

One of the core defining characteristics of New Atheism is its emphasis on rationality and its vehemently held view that faith and religion are irrational. Dawkins argues that religion involves faith, and faith by nature is opposed to evidence. He considers that all faith is blind trust, in the absence of evidence, even in the teeth of evidence. Faith is intellectually irresponsible. According to Dawkins, 'Faith is the great cop-out, the great excuse to evade the need to think and evaluate evidence ... Faith is not allowed to justify itself by argument'.

In *The God Delusion*, Dawkins argues that religious people are non-thinking. He claims that religious people know, without evidence, that the faith of their birth is the one true faith, all others being aberrations or downright false. Faith is infantile and so Dawkins points out that Christian and Muslim children are brought up to believe unquestioningly. Belief in God is something forced upon children by adults and so should be rejected. Dawkins likens faith in God to believing in Santa Claus and the Tooth Fairy. When you grow up, you grow out of it. His analogy contends that both represent belief in non-existent entities.

For New Atheists, the accusation about non-thinking goes far beyond just sloppy thinking or irrationality. It is dangerous and leads to fanaticism. Even mild and moderate religion helps to provide the climate of faith in which extremism naturally flourishes. In *The God Delusion* Dawkins asks why nineteen well-educated middle-class men traded their lives in this world for the privilege of killing thousands. His conclusion was that they believed they would go straight to paradise for doing so. It is religion itself that is to blame not religious extremism. In contrast, though atheists have also done terrible things, they did not do them because of atheism but for other reasons.

Sam Harris

Richard Dawkins

Daniel Dennett

Christopher Hitchens

The key voices of New Atheism – known as the Four Horsemen.

Its main criticisms – infantile world-view

New Atheism sees the religious view of reality as deficient and impoverished compared with its own world-view. They claim that the kinds of views of the universe which religious people have traditionally embraced have been puny, pathetic and measly in comparison to the way the universe actually is.

In contrast to the impoverished vision of the world that religion offers, science offers a bold and brilliant vision seeing the universe as grand, beautiful and awe-inspiring. Dawkins sees the universe presented by organised religion as 'a poky little medieval universe, and extremely limited'.

Great store is put on science by New Atheism. They claim that deep space, the billions of years of life's evolution, and the microscopic workings of biology and heredity contain more beauty and wonder than do 'myths' and 'pseudoscience'. Natural selection is regarded as sufficient to explain the apparent functionality and non-random complexity of the biological world. New Atheism rejects the idea of the supernatural. They claim that such beliefs fail to do justice to the sublime grandeur of the real world. These beliefs represent a narrowing down from reality, an impoverishment of what the real world has to offer.

God is not required as an explanation for the existence of the universe. God's existence cannot explain the world because he must be at least as complex, and

The trigger for rise of New Atheism – the attack on the Twin Towers.

Key quotes

Many of us saw religion as harmless nonsense. Beliefs might lack all supporting evidence but, we thought, if people needed a crutch for consolation, where's the harm? September 11 changes all that. **(Dawkins)**

I'm not even an atheist so much as I am an antitheist; I not only maintain that all religions are versions of the same untruth, but I hold that the influence of churches, and the effect of religious belief, is positively harmful. **(Hitchens)**

'New Atheism' is neither a movement nor new. What is new is the publication of atheist material by big-name publishers, read by millions, and appearing on bestseller lists. **(Flynn)**

Those who can make you believe absurdities can make you commit atrocities. **(Voltaire)**

For God so loved the world, that he gave his only begotten Son, that whosoever believeth in him will believeth in anything. Hitchens 3:16 **(Hitchens)**

Faith, being belief that isn't based on evidence, is the principal vice of any religion. **(Dawkins)**

Only religious faith is a strong enough force to motivate such utter madness in otherwise sane and decent people. **(Dawkins)**

quickfire

2.24 What three main criticisms does New Atheism raise against religion?

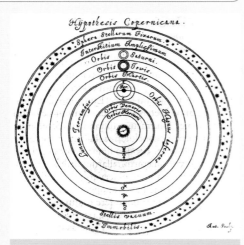

An ancient diagram of the universe

therefore as improbable, as the world itself; and such an improbable entity would also require explanation. Indeed, in *The God Delusion*, Dawkins launches into a long list of the supposed faults of Yahweh, including, 'jealous and proud of it; a petty, unjust, unforgiving control-freak; a vindictive, bloodthirsty ethnic cleanser; a misogynistic, homophobic, racist, infanticidal, genocidal, filicidal, pestilential, megalomaniacal, sadomasochistic, capriciously malevolent bully'.

Its main criticisms – impedes scientific progress

New Atheism affirms a materialist world-outlook. Since matter is law-governed, it can be subject to scientific investigation. Hence, scientific theories are based only on evidence, while religion, they claim, runs away from evidence. Atheism is rational and scientific, while religion is irrational and superstitious. Just as non-thinking and blind faith lead to fanaticism and violence, so blind faith and religious fundamentalism subvert science.

New Atheists see blind faith in the truth of the holy book as axiomatic for religions. Therefore, if the book is true and evidence seems to contradict it, then the evidence, rather than the book, needs to be thrown out. Dawkins argues that when a science book is wrong, someone eventually discovers the mistake and it is corrected in subsequent books. However, that does not happen with holy books.

Religion impedes scientific progress because it teaches us not to change our minds. It saps the intellect. Dawkins sees fundamentalist religion being hell-bent on ruining the scientific education of thousands of young minds and religion in general furthering the idea that unquestioning faith is a virtue.

Religious responses to the challenge of New Atheism

The views expounded by New Atheism have been widely challenged. The fundamental criticism of New Atheism is that it simply attacks easy and lazy caricatures or degenerate forms of religion, ignoring the mainstream reality. It also fails to forward a positive and compelling approach of its own. Its aggressively negative stance led Paul Kurtz to describe it as 'atheist fundamentalism'.

One of the most prolific writers who has addressed the challenges posed by New Atheism is Alister McGrath, a former atheist and now a Christian, who presently holds the Andreas Idreos professorship in Science and Religion at Oxford University as well as professor of Divinity.

Rejection by religious groups of New Atheist claims regarding incompatibility of science and religion

As was noted above, New Atheism takes a strongly positivist view of science, arguing that it explains (or has the potential to explain) everything, including matters traditionally regarded as lying within the religious realm. It denies the idea of multiple explanations of the same things, arguing that only the scientific explanation can be valid. Therefore science and religion are depicted as offering competing explanations.

However, John Polkinghorne sees no competition. He argues that different levels of explanation need weaving together to provide a rich and comprehensive whole. For example, a scientific description of the world may describe the Big Bang and the evolving of living creatures. The religious may speak of God bringing the world into existence and directing it towards its intended outcome. For some it will be seen as a process involving divine action. For others it will be God creating and working through natural forces.

These two accounts supplement rather than contradict each other. The natural world can be interpreted, without any loss of intellectual integrity, in a number of different ways. Indeed, two areas of thought that lie beyond the scope of the natural sciences are the notions of value and meaning – since they are non-empirical.

Alister McGrath argues that evidence and belief in religion is akin to evidence and belief in the natural sciences. Both involve showing that there are good reasons for thinking something is right, without having total confirmation. Dawkins wrongly defines religious faith as believing in something that has no supporting evidence. He fails to make the distinction between the 'total absence of supporting evidence' and the 'absence of totally supporting evidence'.

Increase in fundamental religious activity relating to morality and community

Religious beliefs involve a world-view which is embedded in a person's thinking and behaviour. Therefore, religion cannot be a purely private matter for religious believers. The public and private dimensions of life can never be truly kept separated. The attack on religion from New Atheism has led to some religious groups being more vociferous in their opposition to atheistic trends within society. They see traditional social norms being undermined.

In particular, there has been an upsurge in Islamic and Christian fundamentalism. The word 'fundamentalism' has the meaning of unwavering attachment to a set of irreducible beliefs. As society is viewed as moving away from these fundamental beliefs, so these religious groups become more active in opposing the changes by seeking to influence law and public policy.

For instance, the Christian Right in the USA is an informal coalition of evangelical Protestants and Roman Catholics who seek to apply their understandings of the teachings of Christianity to politics and to public policy. They try to influence and motivate the electorate on particular social issues. The key social issues have been homosexuality, same-sex marriage, abortion and embryonic stem cell research.

In the UK, organisations such as The Christian Institute promote a conservative Christian viewpoint founded on a belief in Biblical inerrancy. The Institute campaigns on social and moral issues seeking to influence Parliament and on occasions taking legal action.

The term 'Islamic fundamentalism' has negative connotations as it is a term associated with groups such as ISIS, designated a terrorist organisation by the United Nations. However, like Christian fundamentalism it can also apply to law-abiding groups following Islam who seek to influence society through social and political action. The implementing of Shari'a law is also a key aim.

Increase in religious apologists in media

The rise of New Atheism has led to much public discussion about Christianity. As a result, it has given a platform for Christian apologists to reaffirm and represent the reasonableness of the Christian faith. It has allowed for a much fuller and more authentic public articulation of the nature and characteristics of Christianity. The church seems to have been prompted to recover an apologetic tradition. The agenda of New Atheism has defined the areas that Christian apologists have had to focus on, e.g. an appeal to the natural sciences in support of faith.

Alister McGrath commented that argument does not create conviction, but the lack of it destroys belief. What seems to be proved may not be embraced; but what no one shows the ability to defend is quickly abandoned.

New Atheism has had a high profile in the media, particularly through the regular television, radio and Internet appearances of Richard Dawkins. The large number of public and university debates featuring one or more of the 'Four Horsemen' has given a platform to various religious apologists such as William Lane Craig debating with Christopher Hitchens. In particular, social media has opened the debate to a wider audience.

Key quotes

The most incomprehensible thing about the universe is that it is comprehensible. (Einstein)

Neither science nor religion can entertain the hope of establishing logically coercive proof of the kind that only a fool could deny. (Polkinghorne)

quickfire

2.25 Name two scientists mentioned who argue that there is no conflict between science and religion.

A Christian Right protest about the treatment of refugees.

AO1 Activity

To help lead you into AO2, hold a class debate gathering from above evidence to support and challenge the view that 'Religion does not have an effective response to the rise of atheism'.

Key skills

Knowledge involves:

Selection of a range of (thorough) accurate and relevant information that is directly related to the specific demands of the question.

This means:

- Selecting relevant material for the question set
- Be focused in explaining and examining the material selected.

Understanding involves:

Explanation that is extensive, demonstrating depth and/or breadth with excellent use of evidence and examples including (where appropriate) thorough and accurate supporting use of sacred texts, sources of wisdom and specialist language.

This means:

- Effective use of examples and supporting evidence to establish the quality of your understanding
- Ownership of your explanation that expresses personal knowledge and understanding and NOT just a chunk of text from a book that you have rehearsed and memorised.

AO1 Developing skills

It is now important to consider the information that has been covered in this section; however, the information in its raw form is too extensive and so has to be processed in order to meet the requirements of the examination. This can be done by practising more advanced skills associated with AO1. The exercises that run throughout this book will help you to do this and prepare you for the examination. For assessment objective 1 (AO1), which involves demonstrating 'knowledge' and 'understanding' skills, we are going to focus on different ways in which the skills can be demonstrated effectively, and also refer to how the performance of these skills is measured (see generic band descriptors for A2 [WJEC] AO1 or A Level [Eduqas] AO1).

▶ **Your task is this:** Below is a **brief summary of the differences between agnosticism and atheism**. You want to explain this in an essay but as they stand at present they are too brief. In order that you demonstrate more depth of understanding, develop this summary by providing examples that will help you explain them further. Aim for 300 words in total.

'Atheism' comes from the Greek word meaning 'without God'. There are various shades of atheism. For instance, 'Protest atheism' is a revolt against God on moral grounds. 'Positive atheism' is the claim that no God or gods exist. 'New Atheism' (antitheism) was coined by Christopher Hitchens.

In contrast, Agnosticism is commonly used to indicate a suspension of the decision to accept or reject belief in God. The term 'agnostic' was first used by the English biologist Thomas Huxley. The word is derived from the Greek, meaning 'without knowledge'. There are different types of agnosticism just as there are different types of atheism.

Agnosticism embraces the idea that the existence of God or any other ultimate reality is, in principle, unknowable. It is not that the evidence is lacking, it is that the evidence is never possible. Some use the word differently.

Many people are convinced that agnosticism is some sort of 'middle way' or 'third way' between atheism and theism. However, Agnosticism is not about belief in God but about knowledge. You can be an agnostic atheist or an agnostic theist.

When you have completed the task, refer to the band descriptors for A2 (WJEC) or A Level (Eduqas) and in particular have a look at the demands described in the higher band descriptors towards which you should be aspiring. Ask yourself:

- Does my work demonstrate thorough, accurate and relevant knowledge and understanding of religion and belief?
- Is my work coherent (consistent or make logical sense), clear and well organised?
- Will my work, when developed, be an extensive and relevant response which is specific to the focus of the task?
- Does my work have extensive depth and/or suitable breadth and have excellent use of evidence and examples?
- If appropriate to the task, does my response have thorough and accurate reference to sacred texts and sources of wisdom?
- Are there any insightful connections to be made with other elements of my course?
- Will my answer, when developed and extended to match what is expected in an examination answer, have an extensive range of views of scholars/schools of thought?
- When used, is specialist language and vocabulary both thorough and accurate?

Issues for analysis and evaluation

The success of atheistic arguments against religious belief

This section covers AO2 content and skills

Specification content
The success of atheistic arguments against religious belief.

New atheism presents atheism as the only option for the serious, progressive, thinking person. Its proponents have focused on the argument that science has disproved God. Indeed, Richard Dawkins argues that religion is 'the root of all evil' for the reason that it goes against all scientific principles and promotes ignorance. It promotes 'non-thinking' and belief is not based on evidence. Rather it is blind faith and religion is seen as irrational. Religion should be abandoned since the human race has progressed and advanced in scientific knowledge.

New Atheism claims that advances in science have now eliminated God from any explanation required of the universe. Science will eventually explain everything. For Dawkins, the 'God of the gaps' is no longer there because the 'gap' is now closed. Science answers our questions about the origin of life and the world without the need for a religious explanation. Although the idea of 'purpose' is used by both science and religion, for the biologist it refers merely to the products of Darwinian natural selection rather than the religious notion of designed for a purpose by an intelligent creator. It is certainly true that science has provided some answers in terms of natural explanations for which previously God had been the explanation.

However, science has serious limitations. The natural sciences are beyond the scope of non-empirical notions such as value and meaning. Science cannot tell us what is right. New Atheism would challenge this response. Atheists such as Sam Harris in his book *The Moral Landscape* argues that moral values are about promoting human well-being and science tells us what promotes well-being . Therefore, science can tell us what is morally right.

Another area connected with science that has been significant in challenging religious belief is empiricism, which is an important aspect of the scientific method. The claim is that God is not open to investigation by means of the senses since God is not a physical object. Science suggests that sense experience is the ultimate source of all our concepts and knowledge. Therefore, scientific theories are based only on evidence while religion, they claim, runs away from evidence. Atheism is rational and scientific while religion is irrational and superstitious.

However, this approach assumes that anything that cannot be verified of falsified is mere private opinion or belief or even delusion. Nonetheless, arguing about the existence of God and the meaning of life is surely open to rational debate even if it is beyond the scientific method. The scientific method draws upon reasonable probabilities rather than certainties, yet Atheists seem to deny any other possibility can occur and so make a deductive error.

The perceived failure of the arguments for God that Dawkins discusses in *The God Delusion* raises doubts about God's existence. At its core, New Atheism views science and religion as in perpetual and principal conflict since any religious explanation operates from the position of faith. Religious faith is seen as a delusion – a fixed false belief. However, such a view appears nonsense since there are many scientists who would claim to hold a religious faith and see no conflict between the two. Another approach might be to claim that science and religion are not in conflict because their relationship is one of independence. Religion deals with ethics and spirituality and science with empirical questions. However, others would argue for a positive and interactive relationship between science and religion, particularly through natural theology. For example, the supposition that the universe has a temporal origin features in contemporary cosmological arguments for the existence of God. The apparent fine-tuning that the universe exhibits is, at the very least, consistent with a religious view of the universe.

AO2 Activity

As you read through this section try to do the following:

1. Pick out the different lines of argument that are presented in the text and identify any evidence given in support.

2. For each line of argument try to evaluate whether or not you think this is strong or weak.

3. Think of any questions you may wish to raise in response to the arguments.

This Activity will help you to start thinking critically about what you read and help you to evaluate the effectiveness of different arguments and from this develop your own observations, opinions and points of view that will help with any conclusions that you make in your answers to the AO2 questions that arise.

Key quotes

To be an empiricist is to withhold belief in anything that goes beyond the actual, observable phenomena. (Fraassen)

[It is as if] a superintellect has monkeyed with physics, as well as with chemistry and biology, and that there are no blind forces worth speaking about in nature (Hoyle)

All religions are versions of the same untruth. (Hitchens)

Rationality is a core part of New Atheism in that it claims that any alternative view is not rational. They claim that religious belief is irrational. However, this is to deny the historical evidence for the faith. For example, in Christianity there is a case to be answered regards the resurrection of Jesus. Even though both sides may disagree it would still be considered a rational debate.

One of the areas where New Atheism has attacked religious belief is the claim that human beings have invented God and that the God they have invented is evil. Dawkins describes the God of the Old Testament as 'arguably the most unpleasant character in all fiction; jealous and proud of it; a petty, unjust, unforgiving control-freak; a vindictive, bloodthirsty ethnic cleanser; a misogynistic, homophobic, racist, infanticidal, genocidal, filicidal, pestilential, megalomaniacal, sadomasochistic, capriciously malevolent bully.'

However, New Atheism's depiction of religion has been accused of being a caricature. It is claimed it misrepresents religion and religious teaching, choosing to focus only on those who are extreme and resort to violence. If God is a human invention, as they argue, then surely that means human beings are the cause of the violence not God. Indeed, religious believers resonate with atheists when it comes to complaints about the behaviour of religious persons. Whether it is the Crusades, religious inquisition, suicide bombings or materialism and the unwillingness to share more than a pittance with those in need – all such actions are unworthy of religious persons. However, no matter how badly religious persons behave, it does not disprove God or particular doctrines. It merely shows that some believers live inconsistently with such doctrines. In fact, it could be argued that such actions demonstrate the truth of most religions that people have a sinful nature.

Questions about the goodness of God are equally problematic for the New Atheist as for the religious believer. Given New Atheists see ethical standards as mere private notions of morality, there can be no objective presence of evil and so blame cannot be laid at the feet of God. If God is a human invention, as New Atheists argue, then surely that means human beings are the cause of violence, not God.

New Atheism also fails to be realistic about the darker side of Atheism (e.g. Lenin and his attempts through violence to eradicate religious belief). It is estimated that atheist and secular regimes in the twentieth century alone, have killed well over 100 million people, more than 100 times the total deaths caused by Christians from the Crusades until the present. New Atheists also ignore the teaching of non-violence and forgiveness in world faiths.

Atheistic arguments against religious experience is another area that has resulted in much debate. Dawkins' approach is to treat religious experiences merely as hallucinations, only differing from madness in the degree to which they are accepted in society. However, such a view ignores fundamental differences between religious revelation and symptoms of mental illness. No account is taken of the mystical experiences reported across time and space and cultural background. Instead, such accounts are dismissed as mere hallucinations or a particular tendency of the human mind to create such experiences.

Atheism's attack on religious belief has also centred around the existence of a multitude of world faiths. Not only do they contradict each other yet at the same time claim divine revelation; but also, it is argued that the religion you follow largely depends on where you are born. It has little to do with truth.

However, religions do not all have the same beliefs. Indeed, people convert from one faith into a different faith. There are great differences between Asian and Western faiths – for example between Buddhism and the Abrahamic faiths.

Perhaps the success of atheistic arguments should be measured not by the persuasiveness of the academic/intellectual arguments but by their influence in the public arena and everyday thinking. Certainly New Atheism has enjoyed a

AO2 Activity

List some conclusions that could be drawn from the AO2 reasoning from the above text; try to aim for at least three different possible conclusions. Consider each of the conclusions and collect brief evidence to support each conclusion from the AO1 and AO2 material for this topic. Select the conclusion that you think is most convincing and explain why it is so. Try to contrast this with the weakest conclusion in the list, justifying your argument with clear reasoning and evidence.

high profile and many feel it has diminished the relevance of religious authority in contemporary society. Anti-theistic views are often at the forefront of public debate via popular media with supporters of New Atheism gaining media attention.

In some ways, New Atheism has actually been instrumental in furthering religious belief. The public debates with well-known figures has attracted more interest in religion and the case for religion has been heard by many who might not previously have been interested. There has been an increase in awareness and interest in spirituality and mindfulness. At the same time membership of some fundamentalist religious groups has increased. The rather hostile, dismissive and caricature depiction of religion by aspects of New Atheism has served to strengthen traditional forms of religion. The growth of faith schools might well be seen as a reaction to perceived threats to religion from movements such as new Atheism.

However, it is interesting that New Atheism has also come under attack from other atheists. For example, C. J. Werleman in *The New Atheist Threat: The Dangerous Rise of Secular Extremists* describes the New Atheists uncritical devotion to science, their childish understanding of religion, their extreme Islamophobia and intolerance of cultural diversity. Many argue that science and rationality are not necessarily on the side of atheism or that these belong uniquely to atheism. It seems clear that atheism has not gone unchallenged in its arguments against religious beliefs.

The extent to which religious responses to New Atheism have been successful

The attack by New Atheism on religious beliefs has not gone unchallenged. New Atheism argues that science has disproved God and religious believers are in denial about the advances of science to explain the universe. However, it is interesting that some of the voices challenging New Atheism have come from scientists themselves. Indeed, many scientists hold a religious belief and see no contradiction between science and religion. Professor Lennox, a Christian, has held many public debates with Dawkins yet neither have been persuaded to change their views.

Stephen Gould commented that based on the religious views of leading evolutionary biologists, 'Either half my colleagues are enormously stupid, or else the science of Darwinism is fully compatible with conventional religious beliefs – and equally compatible with atheism.' Gould was making the point that nature can be interpreted in a theistic or in an atheistic way – but demands neither of these. As Alister McGrath notes 'Both are genuine intellectual possibilities for science'.

The religious response to New Atheism is that they ignore the limitations of science. The natural sciences use the scientific methodology of observation and experiment, which are empirical in their approach. But empiricism cannot speculate about realities beyond the observable world.

However, it is also true, that many scientists are not religious and see religions' world-view as very different from their 'scientific' understanding. They might well claim that the religious world-view includes aspects that cannot be known and so question their inclusion.

New Atheism attacks faith, claiming it is a belief that is held in the total absence of evidence, whilst science is based on evidence and so compels us to accept the truth. Alister McGrath challenges this view of both faith and science. He accuses the New Atheists of failing to make the distinction between 'the total absence of supporting evidence' and 'the absence of totally supporting evidence'. Faith is acting on what you have good reason to believe is true. The evidence in science does not lead automatically to one conclusion. For example, scientists disagree about whether there is a single universe or a series of universes.

However, it might be claimed that the truth of the scientific disagreement can be resolved in the future, whilst the religious claims cannot. In response, the religious

Study tip

It is vital for AO2 that you actually discuss arguments and not just explain what someone may have stated. Try to ask yourself, 'was this a fair point to make?', 'is the evidence sound enough?', 'is there anything to challenge this argument?', 'is this a strong or weak argument?' Such critical analysis will help you develop your evaluation skills.

Specification content

The extent to which religious responses to New Atheism have been successful.

AO2 Activity

As you read through this section try to do the following:

1. Pick out the different lines of argument that are presented in the text and identify any evidence given in support.

2. For each line of argument try to evaluate whether or not you think this is strong or weak.

3. Think of any questions you may wish to raise in response to the arguments.

This Activity will help you to start thinking critically about what you read and help you to evaluate the effectiveness of different arguments and from this develop your own observations, opinions and points of view that will help with any conclusions that you make in your answers to the AO2 questions that arise.

person might argue that if there is a God, then there is a possible eschatological verification or God may even make himself known on earth or through religious experience.

Religious responses about the arguments for the existence of God point out that they are not proofs nor were ever claimed to be. They are *a posteriori* (reasoning based in observation) demonstrations of the coherence of faith. Nevertheless, religious believers such as the Christian William Lane Craig and Richard Swinburne have recently defended the traditional arguments for God, showing them to be justifiable rather than proven. It is also noted by Alister McGrath that the cosmology of the 21st century is much more sympathetic to Christian belief than a century ago.

Another major attack on religion from New Atheism has been the charge that religion is the root of all evil, especially regarding violence. The religious response has been to challenge the use of the word 'religion' and to challenge the claim that religion causes violence. 'Religion' is a false universal in that 'religion' as such does not exist, but rather individual religions exist. The individual religions also have teachings about peace, non-violence and forgiveness as major aspects of their beliefs, for example, ahimsa in Asian faiths or forgiveness in Christianity and Islam. New Atheists focus just on a small group of extremists and label all with the same charge. However, it cannot be denied that religious belief seems to have led some to such violent acts as suicide bombings. In response, it is said that the violence is more politically inspired than religiously motivated, but is that true? The letters left behind by such people may suggest otherwise. Religious people often claim that someone who murders in the name of religion has misinterpreted the true tenets of religion. However, Sam Harris asserts that wrong beliefs and principles of action that do not correctly represent the world around them, are intrinsically dangerous. They become deadly, however, with the addition of faith. For New Atheists, faith means the rejection of evidence-based thinking.

The philosophy of religion has enjoyed a part revival in attempting to address some of the arguments forwarded by the New Atheists. As well as a new defence of the traditional arguments for God by people such as Craig and Swinburne, philosophers have debated the issue of objective morality. Atheism seeks to remove any religious claims to moral authority and looks to science to guide us. But given that atheism views ethical standards as mere private notions of morality, they cannot appeal to any form of objective morality. Morality becomes more a case of individual personal taste. Therefore, religion has responded to atheism's attacks on morality and evil.

If anything, the attacks by atheism seem to have led to a strengthening of religious belief rather than a decline. Religious believers have been forced to address the charges and it has provided an unexpected public platform and welcome interest in the whole area of religious beliefs. Faiths have had opportunities to express their beliefs and to justify them. One wonders if it would have been more effective for atheism to say nothing rather than engage in high profile debate. Many books have appeared defending the rationality of religious belief. However, it is also true that traditional religion if measured by attendance at worship is declining, at least in the West, although there has been growing interest in Asian faiths.

It does seem that the religious responses have been successful since New Atheism has failed to create the knockout blow to religion that it had sought. Instead, possibly because of its caricatures or possibly because of religious responses, New Atheism seems in decline. To many it has come to be seen as a form of intolerant fundamentalism that focussed more on ridiculing opposition than engaging in intellectual debate.

New Atheism does not clearly define religion which may explain why it has focused on extremists as examples of religious belief. It is perhaps in this area that the religion should begin its response if it is to be successful.

Key quote

Some atheists start believing in anything after they give up believing in God. (Nanda)

AO2 Activity

List some conclusions that could be drawn from the AO2 reasoning from the above text; try to aim for at least three different possible conclusions. Consider each of the conclusions and collect brief evidence to support each conclusion from the AO1 and AO2 material for this topic. Select the conclusion that you think is most convincing and explain why it is so. Try to contrast this with the weakest conclusion in the list, justifying your argument with clear reasoning and evidence.

AO2 Developing skills

It is now important to consider the information that has been covered in this section; however, the information in its raw form is too extensive and so has to be processed in order to meet the requirements of the examination. This can be done by practising more advanced skills associated with AO2. The exercises that run throughout this book will help you to do this and prepare you for the examination.

For assessment objective 2 (AO2), which involves 'critical analysis' and 'evaluation' skills, we are going to focus on different ways in which the skills can be demonstrated effectively, and also refer to how the performance of these skills is measured (see generic band descriptors for A2 [WJEC] AO2 or A Level [Eduqas] AO2).

▶ **Your task is this:** Below is **an argument concerning science eliminating God**. You need to respond to this argument by thinking of three key questions you could ask the writer that would challenge their view and further defend their argument.

New Atheism claims that advances in science have now eliminated God from any explanation required of the universe. Science will eventually explain everything. It cannot be denied that science has provided some answers in terms of natural explanations for which previously God had been the explanation. For example, Darwin's theory of natural selection has shown nature to be a battleground. Previously, it had been argued that nature was a mechanism and hence intelligently designed. God had created all things good and hence they required no modifications. This was in conflict with Darwin's theory. However, Darwin's theory had evidence to support it. Religion does not have any evidence. Religious belief is all about faith. But now people began to require evidence for belief. Those who had faith now had to defend their position. As there is no evidence then hence the spread of atheism.

New Atheists see blind faith in the truth of the holy book as axiomatic for religions. Therefore, if the book is true and evidence seems to contradict it, then the evidence, rather than the book, needs to be thrown out. Dawkins argues that when a science book is wrong, someone eventually discovers the mistake and it is corrected in subsequent books. However, that does not happen with holy books.

In addition, the ultimate source of all our concepts and knowledge is our sense experience. The scientific method is based on this view that knowledge is restricted to what can be known by sense experience. The methodology involves collecting data, forming a hypothesis, making a prediction based on the hypothesis and testing the prediction. When it comes to God, it is clear why scepticism arises. God is not open to investigation by means of the senses. God is not a physical object.

Science and the scientific method has whittled down irrational beliefs about the supernatural. That is why most scientists do not believe in God.

Indeed, science and religion are at war, because science has wrecked faith in God, relegating God to the margins of culture. Dawkins notes that 'one of the truly bad effects of religion is that it teaches us that it is a virtue to be satisfied with not understanding'. Religion impedes scientific progress because it teaches us not to change our minds. It saps the intellect.

When you have completed the task, refer to the band descriptors for A2 (WJEC) or A Level (Eduqas) and in particular have a look at the demands described in the higher band descriptors towards which you should be aspiring.

Key skills

Analysis involves identifying issues raised by the materials in the AO1, together with those identified in the AO2 section, and presents sustained and clear views, either of scholars or from a personal perspective ready for evaluation.

This means:

- That your answers are able to identify key areas of debate in relation to a particular issue
- That you can identify, and comment upon, the different lines of argument presented by others
- That your response comments on the overall effectiveness of each of these areas or arguments.

Evaluation involves considering the various implications of the issues raised based upon the evidence gleaned from analysis and provides an extensive detailed argument with a clear conclusion.

This means:

- That your answer weighs up the consequences of accepting or rejecting the various and different lines of argument analysed
- That your answer arrives at a conclusion through a clear process of reasoning.

T3 Religious experience

Specification content

The influence of religious experience on religious practice.

Alister Hardy (1896–1985)

Key terms

Belief-in: a belief that conveys an attitude of trust or commitment

Belief-that: a belief that claims to be an objective fact

quickfire

3.1 Who founded the Religious Experience Research Unit (RERU)?

Specification content

The influence of religious experience on faith.

D: The influence of religious experience on religious practice and faith

Religious experience and religious practice

In 1969 the English marine biologist, Alister Hardy, set up the Religious Experience Research Unit in Oxford with the objective of examining the extent and nature of the religious experiences of people in Britain. Hardy had just retired from his Chair at Oxford as a scientist but had a lifelong interest in religion. In particular, although he had a biological approach to how religion had 'evolved', he did see this development as being in response to another dimension of reality.

In compiling a database of religious experiences, what soon became obvious to Hardy and others involved was the sheer breadth and variety of such experiences. Amongst those accounts were reported the more traditional religious experiences which were centred on followers of various religions.

According to Hardy, a religious experience:

'... usually induces in the person concerned a conviction that the everyday world is not the whole of reality; there is another dimension to life ... awareness of its presence affects the person's view of the world. It alters behaviour and changes attitudes.'

This theme in the specification focuses on the influence of religious experience on religious practice and faith. Religious practice includes ritual, religious ceremonies, religious festivals but also daily life which often involves religious duties and reflections.

Ritual, as well as being a religious experience in itself, can also be a trigger for further religious experience. In addition, prayer and fasting are often preparation for certain ritual actions, ceremonies or festivals and are also personal or communal religious experiences.

Often festivals are celebrations of a past event that is grounded in a significant religious experience. For example, during Ramadan, Muslims celebrate the time when the verses of the Qur'an were revealed to the prophet Muhammad. All these forms of religious practice and faith have both been influenced by religious experience and can lead to religious experience.

Religious experience and faith

Most thinkers define faith in terms of some mixture of an action of the will, trust and belief in a body of truths expressed in statements or propositions. Aquinas viewed the Christian faith as rational, in that it could be supported and explored by reason. However, he did not think that reason alone could discover its truths and insights. Divine revelation was also required.

Many view faith as both a **belief-that** and a **belief-in**.

A typical belief-that statement is 'I believe that in Sikhism the first Guru is Guru Nanak'. The statement is making a claim that is objectively true and that something is a fact. This sort of a belief is grounded in physical, often historical, events but can also include some interpretation. For example, Buddhists may observe that they believe that Siddhartha Gautama was a wise teacher; however, this is still grounded in the world that we experience.

An example of a belief-in statement, however, would be 'I believe in Jesus'. This usually means more than just belief that Jesus was an historical figure. It implies trust in Jesus. It extends beyond the world of our experience into the sphere of faith. The belief and trust in Jesus is inherently linked to faith claims of salvation, resurrection and future hope of an 'other worldly' existence. Belief-in tends to extend the interpretation of the belief-that into a metaphysical statement. Again, Buddhists would believe that Siddhartha Gautama was wise because he taught meditation and claimed the experience of **enlightenment** (**nirvana**) and became the Buddha; however, belief in the Buddha as an inspirational figure due to the faith in (Buddhists use the word **sraddha** meaning 'trust') the other worldly concept of nirvana as a realistic aspiration for all, is belief-in.

For many people, the move from a belief-that to a belief-in, is brought about by a personal religious experience. Equally, other people's religious experience can also be a source of one's own faith. For example, someone can read all about the life of the Buddha or the life of Muhammad and it could lead to conversion. Cat Stevens reading of the Qur'an and of the life of Muhammad led to his conversion to Islam.

Another role of religious experience related to faith is that of encouragement or strengthening faith. For example, in charismatic Christianity the gifts of the Holy Spirit are for edification of the community of believers.

It seems that a religious experience can move people into faith and faith can lead people into a religious experience. In addition, there are many types of religious experiences that have a wide range of manifestations, from quiet reflection and contemplation of the divine, for example private prayer or meditation, to overt, public expressions of faith, for example through the exuberant and euphoric 'speaking in tongues'.

Religious experience and revelation

Through **revelation**, the divine (or ultimate truth for Buddhists) becomes known to humanity. Any type of religious experience can be a revelation. A revelation of religious truth can be communicated (either directly or indirectly by God or by gaining insight) to human beings through a religious experience. For example, many people within religious traditions, in particular the founders, claim to have experienced this.

The content of this revelation is a body of truths usually expressed in statements or propositions. Judaism has the revelation of the Law to Moses on Mount Sinai (Exodus 19–23).

Revelation through religious experience can also be about a moment of 'realisation' coming at the end of a period of reflection. In contrast to the propositional view that produces a body of truths about God or ultimate reality, the non-propositional concept of revelation represents human attempts to understand the significance of revelatory events or experiences. It involves seeing or interpreting events or experiences in a special way, as having spiritual significance rather than just political or sociological importance.

Key terms

Enlightenment: in Buddhism, the experience of awakening to insight into the true nature of things

Nirvana: Buddhist enlightenment

Revelation: a supernatural disclosure to human beings

Sraddha: the closest term to 'faith' in Buddhism sometimes translated from the Sanskrit as 'trust' or 'confidence'

quickfire

3.2 What is the difference between a 'belief-that' and a 'belief-in'?

Key quotes

A faith which evades critical questions is a faith that lacks confidence, which is not truly assured it has found truth. (**Evans**)

Then Moses went up to God; the Lord called to him from the mountain, saying, 'Thus you shall say to the house of Jacob, and tell the Israelites: You have seen what I did to the Egyptians, and how I bore you on eagles' wings and brought you to myself. Now therefore, if you obey my voice and keep my covenant, you shall be my treasured possession out of all the peoples. Indeed, the whole earth is mine, but you shall be for me a priestly kingdom and a holy nation. These are the words that you shall speak to the Israelites.' (**Exodus 19:3–6**)

'Moses Smashing the Tablets of the Law',
Rembrandt (1659)

Specification content

The influence of religious experience on religious practice and faith: value for religious community including: affirmation of belief system.

Key quotes

Praise be to Allah, Who hath sent to His Servant the Book, and hath allowed therein no Crookedness: (He hath made it) Straight (and Clear) in order that He may warn (the godless) of a terrible Punishment from Him, and that He may give Glad Tidings to the Believers who work righteous deeds, that they shall have a goodly Reward, Wherein they shall remain for ever. (Sura 3:18)

The True One and only Omnipresent Immortal Essence of reality. The Creator, the Omniscient and Omnipotent, the Incomprehensible (the fearless). Before all Beginnings and after all Endings, Beyond Time, Space and Form (and enmity). Free from the cycle of Births and Deaths, the Self-manifested. The Loving Merciful Enlightener (Realised with His Grace through total Submission to His Will). (Mool Mantra)

For example, the Old Testament prophets saw the Fall of Jerusalem as an experience of judgement on its people because of disobedience. This reflected a belief that God was active in the world.

Study tip

When writing an answer about religious experience and faith it is always important to support your points with examples. There are some given in the book but draw from your own study of a world religion as well.

AO1 Activity

Try explaining in 30 seconds to a fellow student what the difference between belief-that and belief-in is by using clear examples from one or more world religions. Listen to your fellow student as they do the same and then compare your responses and write down a brief summary.

Value for religious community – affirmation of belief system

In most religions, there is often a pivotal figure who is linked to the founding of that religion. Usually these figures experience a particularly significant event that marks the start of their ministry. Their authority derives from their religious experience as it is seen as confirmation and affirmation of their message.

For example, the angel Gabriel is said to have appeared to Muhammad when he was praying alone in a cave. The angel commanded Muhammad to recite verses that would be included in the Qur'an. The revelations continued for twenty-three years forming the Qur'an which is regarded as the entire revelation of God. The revelations that he received were sometimes a few verses, a part of a chapter or the whole chapter. Muhammad is seen as a passive channel through whom Allah communicated the final message to humanity.

Likewise, in Sikhism Guru Nanak received a revelation, which is at the start of every chapter and sub-chapter in the Sri Guru Granth Sahib (the sacred Scripture of the Sikhs). Guru Nanak recounts how he took a dip in the river and disappeared into the waters. He was missing for two days and nights. On the third day he re-appeared from out of the water with a verse on his lips that is now referred to as the Mool Mantra.

Guru Nanak at the riverside where he had his religious experience.

Buddhism recounts how Siddhartha Gautama was seated under a pipal tree (now known as the Bodhi tree) when he vowed never to arise until he had found the truth. After a reputed 49 days of meditation, he is said to have attained Enlightenment and became known as the Buddha (Awakened One or The Enlightened One).

Key quotes

When I knew and saw thus, my mind was liberated from the taint of sensual desire, from the taint of being, and from the taint of ignorance. When it was liberated there came the knowledge: 'It is liberated'. I directly knew: 'Birth is destroyed, the holy life has been lived, what had to be done has been done, there is no more coming to any state of being.'

This was the third true knowledge attained by me in the last watch of the night. Ignorance was banished and true knowledge arose, darkness was banished and light arose, as happens in one who abides diligent, ardent, and resolute. But such pleasant feeling that arose in me did not invade my mind and remain. **(Majjhima Nikaya 36)**

Now the birth of Jesus the Messiah took place in this way. When his mother Mary had been engaged to Joseph, but before they lived together, she was found to be withchild from the Holy Spirit. Her husband Joseph, being a righteous man and unwilling to expose her to public disgrace, planned to dismiss her quietly. But just when he had resolved to do this, an angel of the Lord appeared to him in a dream and said, 'Joseph, son of David, do not be afraid to take Mary as your wife, for the child conceived in her is from the Holy Spirit. She will bear a son, and you are to name him Jesus, for he will save his people from their sins.' **(Matthew 1:18–21)**

In Christianity, the revelation through the appearance of angels to Mary and Joseph affirms the doctrine of the **incarnation** and virgin birth. The experience of the disciples of the resurrected Jesus affirms beliefs about life after death and the efficacy of Jesus' sacrifice to forgive sin.

Paul is also seen as an influential figure of the Church. Fourteen of the twenty-seven books in the New Testament have traditionally been attributed to him. These contain the core of Christian theology. Paul changed from being someone on a mission to arrest Christians, to someone preaching and suffering for proclaiming Jesus of Nazareth as the Jewish Messiah and Son of God. What triggered the change were a number of religious experiences including a conversion experience when the resurrected Jesus allegedly appeared to Paul on the road to Damascus, Ananias receiving a vision about Paul and Paul being filled with the Holy Spirit.

In such accounts, God is seen confirming a particular person for a task by means of some type of religious experience. Through those individuals, revelation is given. It is the religious experiences that convince followers that the person is God appointed and so affirms their role and status of authority and trustworthy receivers of revelation.

Key quote

Meanwhile Saul, still breathing threats and murder against the disciples of the Lord, went to the high priest and asked him for letters to the synagogues at Damascus, so that if he found any who belonged to the Way, men or women, he might bring them bound to Jerusalem. Now as he was going along and approaching Damascus, suddenly a light from heaven flashed around him. He fell to the ground and heard a voice saying to him, 'Saul, Saul, why do you persecute me?' He asked, 'Who are you, Lord?' The reply came, 'I am Jesus, whom you are persecuting'. **(Acts 9: 1–5)**

quickfire

3.3 Who received the revelation of the Mool Mantra?

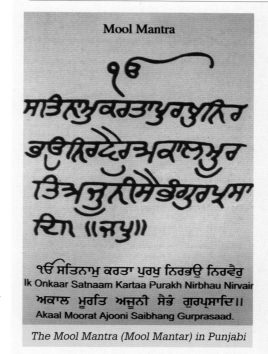

The Mool Mantra (Mool Mantar) in Punjabi

Key term

Incarnation: the embodiment of God the Son in human flesh as Jesus Christ

quickfire

3.4 Which event is said to have changed Paul's life from persecuting Christians to being a follower?

Specification content

The influence of religious experience on religious practice and faith: value for religious community including: promotion of faith value system.

Key quotes

'The cry of the Israelites has now come to me; I have also seen how the Egyptians oppress them. So come, I will send you to Pharaoh to bring my people, the Israelites, out of Egypt.' But Moses said to God, 'Who am I that I should go to Pharaoh, and bring the Israelites out of Egypt?' He said, 'I will be with you; and this shall be the sign for you that it is I who sent you: when you have brought the people out of Egypt, you shall worship God on this mountain.' (Exodus 3: 9–12)

The Lord said to Moses, 'Come up to me on the mountain, and wait there; and I will give you the tablets of stone, with the law and the commandment, which I have written for their instruction.' (Exodus 24:12)

Specification content

The influence of religious experience on religious practice and faith: value for religious community including: strengthening cohesion of religious community.

Value for religious community – promotion of faith value system

As well as religious experiences being seen as the guarantor of received revelation about doctrine and beliefs, religious experience can also be the source of revealing ethical standards. Moses is honoured among Jews as the 'lawgiver of Israel'. Exodus 3 recounts how Moses saw a burning bush which was not consumed. God spoke to him from the bush and commissioned Moses as a prophet and liberator of the people of Israel.

Later Moses received the Ten Commandments inscribed on two stone tablets, along with the laws of the covenant, which included both customary law and ritual ordinances. These provide explicit moral guidance and so govern behaviour of the believer.

Likewise the Buddha's enlightenment experience is an example of meditation to be emulated by others. The Buddha placed great emphasis on searching and testing for oneself just as he did, and the various practices of meditation are examples of this.

Christianity sees Jesus and Paul as revealing and clarifying ethical standards and behaviour. The Gospels record that Jesus summarised Jewish Law in the words, 'Love the Lord your God with all your heart, with all your soul, with all your mind and with all your strength and love your neighbour as yourself'. Jesus is seen by Christians as the Son of God whose authority was confirmed by his miracles, death and resurrection.

Key quote

Develop the meditation of compassion. For when you are developing the meditation of compassion, cruelty will be abandoned. (Maha Rahulovada Sutta 62)

As discussed above, Muhammad received revelations which formed the verses in the Qur'an around which the religion of Islam is based. Muhammad's teachings and practices are also upheld by Muslims and used as sources of Islamic Law.

Key quote

This is the Book; in it is guidance sure, without doubt, to those who fear Allah. Who believe in the Unseen, are steadfast in prayer, and spend out of what We have provided for them; And who believe in the Revelation sent to thee, and sent before thy time, and (in their hearts) have the assurance of the Hereafter. They are on (true) guidance, from their Lord, and it is these who will prosper. (Sura 2:2–5)

Strengthening cohesion of religious community

A religious community celebrating a past religious experience or a religious community together expressing worship, for example, can be occasions when a religious community is strengthened by religious experience. The very act of coming together as a religious community to participate in worship or to commemorate an event of significance has essential value for the religious community and is the lifeblood of religious living.

Such community gatherings provide opportunity for further religious experiences and spiritual benefits such as:

- Strengthening the community spiritually through collective worship
- Creating a greater sense of unity through fellowship

- Establishing a common identity
- Highlighting a common purpose through specific events, e.g. festivals and rites of passage
- Reaffirming faith, e.g. creeds, reading religious texts, rituals, hymns
- Expressing and sharing one's spirituality with others, e.g. testimonies, personal experiences.

The value in celebrating a past religious experience

This is usually by means of festivals or pilgrimage. For many Buddhists, Wesak celebrates the Buddha's enlightenment. Homes are decorated and there are special temple services.

In Islam, the festival of Ramadan celebrates the time when the Qur'an was first revealed to Muhammad. Fasting during the month of Ramadan is obligatory for Muslims. Ramadan is seen as a time to spend with friends and family. The fast will often be broken by different Muslim families coming together to share in an evening meal.

Eid ul Adha is another Muslim festival. It remembers Abraham's willingness to sacrifice his son when Allah ordered him to. Eid usually starts with Muslims going to the mosque for prayers. It is also a time when they visit family and friends as well as offering presents. In both these Islamic festivals there is a coming together of the religious community – sharing in the same rituals and beliefs.

In Judaism, the festival of Pesach remembers the events of the Passover where the enslaved Israelites were spared from the plague of the death of all the firstborn and escaped from Egypt. The Seder meal that takes place over a meal with family and friends involves the retelling of the story in which everyone takes part. This sharing together expresses their common identity as a member of the religious community.

Present day worship and rituals

The experience of present day religious followers as they gather for worship each week can be seen as a religious experience. Shared worship can lead to a special kind of communal experience. The reading and preaching of the sacred text can be a trigger for religious experience. Most religions consider their scriptures as the revealed word of God. Through these texts and others, God speaks to the individual.

Jesus said that where two or three are gathered together for prayer, there he is also. This suggests that there is something special about the gathering together of religious believers. The Friday prayer at the mosque and the Sabbath gathering at the synagogue are specific occasions that strengthen the cohesion of that particular religious community.

Ritual also reinforces the communal experience. It gives a feeling of group solidarity and unity and a sense of belonging to something that is greater than the individuals who comprise it. The rituals that take place such as the Eucharist (Mass or Holy Communion) in Christianity also are special times when as a community worshipping together, there is that experience and mystery that Hardy described – 'the everyday world is not the whole of reality ... there is another dimension to life'. Christian **charismatic worship** has an emphasis and expectation of the Holy Spirit at work amongst the worshippers. This group expectation of a meeting with God is a sharing of religious experiences and so can strengthen the cohesion of that religious community.

Key quote

Ritual is probably the most common source of religious experience for the majority of people. (Momen)

Key quote

All who believed were together and had all things in common; they would sell their possessions and goods and distribute the proceeds to all, as any had need. Day by day, as they spent much time together in the temple, they broke bread at home and ate their food with glad and generous hearts, praising God and having the goodwill of all the people. And day by day the Lord added to their number those who were being saved. (Acts 2:44–47)

quickfire

3.5 Which world religion celebrates Wesak Day?

Wesak Day celebration

Key term

Charismatic worship: exuberant and expressive forms of worship often involving ecstatic religious experiences such as speaking in 'tongues' and healing miracles

Specification content
Value for individual including faith restoring; strengthening faith in face of opposition; renewal of commitment to religious ideals and doctrines.

quickfire

3.6 What is Hajj?

Key quotes

Remember that you were a slave in Egypt and the Lord your God redeemed you from there. (Deuteronomy 24:18)

Then Jesus told his disciples, 'If any want to become my followers, let them deny themselves and take up their cross and follow me'. (Matthew 16:24)

In this you rejoice, even if now for a little while you have had to suffer various trials, so that the genuineness of your faith – being more precious than gold that, though perishable, is tested by fire – may be found to result in praise and glory and honour when Jesus Christ is revealed. (1 Peter 1:6–7)

Key term

Khalsa: the name for those who have undergone the Amrit ceremony – the word 'khalsa' literally means 'pure'

Value for individual – faith restoring

Both one's own religious experience and the testimony and accounts of the religious experience of others can be of value to the individual. If one's own faith is struggling and doubt setting in, then having a religious experience, a meeting with God, can clearly remove doubts and renew faith. Such an experience might come from a time of prayer or meditation or the reading of a sacred text. It might come from being with others of the religious community. The experience may come through participating in a religious ritual such as the Eucharist. It can be any occasion that a person opens themselves up to seeking or listening to God.

The faith restoring experience may also come through others. A testimony of someone's religious experience may lead to one's own renewal of faith as they hear how God has influenced that person's life. The religious experience gained from going on a pilgrimage can rekindle that dwindling faith and commitment. For example, in Islam the Hajj is one of the five pillars and each Muslim is expected to undertake this pilgrimage at least once in their life.

Key quotes

Therefore encourage one another and build up each other, as indeed you are doing. (1 Thessalonians 5:11)

The sangha is a community where there should be harmony and peace and understanding. That is something created by our daily life together. If love is there in the community, if we've been nourished by the harmony in the community, then we will never move away from love. (Thich Nhat Hhan)

Value for individual – strengthening faith in face of opposition

An individual may be strengthened in their faith in the face of opposition as they hear of religious experiences that believers experienced when they faced opposition. It may include some account of an act of God whereby they were rescued from a situation or an account where a believer was given strength to face and overcome the opposition.

It may even be accounts of martyrs that inspire faith in the face of opposition. There are often stories in the sacred texts of followers who faced persecution. In Christianity the supreme example is Jesus, who went through suffering and death and warns his followers that they also will suffer if they follow him.

The story of the origin of the Khalsa in Sikhism, where five Sikhs were willing to die for their faith can be a source of inspiration and trigger for a religious experience.

The founding of the Khalsa

After his inspirational discourse, he flashed his unsheathed sword and said that every great deed was preceded by equally great sacrifice. He asked, with a naked sword in his hand, 'I need one head. Is there anyone among you, who is ready to die for his faith?' When people heard his call, they were taken aback. Some of the wavering followers left the congregation, while other began to look at one another in amazement. After a few minutes, a brave Sikh from Lahore named Daya Ram stood up and offered his head to the Guru. The Guru took him to a tent pitched close by, and after some time, came out with a blood dripping sword. The Sikhs thought Daya Ram had been slain.

The Guru repeated his demand calling for another Sikh who was prepared to die at his command. At this second call, even more people were shocked and some were frightened. A few more of the wavering followers discreetly began to filter out of the congregation.

However, to the shock of many, another person stood up. The second Sikh who offered himself was Dharam Das. This amazing episode did not end there. Soon three more, Mohkam Chand, Sahib Chand and Himmat Rai, offered their heads to the Guru. Each Sikh was taken into the tent and some though that they could now hear a 'thud' sound – as if the sword was falling on the neck of the Sikh.

Now the five Sikhs were missing with the Guru in the tent. It was a nerve-racking time for the sangat (congregation). There was pin-drop silence as all focussed intensely on the tent opening. After what seemed an eternity, the tent opening moved and the Guru came out of the tent. No naked sword this time!

Soon the five Sikhs were presented alive to the congregation wearing brand new decorated robes. They constituted the Panj Pyare: the Five Beloved Ones, who were baptised as the Khalsa or the Pure Ones with the administration of Amrit. The Guru declared: 'From now on, the Khalsa shall be baptised with Amrit created with water stirred with a double-edged sword – Khanda while the words of Gurbani are uttered.' (SikhiWiki)

Prayer and meditation in the face of opposition can lead to a religious experience in which the person gains strength and faith to confront the situation. The sense of God being with the believer because of a religious experience they have had enables the person to stand firm and continue despite threats of persecution. In the early church there is the account of a religious experience at Pentecost when the Holy Spirit was claimed to have come upon the disciples. The result of this was that they proclaimed about Jesus and when facing persecution they said that they couldn't stop. They had to obey God rather than human beings.

Value for individual – renewal of commitment to religious ideals and doctrines

Most religions have occasions where adherents to the faith have an opportunity to renew their commitment to the faith and ideals. Often it takes the form of a public commitment in which the person confirms their faith. This decision to make such a commitment can be a religious experience – a sense of being called. Initiation into a faith can be a time of renewal of commitment. Most religions have some initiation ceremony.

In Sikhism, the **Amrit** ceremony is the initiation rite. During the ceremony, hymns are recited from the Sikh scripture, prayers are said and the principles of Sikhism are affirmed. The candidates then drink some of the amrit from the same bowl, and have it sprinkled on their eyes and hair. Then each recites the Mool Mantra. Undergoing the Amrit ceremony means the person has joined the Khalsa.

The original Sikh Amrit ceremony

Upon administering amrit to the Five Beloved Ones (Panj Pyare), the Guru asked them to baptise him in the same manner, thus emphasising equality between the Guru and his disciples.

Guru Gobind Singh named the new ceremony, Khande di Pahul, namely the baptism of the double-edged sword, which is also known as Amrit-Sanchar. He stirred water in an iron bowl with the sword, reciting five major compositions, Japji, Jaap, Savaiyye, Benti Chaupai and Anand Sahib, while the five Sikhs stood facing him. The Guru's wife, Mata Sahib Kaur put some sugar-puffs into the water. The nectar thus obtained was called 'Khanday-da-Amrit' or simply just 'Amrit'. This implied that the new Khalsa brotherhood would not only be full of courage and heroism, but also filled with humility. (SikhiWiki)

Key quotes

Then they called them in again and commanded them not to speak or teach at all in the name of Jesus. But Peter and John replied … 'For we cannot help speaking about what we have seen and heard'. (Acts 4:21–22)

Abolition of prejudice, equality of privilege amongst one another and with the Guru, common worship, common place of pilgrimage, common baptism for all classes and lastly, common external appearance – these were the means besides common leadership and the community of aspiration which Gobind Singh employed to bring unity among his followers and by which he bound them together into a compact mass. (Narang)

Key term

Amrit: the name of the holy water that is drunk in the baptism ceremony into the Khalsa in Sikhism – the word 'amrit' literally means 'immortality'

The Khalsa ritual

Adult baptism and conversion are similar religious experiences where public commitment to a faith is often made, often with a testimony from the person describing their journey of faith.

Festivals can also be occasions where religious believers are moved to renew their commitments to a religious way of life. In Judaism, **Rosh Hashanah** marks the beginning of the 10-day period of atonement leading to **Yom Kippur** during which Jews are commanded to search their souls and make amends for sins committed. Yom Kippur is the holiest day of the Jewish year and many Jews spend the entire day in prayers at the synagogue.

A similar opportunity for reflection and renewal of commitment is observed in Christianity during the time of **Lent**. It is a period of six weeks during which many Christians observe a period of fasting, repentance, self-denial and spiritual discipline. The goal, as in other religions, is to develop a closer relationship with God.

A common feature of religions is the act of fasting, which is intended to help teach self-discipline. It is seen as a time to take our eyes off the things of this world and instead focus on God. Therefore, it is often associated with religious experiences.

Holy places can also be seen as triggers for a religious experience that leads to renewal and recommitment to religious beliefs. Usually they are places where either something happened or people feel something sacred, possibly worship having taken place there for a great length of time. For example, Jerusalem and the Western wall or the Sikh Golden Temple at Amritsar. Often they become places of pilgrimage such as Makkah. Such locations are seen as places where there is a sacred meeting between the spiritual and the physical.

Key terms

Lent: in Christianity, it is a season of forty days before Easter of prayer and fasting

Rosh Hashanah: the Jewish New Year

Yom Kippur: in Judaism, it refers to the day of Atonement and is the holiest day of the year

quickfire

3.7 During which festival do Jews search their souls and make amends for sins committed?

Key quote

… a process of religious change, which transforms the way the individual perceives the rest of society and his or her personal place in it, altering one's view of the worlds. (**McGuire – referring to conversions**)

Study tip

When you are answering a question under timed conditions keep reviewing each paragraph and make sure that you don't repeat yourself by having a clear plan and a range of examples to cross out once you have used them.

AO1 Activity

Complete the following table from the information you have read in this chapter:

Religious experience influences	Example

AO1 Developing skills

It is now important to consider the information that has been covered in this section; however, the information in its raw form is too extensive and so has to be processed in order to meet the requirements of the examination. This can be achieved by practising more advanced skills associated with AO1. The exercises that run throughout this book will help you to do this and prepare you for the examination. For assessment objective 1 (AO1), which involves demonstrating 'knowledge' and 'understanding' skills, we are going to focus on different ways in which the skills can be demonstrated effectively, and also refer to how the performance of these skills is measured (see generic band descriptors for A2 [WJEC] AO1 or A Level [Eduqas] AO1).

▶ **Your next task is this:** Below is an outline of **how religious experience of the resurrection of Jesus is of value affirming the belief system of Christianity**. At present, it has no quotations at all to support the points made. Accompanying the outline are three quotations that could be used in the outline in order to improve it. Your task is to rewrite the outline but make use of the quotations. Such phrases as 'according to …', 'the scholar … argues', or, 'it has been suggested by …' may help.

Christianity has many accounts of religious experience. Indeed, Christianity is claimed to be God's revelation to his people. It includes the belief that not only does God communicate with his people, can be known and is active in the world; but that God also lived on earth in the form of Jesus.

Both the entry and the exit of Jesus in this world have accounts of the supernatural. Dreams, visions, revelations and appearances are recorded. Christians often claim that the resurrection of Jesus, is good evidence for the truth of the Christian faith. It clearly affirms that there is life after death, that Jesus' sacrificial death was sufficient and that our sins can be forgiven. Without the disciples' experience of Jesus' resurrection, there would have been no evidence to affirm the truth of Jesus' teaching and prophecies. Many Christians regard the physical resurrection as the basis for their belief in Christianity.

1. The New Testament writers speak as if Christ's achievement in rising from the dead was the first event of its kind in the whole history of the universe. He is the 'first fruits', the 'pioneer of life'. He has forced open a door that has been locked since the death of the first man. He has met, fought, and beaten the King of Death. Everything is different because He has done so. This is the beginning of the New Creation: a new chapter in cosmic history has been opened. (C. S. Lewis)

2. There is no justification for reducing the meaning of 'the resurrection of Jesus' to something like 'the continuing significance of Jesus' or 'the disciples' realisation that Jesus' message could not die'. By 'resurrection' they clearly meant that something had happened to Jesus himself. God had raised him, not merely reassured them. He was alive again. (Dunn)

3. Faith in the resurrection is really the same thing as faith in the saving efficacy of the Cross. (Bultmann)

When you have completed the task, try to find another quotation that you could use and further extend your answer.

Key skills Theme 3 DEF

This theme has tasks that concentrate on a particular aspect of AO1 in terms of using quotations from sources of authority and in the use of references.

Key quote

While they were still talking about this, Jesus himself stood among them and said to them, 'Peace be with you'. They were startled and frightened, thinking they saw a ghost. He said to them, 'Why are you troubled, and why do doubts rise in your mind? Look at my hands and my feet. It is I myself! Touch me and see; a ghost does not have flesh and bones, as you see I have' … Then he opened their minds so they could understand the Scriptures. (Luke 24:36–45)

Key skills

Knowledge involves:

Selection of a range of (thorough) accurate and relevant information that is directly related to the specific demands of the question.

This means:

- Selecting relevant material for the question set
- Being focused in explaining and examining the material selected.

Understanding involves:

Explanation that is extensive, demonstrating depth and/or breadth with excellent use of evidence and examples including (where appropriate) thorough and accurate supporting use of sacred texts, sources of wisdom and specialist language.

This means:

- Effective use of examples and supporting evidence to establish the quality of your understanding
- Ownership of your explanation that expresses personal knowledge and understanding and NOT just reproducing a chunk of text from a book that you have rehearsed and memorised.

Specification content

The impact of religious experiences
upon religious belief and practice.

Key quote

The resurrection of Christ is
therefore emphatically a test
question upon which depends the
truth or falsehood of the Christian
religion. It is either the greatest
miracle or the greatest delusion
which history records. (Schaff)

AO2 Activity

As you read through this section try to
do the following:

1. Pick out the different lines of
   argument that are presented in
   the text and identify any evidence
   given in support.

2. For each line of argument try to
   evaluate whether or not you think
   this is strong or weak.

3. Think of any questions you may
   wish to raise in response to the
   arguments.

This Activity will help you to start
thinking critically about what you
read and help you to evaluate the
effectiveness of different arguments
and from this develop your own
observations, opinions and points
of view that will help with any
conclusions that you make in your
answers to the AO2 questions
that arise.

Issues for analysis and evaluation

The extent to which religious experiences impact upon religious belief and practice

It could be argued that it is difficult to separate religious experience from religious belief and practice, if religious experiences are understood to refer to those experiences that are recognisably religious (e.g. religious assembly, reading of sacred writings).

In support of this, an individual's prayer to God is clearly a religious experience for him or her. Although, arguably, it does not compare to the prayer of Jesus in the Garden of Gethsemane, or the prayer of Paul for a miraculous healing, it is still a religious experience. The practice of prayer, then, in itself is a religious experience. Indeed, private prayer often is not just claimed to be a one-way experience as many religious people believe that it is also an exercise in listening to the 'voice' of God. Prayer, for such religious believers, is therefore about communion with God. William James described prayer as 'the very soul and essence of religion' and so its impact upon religious belief and practice is significant.

Many who are deeply committed to a religious faith may spend much time each day in prayer. There is also meditation and one of the goals of meditation is to obtain a religious experience, whether it be nirvana or simply a state of tranquillity in Buddhism or a state of unity with the divine in Hinduism.

Theistic religions seek union with God, while non-theistic religions seek the loss of self, but both are essentially a religious experience and the very foundation of their practice.

In India the training in mystical insight is yoga. By means of exercise based on such things as diet, posture, breathing and intellectual concentration, the person practices bhavana (mental development) in order to be more perceptive of the spiritual realm.

Just as prayer is a religious experience, a baptism or participation in a rite of passage is equally a religious experience. Although the Eucharist for an individual may not be as notable to others as was the baptism of Jesus, or the Eucharist experience the same as the breaking of bread at the last supper, again, it can still be a religious experience. Indeed, it could be argued that the Roman Catholic understanding of the meaning of Eucharist, that is transubstantiation, brings with it the religious experience of the transformation of the bread and wine into the body and blood of Christ.

Therefore, the very act of a religious practice may itself be considered a religious experience and so have significant impact.

However, others might question this view. Just participating in a religious practice does not guarantee that the person participating is the receiver of a religious experience. The participation could be almost mechanical, particularly if it is an act that is often repeated. For instance, saying the Mool Mantra or the Lord's Prayer could be acts where the actual words are repeated by rote, almost unconsciously.

Indeed, if this line or argument is taken then the impact of such experiences is significantly less than those that have true intent, or, as Muslims would express, niyyah or niyat, which is the only things that validates a religious act.

In Christianity, the creed is recited at most Catholic and Anglican services. The creed has been formulated from some key religious experiences (e.g. visions or miracles) that have affirmed the religious beliefs. In that sense, the religious experiences are vital for the religious beliefs. Restating the beliefs allow both individuals and communities to demonstrate what is important to them and may even serve as a means by which others outside of the religious community might come to appreciate what is believed/practised.

For many religious believers, these beliefs can be deepened by an associative religious experience and so enhance their value. However, repetition of the words, even when recited together by a large congregation, need not itself be a religious experience. Nevertheless, the affirmation of beliefs can still be valid even if a religious experience does not occur.

Religious experiences influence belief and practice since they are often the reason for the religious practice, such as a religious pilgrimage or a religious festival. For example, during Ramadan, Muslims celebrate the time when verses of the Qur'an were revealed to the prophet Muhammad. Wesak (Buddha Day) is when Buddhists celebrate the life of the Buddha and his teachings and his revelations about the nature of death, karma and rebirth, suffering and desire.

Clearly these beliefs and practices are important to religious believers. They are reminders to them of why and what they believe – the affirmation of their faith. They demonstrate what is important to them and are a witness to others outside the faith. They serve to unite the religious community and give it a distinctive identity. They strengthen the religious community.

However, it might be argued that in the 21st century, many have called into question the truth of these claimed past religious experiences. For instance, in Christianity many modern scholars dispute the literal interpretation of the virgin birth and the physical resurrection of Jesus. They see them as mythological and later additions – symbolic rather than historical and literal. Nevertheless, it could be argued that the symbolism has significance and value to the religious believer.

Some might argue that religious experiences are not necessary for belief and practice. Assembling at a place of worship is not a religious experience but can be considered of value in strengthening cohesion within the religious community. This is important as a means of preserving identity and reinforcing common bonds between those who belong to the religion. However, the reason for assembling at a place of worship is usually linked to some religious experience of the past. Hence, it is does seem that religious experiences do have a significant impact upon religious belief and practice. Conversion experiences are clearly examples of religious experience that have an impact on the religious belief of the individual. They have changed the beliefs and practices of the person who has had the experience. Examples might include John Wesley, St Paul and Yusuf Ali (formerly known as Cat Stevens). The conversion might be from one denomination to another within the same religion, for example from Baptist to Catholic or Sunni to Shi'a. Alternatively, the conversion might be from one religion to another, or from no religion to a religion. Joining a religion often involves some initiation ceremony marking membership. For instance, in Christianity it may involve baptism, and in Sikhism it is the Amrit ceremony. Usually members of the religion witness or participate in the ceremony and this can have an impact on them in terms of renewing their own religious commitment. Such practices may strengthen faith in the face of opposition from those not part of the religion.

Another line of argument may be questioning the extent to which a religious experience changes belief. Some may argue that conversion experiences are really inner battles and the conclusions reached would have occurred regardless of the religious experience.

William James emphasised the fruits of the religious experience as evidence that religious experiences impact positively on a person's life. The effects can be seen in a change in their behaviour. However, it is difficult to prove that the changes are due to the religious experience rather than psychological reasons. In either case, religious experiences do not prove that God is real.

Key quote

If conversion to Christianity makes no improvement in a man's outward actions – if he continues to be just as snobbish or spiteful or envious or ambitious as he was before – then I think we must suspect that his 'conversion' was largely imaginary. (C S Lewis)

AO2 Activity

List some conclusions that could be drawn from the AO2 reasoning from the above text; try to aim for at least three different possible conclusions. Consider each of the conclusions and collect brief evidence to support each conclusion from the AO1 and AO2 material for this topic. Select the conclusion that you think is most convincing and explain why it is so. Try to contrast this with the weakest conclusion in the list, justifying your argument with clear reasoning and evidence.

Specification content

Whether religious communities
are entirely dependent on religious
experiences.

Whether religious communities are entirely dependent on religious experiences

Religious faiths have various beliefs and practices that derive from past religious experiences. Certainly, the foundation of the faith usually has some sort of religious experience to show the authority of the central figure of the faith. In Judaism, we have Abraham's covenant experience, Moses experiencing the burning bush and many other instances of religious experience peppered throughout the Hebrew scriptures. Christianity is based on the resurrection of Jesus, the miracles of Jesus and such accounts as the baptism and the transfiguration of Jesus. The Buddha's whole enlightenment experience is the very basis of Buddhist teaching and practice. Not only is the revelation of the Qur'an to Muhammad through angel Jibril a religious encounter, the Qur'an itself is seen as the final miracle to humanity from Allah. The Vedas in Hinduism are the product of the insights of the rsis (seers) of ancient Hinduism and the whole purpose and climax of puja is to experience the darshan (divine glimpse). In Sikhism, Guru Nanak's religious experience in the river where he disappeared for three days is the turning point in his ministry. All are clear examples of the primary, albeit indirect level of dependency of religious communities on the religious experience of their founders.

In a similar way, particular events in the religious faith are often associated with a religious experience. These are remembered and celebrated through festivals and pilgrimages. For instance, the festival of Pesach remembers the events of the Passover where the enslaved Israelites were spared from the plague of the death of all the first born and escaped from Egypt. This establishes a common identity and reaffirms faith. Family and friends meet together for the Seder meal where they retell the story and everyone takes part. This coming together to remember the past religious experience and sharing in the same rituals and beliefs, creates a great sense of unity.

However, in the 21st century, many of these religious experiences have been challenged and doubted as historical happenings. Rather they are interpreted as symbolic or mythological. The extent to which this makes such religious experiences vital to religious communities is difficult to gauge. If the events never happened and there was no religious experience, can the account still be vital to the religious community? Some may argue, for instance, that the account of the resurrection of Jesus, if interpreted as symbolic, can still inspire and be meaningful to the religious community.

Private religious experiences like prayer and God speaking to believers is central to a religious community. The experience of present-day religious followers as they gather for worship each week can be seen as a religious experience. Muslims gather in unity for Friday prayers, Buddhists meet and practise as a sangha in monasteries to meditate. The examples are numerous. This shared worship can lead to a special kind of communal experience. Jesus said that where two or three are gathered together for prayer, there he is also. This suggests there is something special about the gathering together of religious believers for prayer and worship. It is also an occasion that strengthens the cohesion of that particular religious community. Therefore, it does seem that religious communities are dependent on religious experiences.

The giving of a testimony of the religious experience is an important means of appealing to others of the validity of the belief and practice of that particular faith. It strengthens and confirms the faith tradition. In some denominations of Christianity a testimony is often an important part of a baptismal service where a person confirms their faith in a public commitment. Indeed the actual decision to make such a commitment can be a religious experience – a sense of being called. The testimony also provides an opportunity to share one's spirituality with others, which can be strength to the religious community.

AO2 Activity

As you read through this section try to do the following:

1. Pick out the different lines of argument that are presented in the text and identify any evidence given in support.

2. For each line of argument try to evaluate whether or not you think this is strong or weak.

3. Think of any questions you may wish to raise in response to the arguments.

This Activity will help you to start thinking critically about what you read and help you to evaluate the effectiveness of different arguments and from this develop your own observations, opinions and points of view that will help with any conclusions that you make in your answers to the AO2 questions that arise.

An alternative line of argument may challenge the validity of all religious experiences and interpret them more in terms of modern psychology. Even if considered genuine, religious experiences can be divisive to a religious community. Religious practices are open to all, but religious experiences, especially mystic ones, can be seen to be exclusive to only a few. Those who do not experience them can feel, or be seen as less spiritual. Those who have undergone a religious experience are often accorded higher status within their religious traditions and are often regarded as being bestowed with a form of divine or special authority.

Indeed, if God is not active in the lives of religious believers, then in what sense is it a religious community. Such a lack of religious experience would suggest that God is just God of the past and not of all times and places. Religious experiences should be part of the experience of religious communities. So, in one sense, religious communities are dependent on religious experiences.

However, beliefs and practices are derived from past experiences, and lack of present day religious experience does not nullify those past events. They are still interpreted as events that promote a faith value system and guide a religious community. If there were no religious experiences from the past then there would be no religious communities.

Another line of argument may involve making some distinction between the different religious experiences. For example, prayer and worship form the basic practice of religious believers worldwide and therefore would be an essential part of what it means to be religious. However, the experiencing of visions and mystical events may not be open to all religious believers and therefore do not constitute an essential element of what it means to be religious.

Religious communities are not entirely dependent on religious experience since religious belief can be the result of rational enquiry. A reasoned faith does not demand a religious experience. However, others argue that being religious is about knowing God and often express it in terms of the need for both head and heart knowledge. It is the heart knowledge that demands a religious experience. In other words, religious believers may argue that individuals need a personal experience of God rather than second-hand accounts. On this view, religious experience may be essential for the individual as much as for a religious community.

However, some religious experiences can be open to different interpretations which imply they are not solely adequate for grounds of belief. Therefore, such religious experiences are not essential for the faith tradition.

Recent debate about the origin of religious experiences has cast some doubt about the whole nature of them. Physiological factors such as drugs and research into stimulation of the temporal lobes, have suggested natural explanations for religious experiences. In a similar way, psychological factors such as certain personality traits and the work of Jung have raised doubts about the validity of religious experiences.

In response, philosophers such as Richard Swinburne have defended their validity through his argument based on the principle of credulity and the principle of testimony which argue that religious experiences can be rationally seen to be genuine given rigorous testing according to certain criteria.

Therefore, the issue may not be so much about whether religious communities *are* dependent on religious experiences but more about whether they should ever be dependent given possible doubts about the validity of any religious experience.

AO2 Activity

List some conclusions that could be drawn from the AO2 reasoning from the above text; try to aim for at least three different possible conclusions. Consider each of the conclusions and collect brief evidence to support each conclusion from the AO1 and AO2 material for this topic. Select the conclusion that you think is most convincing and explain why it is so. Try to contrast this with the weakest conclusion in the list, justifying your argument with clear reasoning and evidence.

Key skills Theme 3 DEF

This theme has tasks that concentrate on a particular aspect of AO2 in terms of using quotations from sources of authority and in the use of references in supporting arguments and evaluations.

Key quotes

The mystic does not give us any information about the external world, he merely gives us indirect information about the condition of his own mind. (Ayer)

When one person suffers from a delusion it is called insanity. When many people suffer from a delusion it is called Religion. (Pirsig)

Key skills

Analysis involves:

Identifying issues raised by the materials in the AO1, together with those identified in the AO2 section, and presents sustained and clear views, either of scholars or from a personal perspective ready for evaluation.

This means:

- That your answers are able to identify key areas of debate in relation to a particular issue
- That you can identify, and comment upon, the different lines of argument presented by others
- That your response comments on the overall effectiveness of each of these areas or arguments.

Evaluation involves:

Considering the various implications of the issues raised based upon the evidence gleaned from analysis and provides an extensive detailed argument with a clear conclusion.

This means:

- That your answer weighs up the consequences of accepting or rejecting the various and different lines of argument analysed
- That your answer arrives at a conclusion through a clear process of reasoning.

AO2 Developing skills

It is now important to consider the information that has been covered in this section; however, the information in its raw form is too extensive and so has to be processed in order to meet the requirements of the examination. This can be achieved by practising more advanced skills associated with AO2. The exercises that run throughout this book will help you to do this and prepare you for the examination. For assessment objective 2 (AO2), which involves 'critical analysis' and 'evaluation' skills, we are going to focus on different ways in which the skills can be demonstrated effectively, and also refer to how the performance of these skills is measured (see generic band descriptors for A2 [WJEC] AO2 or A Level [Eduqas] AO2).

▶ **Your next task is this:** Below is an evaluation of **whether a religious experience can affirm a belief system**. At present it has no quotations at all to support the argument presented. In the margin are two quotations that could be used in the outline in order to improve it. Your task is to rewrite the outline but make use of the quotations. Such phrases as 'according to …', 'the scholar … argues', or, 'it has been suggested by …' may help.

In most religions, there is often a pivotal figure who is linked to the founding of that religion. Usually these figures experience a particularly significant event that marks the start of their ministry. Their authority derives from their religious experience as it is seen as confirmation and affirmation of their message. As a result, their revelation is trusted and forms the basis of the faith. It is embraced as the individual believer's own belief. However, modern scholarship has raised doubts as to the reliability of such accounts. On psychological and physiological grounds, it seems that religious experiences have natural explanations rather than supernatural.

In addition, historical critical method such as that involved in Biblical criticism has questioned the reliability of ancient sacred texts. It seems likely that the accounts of religious experiences should be interpreted more as symbolic or mythological rather than historical and literal.

David Hume drew attention to the fact that religious experiences, miracles, in particular, cannot be used as affirming a belief system since many religions have such accounts and they therefore contradict each other. If a religious experience is appealed to, to confirm a belief then what about all those other religious experiences in other faiths that confirm their beliefs?

Affirming belief through religious experiences assumes that there are already reasons for believing in God and the supernatural. Therefore, religious experiences cannot be appealed to show that God exists.

Others question such views appealing amongst other things to Swinburne's principle of credulity and principle of testimony. Also, just because other faiths claim religious experiences does not exclude the fact that God is not active in other faiths. Another approach might be to question whether all the accounts in other faiths are of the same strength of testimony. If the experience is consistent with the nature of God, then there seems no valid reason for rejecting the religious experience.

When you have completed the task, try to find another quotation that you could use and further extend your evaluation.

E: Different definitions of miracles

Introduction

At the start of a philosophical discussion on miracles, some definition would normally be expected. However, the question as to what exactly is involved in a proper conception of the miraculous is part of the controversy. Another area of controversy involves the grounds for deciding whether a miracle has taken place.

For instance, would you regard the following story as an example of a miracle? Why/why not?

You have to be pretty brave to jump out of a plane – but you also have to be lucky to survive the leap with a faulty parachute. Lareece Butler had fate on her side in March, when she escaped a free fall of 3,000 feet with only a broken leg, a fractured pelvis, and a concussion. As Butler plummeted, the chute's ropes twisted around her. She later told reporters she had prayed, 'God save me, please; I have a son', but could recall nothing else until she woke up in the hospital, surrounded by her amazed and grateful family. (from http://www.oprah.com/spirit/real-life-miracles_1#ixzz4oK1ubF7t)

The word miracle is derived from the Latin word for 'wonder'. The main characteristic of a miracle is that in some way it is unusual or extraordinary such that it provokes wonder. There have been a number of different philosophical definitions of a miracle and four of the main ones are discussed below.

St Thomas Aquinas

An early definition of a miracle was given by St Augustine (354–430) who held that a miracle is not contrary to nature because the hidden potentials in nature that make miracles possible have been placed there by God. Hence it is only contrary to our knowledge of nature.

St Thomas Aquinas (1225–1274) developed this understanding. He defined a miracle as 'That which has a divine cause, not that whose cause a human person fails to understand'. He believed that everything that existed had a nature, i.e. the things that it is able to do. A miracle is an event beyond the natural power of any created being. It has a 'divine cause' and so is not a normal part of the nature of things. God alone can do miracles since he is un-created. He distinguished between three kinds of miracle:

- Events in which God does something which nature could never do. For example, the sun going back on its course across the sky.

- Events in which God does something which nature can do, but not in this order, for example, someone living after death.

- Events in which God does something that the working of nature usually does, but without the operation of the principles of nature. For example, someone being instantly cured of an illness that usually takes much longer to cure.

In all three events God is active.

Thomas Aquinas (1225–1274)

This section covers AO1 content and skills

Specification content

Miracles the definitions of.

Key quote

A miracle is …. that which has a divine cause, not that whose cause a human person fails to understand. (Aquinas)

Specification content

St Thomas Aquinas (miracles different from the usual order).

quickfire

3.8 Name two key areas of controversy about miracles.

quickfire

3.9 What argument did Aquinas give to explain why miracles were not contrary to nature?

Specification content

David Hume (transgression of a law
of nature).

David Hume

Aquinas' understanding of miracles was couched in terms of objects being governed by their nature which gave them certain powers to act. However, since the 17th century, any talk concerning the behaviour of things became expressed in terms of the laws of nature or natural laws. By the time of David Hume it was thought that natural laws were universal and governed all events. In Section X of Hume's book *Enquiry Concerning Human Understanding* he defines a miracle as 'a violation of natural law'.

Hume then develops this by offering a fuller definition: 'a transgression of a law of nature by a particular volition of the Deity, or by the interposition of some invisible agent'. For Hume, a miracle not only had to be an event that broke the laws of nature but also had to express divine cause.

An example of this would be the raising of a person from the dead. It breaks our regular experience of the law of nature and demands an intervention by God or some supernatural agent. It is a miracle regardless of whether anyone recognises it or not.

Other examples might include the healing of a man with a withered arm, restoring the limb to its normal state, or walking on water with no support under the water and without the feet sinking into the water.

Key quote

The idea of a suspension of natural law is self-contradictory… This contradiction may stand out more clearly if for *natural law* we substitute the expression *the actual course of events*. *Miracle* would then be defined as 'an event involving the suspension of the actual course of events'. And someone who insisted on describing an event as a miracle would be in the rather odd position of claiming that its occurrence was contrary to the actual course of events. (McKinnon)

Jesus walking on water

Laws of nature

Hume's understanding of a law of nature has been understood by philosophers in two different ways. The first is often referred to as the 'hard' interpretation. This assumes that laws of nature are unalterably uniform. If miracles are a 'violation' of what cannot be altered, then miracles are impossible.

A similar 'hard' interpretation argues that what appears to be a violation of a law of nature is a misstated law of nature. The laws postulated need to be adjusted to take in the new circumstance, so that a new law of nature is now derived that now has no exceptions. Once again, the view is that there can be no violation of a law of nature.

An alternative understanding of a violation of a law of nature is referred to as the 'soft' view. This sees natural laws not as fixed laws that are unalterable in any circumstance, but rather natural laws that can have exceptions. Therefore, natural laws are seen as regular normal patterns of events but can be altered, for example, by the intervention of God. This then makes the issue for belief in miracles not about a logical impossibility but about whether the evidence for the altered law is credible and convincing.

quickfire

3.10 In what key way did Hume's definition of miracles differ from that of Aquinas?

quickfire

3.11 In which of Hume's books does his famous essay on miracles appear?

quickfire

3.12 State the definition of 'miracles' given by Hume.

David Hume (1711–1776)

Key quote

Nothing is esteemed a miracle, if it ever happens in the common course of nature. (Hume)

quickfire

3.13 What is meant by the 'soft' interpretation of a law of nature?

Study tip

When you are answering a question under timed conditions it is important to stay focused on the precise words of the question. Make sure you keep referring to this as you answer.

AO1 Activity

Close the book and see if you can explain to a fellow student three things about each of the two definitions you have read about so far (Aquinas and Hume). After listening to your fellow student do the same, between you try to come up with the best three points for each (it may be a combination of both answers).

R. F. Holland

Ray Holland (1923–2013) presents a completely different approach to defining a miracle. He argued that a miracle need neither involve a breaking of the laws of nature, nor an intervention by God. A miracle can only be spoken about against a religious background where the miracle is taken as a sign. Hence, a miracle can be defined as 'a remarkable and beneficial coincidence that is interpreted in a religious way'. Holland refers to this as a '**contingency miracle**'.

The illustration that Holland used was of a child caught between the rail tracks in his toy car, with a train fast approaching out of sight of the boy. The mother could see both the boy on the tracks and the train approaching. She realised that the boy would be hit by the train as there was too little distance for it to stop, once the driver saw the boy. However, the train suddenly started to slow down and eventually stopped about a metre away from the boy. The mother still said it was a miracle, even when she was later told that the reason for the train stopping was that the driver had suffered a heart condition and passed out, causing the automatic braking system to come into play and so stop the train.

In Holland's illustration, the mother thanks God. A non-religious person would describe the event as extraordinarily lucky. However, to the religious person, even though it doesn't break the laws of nature, it is seen as a miracle. It is not about a real action undertaken by a supernatural being. It is an interpretation of an ordinary event that makes it a miracle. Only if a person interprets the event as a miracle can the event be called a miracle.

Richard Swinburne

Richard Swinburne (b1934) endorses Hume's definition and accepts that a miracle is an objective event in which God intervened. However, he also makes two significant changes/additions:

(i) He borrows a phrase from Ninian Smart, to overcome what he regards as a misleading phrase that Hume used. Instead of Hume's phrase, 'a violation of a law of nature', Swinburne uses the phrase 'an occurrence of a non-repeatable counter-instance to a law of nature'. By this, he meant that given a law of nature (L), suppose an event (E) happens, i.e. a counter-instance. Then it is not possible that E could be predicted by replacing law L with a more successful law. It would also have to be the case that for any modified law which would successfully allow the prediction of event E, it would mean that the modified law would give false predictions in all other events. Whereas if we leave law L as it is, we have good reason to believe it would give correct predictions in all other conceivable circumstances.

(ii) Miracles hold some deeper religious significance than just breaking laws of nature. To be a miracle an event must contribute significantly towards a holy divine purpose for the world. Miracles are also seen as signs from God. The word 'sign'

Key term

Contingency miracle: a remarkable and beneficial coincidence that is interpreted in a religious fashion

Specification content

R. F. Holland (contingency miracle).

Holland's example of a miracle.

Specification content

Richard Swinburne (religious significance).

quickfire

3.14 What term does Holland use to define his type of miracle?

is used in John's Gospel to refer to Jesus' miracles which always seem to point to something beyond the actual event. The miracles are not seen as an end in themselves.

Considerations of why religious believers accept that miracles occur

A religious believer accepts that God exists. God's existence may be independently supported by traditional theistic arguments such as the design argument. If there is strong historical evidence that a miracle has occurred, then it seems reasonable to believe that it has, as long as there seems a suitable motive for God acting in this particular way.

Swinburne argues that natural theology establishes the probability that God would produce a revelation, which would need to be confirmed as authentic. Miracles could be the vehicle for this as long as the miracle could be judged as actual on the basis of historical investigation.

The nature of God as loving and compassionate may be another reason why religious believers may accept that miracles occur. God in his love might be expected to intervene through compassion. The various world religions understand God to be loving and caring for his people. Therefore, God may be expected to intervene on occasions through miracles to show that love and care.

Healing service

Swinburne also suggests that additional evidence for believing a miracle occurs could include the miracle happening in answer to a prayer and if the prayer was addressed to a named person (e.g. Jesus, Allah). If the world is God's creation, it becomes much more likely that he would wish to intervene and respond to requests to do so.

Evidence from sacred writings

The sacred writings of many religions record supernatural events to vindicate the claims of those who are accepted as God's messengers on Earth. In Christianity, for example, there are accounts of Moses and the parting of the Red Sea to let the Israelites escape from the pursuing Egyptians; the miracles of Jesus, Jesus' resurrection, the miracles performed by the Apostles Peter and Paul.

Some historians, such as Carl Becker, argue that miracles cannot be the object of historical investigation since miracles claim to involve a supernatural being. However, this has been challenged. Consider the resurrection of Jesus, which Christians claim was performed by God. The event can be checked out by historians since it is associated with other historical data. For example, the crucifixion, death and entombment of Jesus; Jesus' tomb discovered to be empty some days after his death; the claim by Jesus' followers that they saw Jesus alive several days after his death and entombment. It is true that the historian cannot identify the supernatural agent who is said to perform the miracle. However, it may be possible to detect through historical investigation various aspects of the supernatural agency of an alleged miracle. For religious believers this is particularly true as their world-view sees God involved in an event as agent.

Buddhism is non-theistic so that it rejects the idea of a miracle as a 'sign of God'. There are examples in early Buddhist texts of people who developed supernatural powers from mystical practices, but the Buddha did not encourage this. Later Tantric practices within Buddhism are associated with experiences of the

Specification content

Considerations of why religious believers accept that miracles occur.

quickfire

3.15 What two significant changes/additions did Swinburne make to Hume's definition?

Key quote

If a god intervened in the natural order to make a feather land here rather than there for no deep ultimate purpose, or to upset a child's box of toys just for spite, these events would not naturally be described as miracles. (Swinburne).

quickfire

3.16 Give three possible reasons why a religious believer may accept that a miracle has occurred.

Specification content

Considerations of why religious believers accept that miracles occur: evidence from sacred writings.

miraculous. Indeed, all the various schools of Buddhism, in one way or another, present views about the supernatural through either stories about the Buddha or the spiritual achievements of advanced practitioners.

Although Islam accepts the supernatural, Muhammad refused to do wondrous signs to strengthen his authority. The performance of miracles for some Muslims is a sign that a person's intention is still directed toward worldly approval, and not exclusively toward God. Although, for many Muslims, the only miracle is the production of the Qur'an, there are some Muslims who believe in miraculous stories associated with Muhammad.

Therefore, religious believers claim they have reason to accept that miracles occur since their sacred writings, which are considered the word of God, contain accounts of miracles.

Affirmation of faith traditions

Many religious believers claim that the only 'true' religion has 'true' miracles whilst other religions have either no miracles or 'false' miracles. Miracles function like a divine signature, confirming the authority and truth claims of a particular faith tradition. The Judaeo-Christian tradition supports this view. For example, Hebrews 2:3–4

'This salvation, which was first announced by the Lord, was confirmed to us by those who heard him. God also testified to it by signs, wonders and various miracles ...'

If God had an interest in communicating with people and if God desired that they be able to recognise some message as being from him, then the occurrence of miracles might be expected. For instance, there is an account in some traditions of Islam that the people of Mecca asked Muhammad to show them a miracle. So Muhammad split the moon into two by a gesture of his index finger. The halves of the moon appeared one behind the mountain and the other in front of it. The miracle confirmed the authority of Muhammad to the people.

Many Christians would argue that the resurrection of Jesus confirms that Jesus is the Son of God and that Christianity is the one true revelation. In both examples, for the religious believer, the miracle affirms the faith tradition.

For Christians the resurrection of Jesus affirms his status as the son of God.

Miracles can also be an essential element of the actual revelation. For example, according to the Christian tradition, Jesus entered our world by means of the Virgin Birth. Jesus died, overcame death by his resurrection and was victorious over evil. Christians see Jesus as the revelation rather than Jesus as the one who receives the revelation.

Some religious believers may take the evidence of miracles in other religions to support the claim that those religions also make valid or true claims. They would argue that there is no reason why God should not work miracles within any religion, as each contains a valid response to the reality of God.

Personal experience

Miracles can generate and support faith in individuals, especially if personally experienced. A good example are the claimed healing miracles at the Roman Catholic Shrine at Lourdes. Since 1858, there have been 69 verified miracles or cures in Lourdes. The most recent case occurred in 1989 but was not officially confirmed until 2013 after extensive investigation by a medical committee. The person healed is Danila Castelli who had a tumour. The medical committee concluded that the way she was healed remains 'unexplained according to current scientific knowledge'.

Key quote
Signs are with Allah only, and I am only a plain warner. (Muhammad)

Specification content
Considerations of why religious believers accept that miracles occur: affirmation of faith traditions.

quickfire
3.17 In what way does a miracle function like a divine signature?

Specification content
Considerations of why religious believers accept that miracles occur: personal experience.

The reason that religious believers go to Lourdes is that they believe in a personal God and they have faith that God answers prayers. Therefore, they pray for God's intervention. The prayer for a miracle usually relates to a prayer for healing. For the religious believer, miracles are not just events in the past that happened to individuals to confirm their authority, but are events that can happen in the present. God is active within his creation and works within the world to answer prayer.

Testimonies to personal healing are often a feature of charismatic Christianity. They have a world-view where miracles, signs and wonders are expected to be present in the lives of believers. Therefore, one reason why religious believers accept that miracles occur is that they claim they have personal experience of them or that they know others who have.

Study tip

It is important to know which scholar proposed which definition. Try not to confuse them by using a simple technique of letter association e.g. **R**ichard **S**winburne = **R**eligious **S**ignificance; **T**homas **A**quinas = **T**hree **A**ctive ways God intervenes, etc.

AO1 Activity

Create a simple table for the four different definitions of miracles. Column headings: scholar; definition; problems with the definition (if any).

Lourdes

AO1 Developing skills

It is now important to consider the information that has been covered in this section; however, the information in its raw form is too extensive and so has to be processed in order to meet the requirements of the examination. This can be achieved by practising more advanced skills associated with AO1. For assessment objective 1 (AO1), which involves demonstrating 'knowledge' and 'understanding' skills, we are going to focus on different ways in which the skills can be demonstrated effectively, and also refer to how the performance of these skills is measured (see generic band descriptors for A2 [WJEC] AO1 or A Level [Eduqas] AO1).

▶ **Your next task is this:** Below is **a summary of different understanding of 'laws of nature'**. At present, it has no references at all to support the points made. Underneath the summary are three references to the works of scholars, and/or religious writings, that could be used in the outline in order to improve the summary. Your task is to rewrite the summary but make use of the references. Such phrases as 'according to ...', 'the scholar ... argues', or, 'it has been suggested by ...' may help. Usually a reference included a footnote but for an answer in an A-Level essay under examination conditions this is not expected, although an awareness of which book your evidence refers to is useful (although not always necessary).

Hume's definition of a miracle refers to violation of a law of nature. However, his understanding of a law of nature was very different from that of Aquinas. Aquinas' understanding was in terms of objects being governed by their nature, which gave them certain powers to act. In contrast, Hume thought that natural laws were universal and governed all events. However, scholars disagree as to whether Hume thought the laws of nature were unalterable and confirmed and hence there was a uniform experience of those laws, or whether there could be exceptions if there was a supernatural intervention.

Key quotes

A miracle is a violation of the laws of nature; and as a firm and unalterable experience has established these laws, the proof against a miracle, from the very nature of the fact, is as entire as any argument from experience can possibly be imagined. **(Hume)**.

The idea of a suspension of natural law is self-contradictory ... This contradiction may stand out more clearly if for *natural law* we substitute the expression *the actual course of events*. *Miracle* would then be defined as 'an event involving the suspension of the actual course of events'. And someone who insisted describing an event as a miracle would be in the rather odd position of claiming that its occurrence was contrary to the actual course of events. **(McKinnon)**

Now of course we must agree with Hume that if there is absolutely 'uniform experience' against miracles, if in other words they have never happened, why then they never have. Unfortunately, we know the experience against them to be uniform only if we know that all the reports of them are false. And we can only know all the reports to be false only if we know already that miracles have never occurred. In fact, we are arguing in a circle. **(Lewis)**

When you have completed the task, try to write another reference that you could use and further extend your answer.

This section covers AO2
content and skills

Specification content

The adequacy of different definitions of miracles.

Issues for analysis and evaluation

The adequacy of different definitions of miracles

The criteria for an event to be called a miracle has long been debated. Views have changed as our scientific understanding and world-views have changed. What in the past may have caused wonder, may in the twenty-first century no longer be a cause for wonder. We may now be able to give explanations to account for the event. But does that necessarily stop it being a miracle?

Certainly, Holland did not think so. His definition was not about a real action undertaken by a supernatural being. It was the interpretation of an ordinary event that made it a miracle. Only if a person interprets the event as a miracle can the event be called a miracle. His story of the mother seeing the train stop before hitting her son, is to her a miracle even when later she learns that the driver had a heart attack and the dead man's handle automatically stopped the train.

In other words, we can identify natural reasons why the event happened and there seems no breaking of the laws of nature or supernatural intervention. Nevertheless, to the mother it was a miracle.

In one sense Holland's definition could be considered adequate since it is consistent with many people's world-view of a non-supernatural universe and the meaning of the word 'miracle' has been changed to fit in with that world-view. However, to other people, it may not be seen as adequate since it appears to call any unexpected beneficial event a miracle without any reference to a supernatural agent causing the event. It has used a term usually applied to the intervention of a supernatural agent and applied it to a natural occurrence albeit an unexpected occurrence. Holland's definition also removes objectivity since defining an event as a miracle rests solely on the decision of the individual. If someone regards an event as unexpected and beneficial, then for them it is a miracle.

One line of argument would be that even Holland's definition is still consistent with the idea of supernatural intervention. It is not a breaking of a law of nature so much as the supernatural agent working with the laws of nature and in the timing of the events. The result is a beneficial outcome. Such a view may then regard the definition as adequate.

Hence, many see some type of intervention and a beneficial outcome, as necessary aspects of a definition of a miracle.

Others feel this is inadequate and demand objective rather than subjective criteria. They point out that it would be impossible to know if God had acted or not since all events could be explained without recourse to God. In response, it could be argued that it is consistent with our understanding of the way God works in the universe, i.e. God working through evolution and free will choices. Also, that if it occurs in response to prayer then it would add weight to this interpretation of the event.

An early definition of miracle was given by Thomas Aquinas. He linked the act of a miracle with divine cause, since miracles were events which were not a normal part of the nature of things. Although Aquinas' definition clearly involves a supernatural agent, many may judge his definition as inadequate. This is because of his understanding that everything that existed had a nature, i.e. the things that it is able to do. Our modern-day understanding is of laws of nature. However, all three Biblical examples that he used (the sun going back on its course across the sky; someone living after death; someone being instantly cured of an illness that usually takes much longer to cure) are examples that Hume and Swinburne would agree with as examples of a miracle. The difference would be that they would express it in terms of laws of nature.

AO2 Activity

As you read through this section try to do the following:

1. Pick out the different lines of argument that are presented in the text and identify any evidence given in support.

2. For each line of argument try to evaluate whether or not you think this is strong or weak.

3. Think of any questions you may wish to raise in response to the arguments.

This Activity will help you to start thinking critically about what you read and help you to evaluate the effectiveness of different arguments and from this develop your own observations, opinions and points of view that will help with any conclusions that you make in your answers to the AO2 questions that arise.

One of the most popular definitions of a miracle is provided by Hume. He referred to 'a transgression of a law of nature by a particular volition of the Deity, or by the interposition of some invisible agent'. His definition has the idea of divine action and objectivity. However, much discussion has arisen over the idea 'violating a law of nature'. To some, this description seems to imply that God is going against his own laws.

It could be argued that laws of nature do not just describe what happens, they describe what happens in a regular and predictable way. When what happens is entirely irregular and unpredictable, then its occurrence is not something describable by natural laws. Hume seems to see a miraculous event as the occurrence of a non-repeatable counter-instance to a law of nature. If the law was left unmodified then we have good reason to think it would give good predictions in all other conceivable circumstances. In this sense it might be judged valid to claim that a law of nature had been violated in this one instance.

Others, such as Alistair McKinnon, maintain that defining miracles as a violation of a law of nature is a contradiction in terms. Laws of nature exert no opposition or resistance to anything. They are simply highly generalised shorthand descriptions of how things do in fact happen. He suggests that it would be more accurate to replace the phrase 'natural law' with 'the actual course of events'. This means that whatever happens is included in his understanding of natural laws. Hence Hume's definition is inadequate.

If such a God were omniscient then they would have foreseen the consequences of the laws of nature and possibly extended them to allow for 'miraculous' events to happen with greater moral consistency. Also, it portrays God as an interventionist rather than as a sustainer. If God is an interventionist then it suggests that God is monster since most miracles are trivial and events such as the holocaust had no intervention.

Hume's view that 'a firm and unalterable experience has established these laws' has also met with criticism. If they are unalterable then it is logically impossible for them to happen. Also, for laws of nature to have a uniform experience seems to deny that no miracle has happened. The question still remains, how could you know that prior to looking at the evidence?

A further criticism of Hume's definition is that it lacks any reference to the purpose of miracles.

Swinburne's definition attempts to overcome the problems of Hume's by its rephrasing of 'violations of a law of nature' to 'an occurrence of a non-repeatable counter-instance to a law of nature'. Swinburne also emphasises the purpose aspect of miracles as 'signs'.

However, many struggle with the idea of a God who intervenes. It suggests a God who is outside of time and it is not at all clear what that means.

Richard Purtill in a chapter in *In Defence of Miracles* identifies five parts to the definition of a miracle. First, the exception to the natural order is temporary. Second, it is an exception to the ordinary course of nature. Third, unless you have the idea of a way things ordinarily happen, then the idea of a miracle cannot be made clear. Fourth, a miracle must be caused by the power of God. Finally, it must address the purpose of miracles – they must be a sign of God acting. On this view, it seems that Swinburne's definition is the most comprehensive.

AO2 Activity

List some conclusions that could be drawn from the AO2 reasoning from the above text; try to aim for at least three different possible conclusions. Consider each of the conclusions and collect brief evidence to support each conclusion from the AO1 and AO2 material for this topic. Select the conclusion that you think is most convincing and explain why it is so. Try to contrast this with the weakest conclusion in the list, justifying your argument with clear reasoning and evidence.

How far different definitions of miracles can be considered as contradictory

The four definitions that are specified for study are those by Aquinas, Hume, Holland and Swinburne. One of the most obvious contradictions between these different definitions is that whilst Hume and Swinburne see God as interventionist and breaking laws of nature, Holland sees natural courses of events and amazing coincidences.

However, this may not be a contradiction. They could be seen to be describing different types of miracles. Holland's definition refers to 'contingency' miracles. It is when several events, all with natural causes, come together that make the event unusual. If the context is of a believer who has an expectation of divine agency acting, possibly because of praying – then the event might well be described as a miracle.

Norman Geisler refers to such events as a 'class two miracle'. The 'violation miracle' is that described by Hume and Swinburne, where it appears that a law of nature has been violated. Both types of miracles involve divine agency but working at different levels. So, is that really a contradiction?

Aquinas' definition also supports divine agency but because of scientific understanding of the times, he does not couch it in terms of breaking a law of nature. However, he does make clear that miracles are events that are different from the usual order. For Aquinas, a miracle is an event beyond the natural power of any created being. It has a 'divine cause' and so is not a normal part of the nature of things. His three kinds of miracles that he lists make this clear: events in which God does something which nature could never do (the sun going back on its course across the sky); events in which God does something which nature can do but not in this order (someone living after death); events is which God does something that nature does but without the operation of the principles of nature (instant healing).

AO2 Activity

As you read through this section try to do the following:

1. Pick out the different lines of argument that are presented in the text and identify any evidence given in support.

2. For each line of argument try to evaluate whether or not you think this is strong or weak.

3. Think of any questions you may wish to raise in response to the arguments.

This Activity will help you to start thinking critically about what you read and help you to evaluate the effectiveness of different arguments and from this develop your own observations, opinions and points of view that will help with any conclusions that you make in your answers to the AO2 questions that arise.

Key quote

It is not against the principle of craftsmanship ... if a craftsman effects a change in his product, even after he has given it its first form. (Aquinas)

Another line of argument might focus on the apparent contradiction between the relative subjectivity and objectivity of the miracle. The 'contingency miracle' is subjective and becomes a miracle when someone interprets events in this way – usually from within the circle of believers. In contrast, the 'violation miracle' is objective in that the breaking of the law of nature is identified by all, both by sceptics and believers.

However, some may disagree. Those who reject the supernatural (naturalism) would argue that no law of nature has been broken. Rather it is that we had an incomplete law and there exists a law of nature that incorporates the particular circumstance that has occurred.

At this point both the sceptic and the believer accuses the other of holding positions that are unfalsifiable. The sceptic accusing the religious believer of admitting no conceivable event to conclude that there is no God. The religious believer accusing the sceptic of admitting no conceivable event to conclude there is a supernatural.

Key quote

It often seems to people who are not religious as if there was no conceivable event or series of events the occurrence of which would be admitted by sophisticated religious people to be a sufficient reason for conceding 'there wasn't a God at all'. **(Swinburne)**

Another line of argument may consider whether the definitions contradict in terms of the extent to which they allow for the possibility of miracles to actually happen. Some contradiction can be seen, depending whether the 'hard' or 'soft' interpretation of Hume's definition is adopted. The 'hard' view understands the definition to rule out any possibility of miracles. Hume's understanding of miracles, in which the laws of nature are said to be violated, seems contrary to the scientific understanding of the universe that is mechanistic, orderly and regular. Given a set of conditions, the same effects will always follow. Therefore miracles cannot happen by definition. In response, it might be argued that the development of quantum physics has challenged this mechanistic understanding of the universe in favour of unpredictability. However, random non-significant events are not the general understanding of 'miracles'.

The 'soft' interpretation of Hume's definition allows for the possibility that miracles could occur rather than that they have occurred. Swinburne sees his understanding of miracles as consistent with the existence of a God and argues that it is reasonable to believe that they occur.

Another possible area of contradiction involves the issue of purpose of miracles. Hume does not consider this in his definition. Therefore, miracles are not linked or associated with some 'sign' from God or some beneficial intervention. In contrast, both Holland and Swinburne make clear that these are key elements of their definitions.

It could be argued that there is no contradiction between any of the definitions. They are merely focussing on different aspects and acknowledging two different types of events that can be called miracles (contingency and violation).

Indeed, this line of argument could accept that every definition of miracle is in itself correct but just not the fullest definition one could offer. Such an argument would say that each definition is useful to a religious believer in the way it is used to strengthen their faith. For instance, Holland's story allows for the religious experience and significance of a miracle to be drawn out from circumstances that are not only explainable by the supernatural.

Overall, perhaps the most important response to this issue would be 'does it really matter?' Different or contradictory does not mean that in a holistic sense this destroys the meaning, purpose or integrity of religious experience. After all, whether or not a miracle violates a law of nature or works within nature, the significance of either definition is what really matters for the religious believer.

AO2 Activity

List some conclusions that could be drawn from the AO2 reasoning from the above text; try to aim for at least three different possible conclusions. Consider each of the conclusions and collect brief evidence to support each conclusion from the AO1 and AO2 material for this topic. Select the conclusion that you think is most convincing and explain why it is so. Try to contrast this with the weakest conclusion in the list, justifying your argument with clear reasoning and evidence.

Key skills

Analysis involves:

Identifying issues raised by the materials in the AO1, together with those identified in the AO2 section, and presents sustained and clear views, either of scholars or from a personal perspective ready for evaluation.

This means:

- That your answers are able to identify key areas of debate in relation to a particular issue

- That you can identify, and comment upon, the different lines of argument presented by others

- That your response comments on the overall effectiveness of each of these areas or arguments.

Evaluation involves:

Considering the various implications of the issues raised based upon the evidence gleaned from analysis and provides an extensive detailed argument with a clear conclusion.

This means:

- That your answer weighs up the consequences of accepting or rejecting the various and different lines of argument analysed

- That your answer arrives at a conclusion through a clear process of reasoning.

Key term

Naturalist: a person who believes that only natural (as opposed to supernatural or spiritual) laws and forces operate in the world

AO2 Developing skills

It is now important to consider the information that has been covered in this section; however, the information in its raw form is too extensive and so has to be processed in order to meet the requirements of the examination. This can be achieved by practising more advanced skills associated with AO2. For assessment objective 2 (AO2), which involves 'critical analysis' and 'evaluation' skills, we are going to focus on different ways in which the skills can be demonstrated effectively, and also refer to how the performance of these skills is measured (see generic band descriptors for A2 [WJEC] AO2 or A Level [Eduqas] AO2).

▶ **Your next task is this:** Below is **an evaluation of whether definitions are suitable for identifying miracles**. At present, it has no references at all to support the arguments presented. Underneath the evaluation are three references made to the works of scholars, and/or religious writings, that could be used in the evaluation in order to improve it. Your task is to rewrite the evaluation but make use of the references. Such phrases as 'in his/her book ... (scholar) argues that ...', 'an interesting argument in support of this is made by ... who suggests that ...', or, 'the work of (scholar) has made a major contribution to the debate by pointing out ... ' may help. Usually a reference included a footnote but for an answer in an A Level essay under examination conditions this is not expected, although an awareness of which book your evidence refers to is useful (although not always necessary).

Before you can decide whether a miracle has happened, you must know how you would identify a miracle. The definitions that involve a violation of a law of nature are usually appealed to by theists. However, it is not clear how you would know a law of nature had been broken. How is it possible to distinguish between an unusual event in nature, a law of nature that is not complete and a miracle? Equally to appeal to a divine agency, as the cause assumes that there is a divine being, assumes that a divine being exists. Some would argue that it is a circular argument that appeals to miracles to prove the existence of God.

In response, some theists argue that events like the resurrection of Jesus are so unusual that a divine cause is the only explanation. However, no historical event can be justifiably identified as an act of God.

Theists may respond by arguing that there are other reasons for believing that there is a God. Others may argue that both the theist and the naturalist argue from a faith position. Neither side being able to falsify the other. Once the naturalists agree that they hold a faith position, then in all fairness they must allow other alternative world-views the same opportunity.

Key quotes

The problem of 'miracles' ... must be solved in the realm of historical investigation, not in the realm of philosophical speculation. (Montgomery)

The odds for getting a perfect bridge hand are 1 in 1,635,013,559,600. But it happened – naturally! The argument from the odd to God amounts to saying that adding more zeros to the end of a probability ratio can transform an unusual event into a miracle. (Geisler)

If a miracle is merely a portent [which] is not contrary to nature, but contrary to our knowledge of nature, it has no real apologetic value. (Flew)

When you have completed the task, try to write another reference that you could use and further extend your evaluation.

F: Contrasting views on the possibility of miracles: David Hume and Richard Swinburne

David Hume's essay and his scepticism of miracles

Although Hume's essay on miracles, chapter ten in his book *Enquiry Concerning Human Understanding* (1777), is scarcely twenty pages long, it is regarded as a major contribution to the debate about miracles. He wrote it to convince people that the appeal to miracles could not demonstrate the truth of Christianity or religion in general. The essay is in two parts. Part 1 attempts to show on philosophical grounds that the evidence against the occurrence of a purported miracle strongly outweighs the evidence in favour of the occurrence. Part 2 attempts to show that although in theory the evidence in favour could outweigh the evidence against, in practice this never happens.

Hume was an **empiricist** and therefore believed that all questions of truth had to be based on experience. This approach therefore required assessing evidence. He felt that this was particularly important for any historical enquiry since a wise person proportions their belief to the evidence. For example, if a particular event is claimed to have happened then an investigator will weigh the evidence in favour of the event happening against the evidence that it did not happen. Part of that evidence will include the testimony of witnesses and our experience of what usually happens.

Hume and his challenge relating to testimony-based belief

Given that a wise person 'proportions' their belief to the evidence, Hume examined the evidence for miracles. He concluded:

- Where the experience has been constant then this constitutes a full proof.
- Where it has been variable then it is a case of weighing the proportionate probability of the experience having happened against not having happened.
- Where the belief is about miracles then a difficulty arose. This was because a miracle (according to Hume) is a violation of the laws of nature that have been established by a firm and unalterable experience. In other words, there must have been a uniform experience against such an event in order for the event to be identified as a miracle. In such a case, even the most impressive testimony would merely balance the improbability of the miracle. Hume concludes that only testimony so strong that its falsehood would itself be more miraculous than the alleged miracle would convince him that a miracle had taken place.

Hume does not seem to deny the possibility of miracles as such but examines the balance of probability. What is more likely: that a miracle occurred or that a witness is either lying or mistaken? Miracles are by definition exceptional events, whilst people lying or being mistaken is common. Therefore, the probability seems against the miracle occurring. However, Hume examines the criteria by which to establish the virtual impossibility that the witnesses are lying or mistaken. He considers the quality of testimony that would be needed to outweigh our present-day experience of the regularity of nature.

This section covers AO1 content and skills

Specification content

David Hume – his scepticism of miracles including challenges relating to testimony-based belief.

Key term

Empiricist: a person who believes that all knowledge is based on sense experience

Tomb and monument to David Hume, Edinburgh

quickfire

3.18 According to Hume, what would convince him that a miracle had taken place?

Specification content

Challenges relating to the credibility of witnesses; susceptibility of belief.

Key quotes

There is not to be found in all history, any miracle attested by a sufficient number of men, of such unquestioned good sense, education and learning …. (Hume)

If the spirit of religion join itself to the love of wonder, there is an end of common sense; and human testimony, in these circumstances loses all pretensions to authority. (Hume)

… if a civilised people has ever given admission to any of them [miracles], that people will be found to have received them from ignorant and barbarous ancestors …. (Hume)

quickfire

3.19 Give three reasons Hume gave to doubt miracles that concerned the credibility of witnesses and susceptibility of belief.

Specification content

Challenges relating to the contradictory nature of faith claims.

Key quote

This argument … is not in reality different from the reasoning of a judge, who supposes, that the credit of two witnesses, maintaining a crime against any one, is destroyed by the testimony of two others who affirm him to have been two hundred leagues distant, at the same instant when the crime was said to have been committed. (Hume)

quickfire

3.20 Give the reason that Hume gave to doubt miracles that concerned faith claims.

Challenges relating to the credibility of witnesses and susceptibility of belief

In Part 2 of his essay, Hume attempts to demonstrate that the quality of the testimony required to establish the occurrence of a miracle can never be forthcoming and so miracles cannot be shown to have happened. He highlighted four reasons against miracles, three of which concern the credibility of witnesses and susceptibility of belief.

1. No miracle has a sufficient number of witnesses. What is required is a quantity of educated, trustworthy witnesses to a public event in 'a celebrated part of the world'. They would have to be 'of such unquestioned good sense as to secure us against all delusions in themselves'. In particular, the witnesses would have to have a lot to lose if they were found to be lying. Hume claims that in all history there have not been found such witnesses to a miracle.

2. People are prone to look for marvels and wonders. The passion and surprise arising from miracles, being an agreeable emotion, gives a tendency toward the belief of those events. Hume contends that a religionist may know the miracle is false but 'perseveres in it, with the best intentions in the world, for the sake of promoting so holy a cause'. They had a vested interest and were biased. These aspects can easily account for delusions about miracles.

3. The sources of miracle stories are from ignorant people. This seems to refer partly to uneducated Galilean peasants, a possible reference to the New Testament gospels. Hume noted that there were no equivalents in his day that compared to the recorded miracles in the Bible. Therefore, he focused on testimony of those in the distant past. The miracle stories acquired authority without critical or rational inquiry. Too often the learned merely deride the absurdity rather than inform themselves and others of the facts by which it can easily be refuted. If they had originated in 'a city renowned for arts and knowledge', rather than in some remote country, Hume maintains they would not have been believed.

Challenges relating to the contradictory nature of faith claims

Hume's final reason against miracles concerns his argument about religious traditions counteracting each other. This is different from the ones about testimony and susceptibility about belief. Unreliability here does not derive from that of the witnesses but rather that evidence is further contradicted by other witnesses. If an Islamic miracle supports Islam and so discredits Christianity as a true religion then, equally, any claim of a Christian miracle will likewise discredit Islam. Therefore, evidence for one is evidence against the other and vice versa. Every supposed miracle is used to establish that particular tradition and therefore is an indirect attempt to destroy the credit of other religions. Miracles are therefore self-cancelling as witnesses to the truth of a religious system.

Hume's conclusions

In Part 1 of his essay Hume concludes 'that no testimony is sufficient to establish a miracle, unless the testimony be of such a kind, that its falsehood would be more miraculous than the fact which it endeavours to establish'. In Part 2, Hume concludes that it is more rational to distrust the testimony about a miracle than to believe that the law of nature had been broken. The reason is that violations of truth are most common in the testimony concerning religious miracles. As a result, no such testimony can outweigh our experience of the regularity of the laws of nature.

Therefore, no testimony will be sufficient to establish a miracle. This also means that no miracle can be a just foundation for a religion.

Many scholars argue that Hume presents an *a priori* argument in Part 1 of his essay, and in Part 2 presents an *a posteriori* argument. Other scholars debate whether an empiricist could have an *a priori* argument, given empiricists argue that knowledge derives from experience. The whole matter rests on the use of the word 'argument' which is sometimes wrongly used instead of the word 'reasoning'. It should be noted that a deductive argument is different from an argument with elements of deductive reasoning. Arguments that contain elements of deductive reasoning are not necessarily deductive.

Study tip

As it is only 20 pages long then it may be possible for you to read Hume's essay for your own wider reading. www.davidhume.org/texts/ehu.html

AO1 Activity

Imagine a friend comes to report a miraculous experience to you. Using Hume's principles when analysing miracles think of five reasons to give to your friend as to why miracles do not occur to help them realise they may have been mistaken.

Swinburne's definitions of natural laws

Whereas Hume seems to reject the possibility of rational belief in miracles, Swinburne argues that there can be evidence that a law of nature has been violated and so accepts that rational belief in miracles is possible. His main writings on miracles can be found in his book *The Concept of Miracle* (1970).

As discussed earlier, Swinburne accepted the basis of Hume's definition of a miracle but instead of violations of the laws of nature, Swinburne used the phrase 'a non-repeatable counter-instance to a law of nature'. He avoids the word 'violation' as he thinks it suggests too close an analogy between laws of nature and civil or moral laws.

Identifying a non-repeatable counter-instance to a law of nature

Swinburne identifies three observations necessary that a non-repeatable counter-instance to a law of nature would have to fulfil:

1. If we have good reason to believe that an event E has occurred contrary to predictions of L (what we assume is a law of nature), and we have good reason to believe that events similar to E would not occur again in similar circumstances, then there is every reason to think that L is indeed a law of nature.

2. It would have to be the case that if we tried to modify the law of nature to try to predict event E then the modified law of nature will give false predictions in other circumstances.

3. If we leave the law of nature unmodified we have good reason to believe that the unmodified law will give correct predictions in all other conceivable circumstances.

Can a non-repeatable counter-instance be believed to have happened?

Swinburne then addresses the question of what would be a good reason for believing that an event E, if it occurred, was a non-repeatable as opposed to a repeatable counter-instance to what we had assumed was the law of nature L. This is crucial because if the event E is in fact a repeatable counter-instance, then all we would need to do would be to modify L to form a true law of nature that could also predict these repeatable counter-instances.

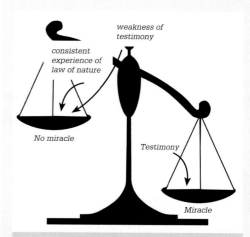

consistent experience of law of nature

weakness of testimony

No miracle

Testimony

Miracle

The issues involved in the weighing up of miracles

Specification content

Richard Swinburne – his defence of miracles, including definitions of natural laws.

Key quote

We have, to some extent, good evidence about what are laws of nature, and some of them are so well established and account for so much data that any modification of them which we could suggest to account for the odd counter instance would be so clumsy and ad hoc as to upset the whole structure of science. (Swinburne)

quickfire

3.21 What did Flew say about Hume's reason for rejecting historical evidence of witnesses in favour of the law of nature not being violated?

Key terms

Sacrament: one of the Christian rites considered to have been instituted by Christ to confer or symbolise grace

Tabernacle: box-like vessel for the exclusive reservation of the consecrated Eucharist

Transubstantiation: the Roman Catholic doctrine that in the Eucharist, the whole substance of the bread and wine changes into the substance of the body and blood of Christ

Specification content

Richard Swinburne's defence of miracles – contradictions of Hume's arguments regarding contradictory nature of faith claims.

A Roman Catholic Mass at consecration of the elements

A tabernacle containing the reserved sacrament

The philosopher Antony Flew commented that the reason Hume rejects historical evidence of witnesses and favours the law of nature not being violated is because the historical evidence is often appealing to a singular past event that is no longer possible to examine directly. In contrast, the supposed law of nature can be tested at any time by any person.

However, Swinburne points out that both historical and scientific evidence give only limited support to any claim. Also, both can be tested at any time by any person. The historical evidence is not just written or verbal testimony. It is also about the character, mind and competence of the original witnesses; physical traces of the event; present effects resulting from the event. He concludes that 'the wise man in these circumstances will surely say that he has good reason to believe that E occurred, but also that L is a true law of nature and so that E was a violation of it'.

As Swinburne comments, 'Whether there is such evidence is, of course, another matter'.

A non-repeatable counter-instance identified as a miracle

For a non-repeatable counter-instance of a law of nature to be a miracle, it has to be caused by a god. To conclude that it was brought about by a rational agent would be to give a different kind of explanation. If there is other evidence for the existence of God, then if event E is the sort of thing that is consistent with a god's character and is otherwise unexplained, then Swinburne argues that it is reasonable to believe that God caused the event. In particular he reasons that if events occur that normally occur by the intentions of human beings but they occur without human beings, then it would be justifiable to claim a non-material being caused it, i.e. a god.

Contradictions of Hume's arguments regarding contradictory nature of faith claims

Hume stated that miracles in different religious traditions were contradictory and self-cancelling. If miracles are appealed to as evidence for the truth of religion, then miracles in another religious tradition would destroy the evidence of that religion and vice versa.

Swinburne responds by pointing out that Hume's argument would only be valid if the two miracles were in conflict and incompatible. Swinburne claims that most alleged miracles do not give rise to conflict. He gives a fictional example of two such miracles that would illustrate a conflicting claim:

1. A devout Roman Catholic priest might be praying for a miracle to demonstrate the truth of the doctrine of **transubstantiation** when the **tabernacle** containing the **Sacrament** levitated.

2. A dedicated Protestant minister might pray for a miracle to happen to show that the doctrine of transubstantiation is idolatrous. Then lightning strikes out of a cloudless sky and destroys the tabernacle.

These are conflicting miracles concerning doctrine and Swinburne makes the point that religious miracles are not of this type.

A miracle in the context of Hinduism and one in the context of Islam will not usually show that specific details of their respective religions are true. Most, if they occurred, would only show the power of God or gods and their concern for the needs of people.

Paper headlines about Shiva milk drinking statue

Contradictions of Hume's arguments regarding credibility of witnesses

Swinburne accepts that Hume's three arguments against miracles involving credibility of witnesses are valid. However, he makes the point that the standards of evidence that Hume sets are very high, questioning what exactly constitutes a sufficient number of witnesses. One of the purported miracles in Hume's essay concerns the Tomb of Abbé Paris.

In the case of the Tomb of Abbé Paris, Hume considers the credibility of the witnesses in terms of their number, integrity and education as irrelevant though it is of an exceptional quality. Hume regards the miraculous nature of the event sufficient to reject it.

The second of Hume's points against miracles concerned the love of gossip and the bias that some people have such that they propagate a miracle story even when they know it isn't true. Again, Swinburne does not deny that happens but comments that there are other people who are scrupulously honest and only historical investigation will show which group the witnesses to any alleged miracle are in. In contrast, Hume seems to assume all believers are either deceivers or deceived.

Hume's third point against miracles centres on the origin of miracles as being from ignorant and barbarous nations. Swinburne comments that Hume seems to identify an ignorant nation as one that believes miracles happen. To make such a connection would seem unjustified.

Swinburne lists three principles for weighing conflicting evidence, besides the most basic principle of accepting as many pieces of evidence as possible:

1. Evidence of different kinds ought to be given different weights. For instance, our own memory ought to count for more than the testimony of another witness unless circumstances suggest otherwise, e.g. I am drunk.

2. Different pieces of evidence ought to be given different weights in accordance with any empirical evidence which may be available about their different reliability. For instance, we can weigh the different conflicting testimonies by looking at how reliable previous testimonies by these witnesses have been.

3. Multiple similar testimony from different witnesses ought to be given more weight against a lesser number of contrary testimonies, unless there is strong evidence of falsehood. For example, if five people all claim the same thing then it is more persuasive than one person saying something contrary, unless we can explain why the five people all said the same, e.g. they had plotted together to give false testimony.

Swinburne argued that these principles for assessing conflicting evidence were relevant to weighing up the evidence for miracles.

Study tip

There are a lot of key terms and different scholars in religious studies. Make sure you know what each term means and what each scholar argues. Try to avoid confusion by compiling your own glossary or flash cards as you go along.

AO1 Activity

Have a go at writing a conversation between Hume and Swinburne about miracles. Each scholar can say one thing in turn and then go back to the first for the second point, etc. Try to think of questions each one would ask the other. This will help you consolidate who said what and the objections they may have towards other definitions.

Specification content

Richard Swinburne's defence of miracles – contradictions of Hume's arguments regarding credibility of witnesses.

quickfire

3.22 Why did Hume reject belief in the miracles at Tomb of Abbé Paris?

Key quote

And what have we to oppose such a cloud of witnesses, but the absolute impossibility or miraculous nature of the events, which they relate? And this surely, in the eyes of all reasonable people, will alone be regarded as a sufficient refutation. (Hume)

Miracles at Tomb of Abbé Paris

quickfire

3.23 State one of Swinburne's principles for weighing conflicting evidence.

Key skills

Knowledge involves:

Selection of a range of (thorough) accurate and relevant information that is directly related to the specific demands of the question.

This means:

- Selecting relevant material for the question set

- Being focused in explaining and examining the material selected.

Understanding involves:

Explanation that is extensive, demonstrating depth and/or breadth with excellent use of evidence and examples including (where appropriate) thorough and accurate supporting use of sacred texts, sources of wisdom and specialist language.

This means:

- Effective use of examples and supporting evidence to establish the quality of your understanding

- Ownership of your explanation that expresses personal knowledge and understanding and NOT just reproducing a chunk of text from a book that you have rehearsed and memorised.

AO1 Developing skills

It is now important to consider the information that has been covered in this section; however, the information in its raw form is too extensive and so has to be processed in order to meet the requirements of the examination. This can be achieved by practising more advanced skills associated with AO1. For assessment objective 1 (AO1), which involves demonstrating 'knowledge' and 'understanding' skills, we are going to focus on different ways in which the skills can be demonstrated effectively, and also refer to how the performance of these skills is measured (see generic band descriptors for A2 [WJEC] AO1 or A Level [Eduqas] AO1).

▶ **Your final task for this theme is:** Below is **a summary of Hume's challenge to miracles based on the contradictory nature of faith claims.** You want to use this in an essay but as it stands it is undeveloped and has no quotations or references in it at all. This time you have to find your own quotations (about 3) and use your own references (about 3) to develop the answer. Sometimes a quotation can follow from a reference but they can also be used individually as separate points.

One of Hume's reasons against miracles concerns his argument about religious traditions counteracting each other. This is different from the ones about testimony and susceptibility about belief. It is not that the witnesses are false but that the claims of miracles in one religion are contradicted by claims of miracles in other religions. It is exactly how a judge reasons. Two witnesses who claim to be eyewitness to a crime and so be good evidence against a suspect, are destroyed by the testimony of two other witnesses who give evidence that the suspect was 200 miles away at the time the crime was committed, and so could not be guilty.

In a similar way the apologetic value of a claimed miracle in Christianity is destroyed by a claimed miracle in Islam.

The result will be a fairly lengthy answer and so you could then check it against the band descriptors for A2 (WJEC) or A Level (Eduqas) and in particular have a look at the demands described in the higher band descriptors towards which you should be aspiring. Ask yourself:

- Does my work demonstrate thorough, accurate and relevant knowledge and understanding of religion and belief?

- Is my work coherent (consistent or make logical sense), clear and well organised?

- Will my work, when developed, be an extensive and relevant response which is specific to the focus of the task?

- Does my work have extensive depth and/or suitable breadth and have excellent use of evidence and examples?

- If appropriate to the task, does my response have thorough and accurate reference to sacred texts and sources of wisdom?

- Are there any insightful connections to be made with other elements of my course?

- Will my answer, when developed and extended to match what is expected in an examination answer, have an extensive range of views of scholars/schools of thought?

- When used, is specialist language and vocabulary both thorough and accurate?

Issues for analysis and evaluation

The effectiveness of the challenges to belief in miracles

This section covers AO2 content and skills

Specification content

The effectiveness of the challenges to belief in miracles.

If miracles are understood in the sense of 'contingency miracles' then many would argue that there is no problem in believing in such events happening. They are just natural events that are amazing coincidences. To the theist, they would see God working through natural events, whilst the naturalists would not interpret the events as involving any divine agency. However, the naturalistic interpretation is open to the charge that the events are merely random, since there is no reason to believe otherwise unless the person has a prior belief in God. If the events are random there is no reason to think the events have any significance.

The main challenges to belief in miracles have come from the more traditional understanding of miracles involving the breaking of a law of nature for a purpose by a divine being. One line of argument might be to challenge the view that a divine agency is the necessary cause of the event. To claim that it must be ascribed to supernatural agents is to say something that no one could possibly have the right to affirm on the evidence of the event alone. To offer an explanation is very different from reporting the evidence of an occurrence of an inexplicable event. No matter how strange an event someone reports, the statement that it must have been due to a supernatural agent cannot be part of that report. Therefore the term 'miracle' should not be used in such instances.

Another challenge has been the problem of being able to identify whether a law of nature has been broken. It could be that the law was just incomplete and there is a law that includes the circumstance that occurred. Swinburne has attempted to address this problem by rephrasing what is meant by the breaking of a law of nature. He defines a miraculous event as the occurrence of a non-repeatable counter-instance to a law of nature. If the law was left unmodified then we have good reason to think it would give good predictions in all other conceivable circumstances. In this sense it might be judged valid to claim that a law of nature had been violated in this one instance. However, many might feel that the problem remains in showing that a law of nature has been broken. It is the case that both the theist and naturalist argue from a position of faith since neither position can be conclusively falsified.

Hume argued that it was unreasonable to believe in miracles. He considered that it will always be more reasonable to believe that the law of nature has not been broken, than to believe testimony that the law of nature has been broken. Testimony to miracles had inherent weaknesses and so was likely to be unreliable and weaker than our everyday experiences of the regularity of nature. Swinburne has responded to the challenge of the credibility of witnesses. However, the extent to which they are persuasive will be influenced by a person's world-view. Hume's claim that no miracle has a sufficient number of witnesses has been challenged as far too stringent and that many events in history would not pass the test. St Paul claimed that the resurrected Jesus was seen by at least five hundred people whilst the Angels of Mons were witnessed by hundreds of people. Nevertheless, most events in history are not claiming to involve the supernatural so maybe it is not unreasonable to demand a higher quality of evidence for claimed miracles. For example, the resurrection accounts may have been written long after the alleged event and may not have been meant to be taken literally. Also they were written by people who may have had a vested interest. A point that Hume draws attention to.

Hume himself gave an example in his essay 'On Miracles' which was witnessed publically by a large number of creditable people – yet dismissed the account as unreliable on the grounds that it was impossible. This suggests Hume decided it was unreasonable to believe in miracles regardless of the evidence.

AO2 Activity

As you read through this section try to do the following:

1. Pick out the different lines of argument that are presented in the text and identify any evidence given in support.

2. For each line of argument try to evaluate whether or not you think this is strong or weak.

3. Think of any questions you may wish to raise in response to the arguments.

This Activity will help you to start thinking critically about what you read and help you to evaluate the effectiveness of different arguments and from this develop your own observations, opinions and points of view that will help with any conclusions that you make in your answers to the AO2 questions that arise.

Another line of argument is that testimony is not the only evidence for miracles. Physical effects can be seen such as a healed withered hand or X-rays.

However, some theists see God as sustainer not interventionist but God as sustainer does not deny the possibility that God also intervenes. This view that miracles are a breaking of a law of nature could be seen as putting God into the role of spectator of events. He is a God who is outside of the universe and who observes events. At times he enters our world to change events by suspending natural laws. Religious believers may argue that prayer is consistent with such a view, in that in praying, believers are asking God to intervene. Some also combine a belief that miracles break laws of nature with a belief that laws of nature are the means by which God sustains the universe.

Another aspect that is a challenge to belief is that miracles appear to limit God in time. Indeed, the idea of an interventionist God is contrary to classical theism where God is seen as sustainer and preserver of the universe where the world is dependent on God's sustaining activity for its existence. In other words, an interventionist God would have to be limited to the time frame of the event in order to intervene. This is incompatible with the idea of God being outside of time. However, it is not clear what being inside or outside time means. Whatever they do mean, it is not obvious why God could not be both inside and outside time.

The idea that miracles are trivial acts and so present God as a monster figure has been challenged by various attempts at providing some sort of theodicy. However, the extent of the success of the theodicies is questionable. The problem of evil remains a major problem for many people. If God is able to intervene, then why doesn't he address the real problems of the world more directly by means of miracles? This is part of the problem of evil and suffering. God has the means (power) and the motivation (love, goodness) to eliminate evil and suffering. Yet there is evil and suffering. God seems indifferent to the continued existence of suffering in the world.

Indeed, a recent professor of divinity at Oxford University, Maurice Wiles, argued that a God who acts in such a trivial way is a God not worthy of worship. This implies that miracles do not happen if belief in a traditional God is to be maintained.

Another challenge to belief in miracles has been that miracles contradict science and that to conclude that an event is caused by God because it appears to break a law of nature is to resort to a 'God of the gaps' argument. Science may have some unanswered questions – things that, as yet, have not been explained. However, it does not justify religious believers to argue that if science can't explain how something happened, then God must be the explanation. Such arguments are called 'God of the gaps' arguments.

However, science is not invalidated if God intervenes and from time to time breaks the laws of nature. It just means that on those occasions science's predictions based on those laws will be incorrect. There is no entity called 'science' that can authoritatively rule whether miracles can or cannot happen. Science is neutral and has limitations.

It could be concluded that it is rational to believe that a miracle has occurred while allowing the possibility that evidence might turn up later to show that we were mistaken.

Perhaps the issue can be solved in looking at our understanding of the laws of nature. If laws of nature are generalisations formulated retrospectively to cover what has happened, then there cannot be miracles. For whenever any event happens that is outside of the established natural laws, it would simply mean that we must widen the law to cover this new case. In this understanding, supposed laws of nature are not broken but are better described as incomplete laws that now have to be adapted to include the new happening. However, this still leaves us with the concept of a miracle that works within the laws of nature.

AO2 Activity

List some conclusions that could be drawn from the AO2 reasoning from the above text; try to aim for at least three different possible conclusions. Consider each of the conclusions and collect brief evidence to support each conclusion from the AO1 and AO2 material for this topic. Select the conclusion that you think is most convincing and explain why it is so. Try to contrast this with the weakest conclusion in the list, justifying your argument with clear reasoning and evidence.

The extent to which Swinburne's responses to Hume can be accepted as valid

Specification content

The extent to which Swinburne's responses to Hume can be accepted as valid.

Swinburne's responses to Hume cover three main areas. The first concerns Hume's actual definition of miracles. Swinburne interprets the definition as the 'soft' meaning rather than the 'hard' meaning. Many feel this is justified as if the 'hard' interpretation was intended by Hume, it is not clear why Hume then argued against the reliability of testimony. Others argue that Hume did mean the 'hard' interpretation and was making clear that there had indeed been 'a firm and unalterable experience [that] has established these laws'. Indeed, Hume records accounts of miracles that were witnessed by people of unquestioned integrity, yet he refused to credit such testimony on the grounds of 'the absolute impossibility or miraculous nature of the events which they relate'. This implies that Hume rejected miracles regardless of the evidence, even though Hume was an empiricist and so should be led by the evidence.

It could be argued that science is not invalidated. If God intervenes and 'from time to time breaks the laws of nature' then it only follows that science's predictions based on those laws will be incorrect 'from time to time'. It must be acknowledged that scientific methodology itself has limitations. There is no entity called 'science' that can authoritatively rule whether miracles can or cannot happen as science is neutral. Indeed, it is quite rational to believe that a miracle has occurred, while allowing the possibility that evidence might turn up later to show that we are mistaken.

Swinburne's rephrasing of 'a violation of a law of nature' again seems helpful. It makes clear that identification of a breaking of the law of nature requires that the exception to the natural order is temporary and it is an exception to the ordinary course of nature.

However, this would still not address the naturalist position.

Many feel that Swinburne's addition to the definition that includes 'purpose' is important. This fits in with the idea of religious 'signs' rather than a God who just 'shows off'.

The second area in which Swinburne responded to Hume concerned claims that miracles in different religious traditions were contradictory and therefore self-cancelling. The reasoning is that if miracles are appealed to as evidence for the truth of a religion, then miracles in another religious tradition would destroy the evidence of that religion. However, it is not clear that miracles do actually give rise to conflict. They tend to show the power of God or gods and their concern for the needs of people. For them to be contradictory would require two opposing doctrines to be authenticated by a miracle. Swinburne claims this has not occurred. A miracle in the context of Hinduism and one in the context of Islam will not usually show that specific details of their respective religions are true. The fact that miracles occur in different faith traditions does not constitute a contradiction. However, many take issue with this argument. For instance, the resurrection of Jesus is often cited as proof of Christianity and by implication affirms that Christianity is the only true faith. In response, many people may argue that God reveals himself in different ways to different people and through different religions. Others may challenge the authenticity of claimed miracles in other faiths or even assume it is the work of other supernatural agents.

AO2 Activity

As you read through this section try to do the following:

1. Pick out the different lines of argument that are presented in the text and identify any evidence given in support.

2. For each line of argument try to evaluate whether or not you think this is strong or weak.

3. Think of any questions you may wish to raise in response to the arguments.

This Activity will help you to start thinking critically about what you read and help you to evaluate the effectiveness of different arguments and from this develop your own observations, opinions and points of view that will help with any conclusions that you make in your answers to the AO2 questions that arise.

Swinburne's third area responding to Hume concerns the credibility of witnesses. Hume cites a number of reasons including the absence of sufficient number of quality witnesses. It could be argued that Hume's argument is reasonable since the witnesses must be trustworthy and reliable. However, a weakness in the argument may be that it is not clear how many witnesses are required to qualify for 'sufficient'. Is belief ultimately based on the number of witnesses? Maybe the nature of the event and the extent it is consistent with the nature of God and his purposes are more significant than how many witnesses there are to the event.

Hume seems to write as if all believers were either deceivers or the deceived. In his chapter on miracles in his book *Enquiry concerning Human Understanding* he cited some miracles that occurred in France which supposedly took place in his own lifetime. Hume acknowledged that the events were witnessed by people of unquestioned integrity. However, Hume refused to credit such testimony on the grounds of 'the absolute impossibility or miraculous nature of the events which they relate'. This implies that Hume rejected miracles regardless of the evidence. However, as an empiricist he surely should go by the evidence. It raises the wider question as to the extent that weight of evidence can persuade us to change our minds.

Another aspect of testimony that Hume raised against miracles concerned the love of gossip and bias of people who tend to spread stories of miracles, especially if the account is used to establish a religion, even though they know the miracles to be false. Hume also claimed that the origins of miracles were from ignorant and barbarous nations resulting in the miracle stories acquiring authority without critical or rational inquiry.

Certainly, Swinburne seems correct in drawing attention to the different weighting that should be given to various witnesses. For instance, multiple similar testimonies from different witnesses ought to be given more weight against a lesser number of contrary testimonies, unless there is strong evidence of falsehood. E.g they had plotted together to give false testimony. Hume does seem to imply that all believers were either deceivers or deceived. However, we do know that accounts can undergo change as they are passed on. It has also been argued that miracles cannot be open to historical research since the agent to which a miracle is ascribed in non-empirical and supernatural and so cannot be detected by historical methods. In response, Francis Beckwith pointed out that disproving the historicity of a miracle is only possible if it is within the bounds of the historical endeavour to investigate a miracle.

Another line of argument might be to follow Swinburne's positive reasons for believing in miracles. He argues that we should actually expect miracles since God needs to communicate with his creatures and to authenticate his message. He further argues that if the event happens in response to prayer and is consistent with the nature of God, then it is acceptable historical evidence.

Others may dismiss testimony on the grounds that God cannot enter time and space since God is outside of time. Hence the debate focuses not just on testimony itself but also on the coherency of what the testimony is claiming.

The alternative definition of miracle as an event of religious significance faces difficulties over testimony. It seems to demand that God providentially orders the world so that natural causes of events are ready and waiting to produce certain other events at the right time. Many would find that difficult to accept and so would regard testimony as insufficient to establish the miracle.

Some may conclude that Swinburne raises valid responses to Hume's arguments. However, it may well be that the believer and the naturalist with their different world-views will remain unconvinced of the other's position.

AO2 Activity

List some conclusions that could be drawn from the AO2 reasoning from the above text; try to aim for at least three different possible conclusions. Consider each of the conclusions and collect brief evidence to support each conclusion from the AO1 and AO2 material for this topic. Select the conclusion that you think is most convincing and explain why it is so. Try to contrast this with the weakest conclusion in the list, justifying your argument with clear reasoning and evidence.

AO2 Developing skills

It is now important to consider the information that has been covered in this section; however, the information in its raw form is too extensive and so has to be processed in order to meet the requirements of the examination. This can be achieved by practising more advanced skills associated with AO2. For assessment objective 2 (AO2), which involves 'critical analysis' and 'evaluation' skills, we are going to focus on different ways in which the skills can be demonstrated effectively, and also refer to how the performance of these skills is measured (see generic band descriptors for A2 [WJEC] AO2 or A Level [Eduqas] AO2).

▶ **Your final task for this theme is:** Below is **an evaluation of whether Hume displayed a contradictory approach to miracles**. You want to use this in an essay but as it stands it is a weak argument because it has no quotations or references in it at all as support. This time you have to find your own quotations (about 3) and use your own references (about 3) to strengthen the evaluation. Remember, sometimes a quotation can follow from a reference but they can also be used individually as separate points.

Scholars disagree as to the extent that Hume's essays contain contradictory ideas. One area that appears contradictory is whether Hume thought that miracles were impossible. Both in his definition and in his assessment of particular miracles he seems ambiguous. Certainly, if one takes a hard interpretation of his definition, it seems that laws of nature cannot be violated regardless of alleged evidence to the contrary. However, if one takes the 'soft' interpretation then it appears it is more an issue of the strength of the evidence as to whether a miracle occurred.

It is not clear if Hume contradicts his supposed empiricist position when he assesses miracles. An empiricist should be led by the evidence yet his approach seems to contain some *a priori* arguments.

The result will be a fairly lengthy answer and so you could then check it against the band descriptors for A2 (WJEC) or A Level (Eduqas) and in particular have a look at the demands described in the higher band descriptors towards which you should be aspiring. Ask yourself:

- Is my answer a confident critical analysis and perceptive evaluation of the issue?

- Is my answer a response that successfully identifies and thoroughly addresses the issues raised by the question set?

- Does my work show an excellent standard of coherence, clarity and organisation?

- Will my work, when developed, contain thorough, sustained and clear views that are supported by extensive, detailed reasoning and/or evidence?

- Are the views of scholars/schools of thought used extensively, appropriately and in context?

- Does my answer convey a confident and perceptive analysis of the nature of any possible connections with other elements of my course?

- When used, is specialist language and vocabulary both thorough and accurate?

Key skills

Analysis involves:

Identifying issues raised by the materials in the AO1, together with those identified in the AO2 section, and presents sustained and clear views, either of scholars or from a personal perspective ready for evaluation.

This means:

- That your answers are able to identify key areas of debate in relation to a particular issue

- That you can identify, and comment upon, the different lines of argument presented by others

- That your response comments on the overall effectiveness of each of these areas or arguments.

Evaluation involves:

Considering the various implications of the issues raised based upon the evidence gleaned from analysis and provides an extensive detailed argument with a clear conclusion.

This means:

- That your answer weighs up the consequences of accepting or rejecting the various and different lines of argument analysed

- That your answer arrives at a conclusion through a clear process of reasoning.

T4 Religious language

Specification content

Limitations of language for traditional conceptions of God such as infinite and timeless.

Communication is complex

quickfire

4.1 What do we mean by communication?

Key term

Metaphysical: that which is beyond, or not found in, the physical world

---

A: Inherent problems of religious language

Limitations of language for traditional conceptions of God such as infinite and timeless

Our communication depends on language – this may sound like an obvious statement to make but the implications are significant and it is important that we set these out from the beginning. Whether we are speaking to someone, listening to someone, writing something or reading something, there are many assumptions that we make about the nature of communication that are taken for granted. One such assumption is that we can be understood. If this is not true, then our communication is ineffective. Our speaking and writing would be nothing more than random sounds and shapes, as our intended audience could not interpret what we are trying to say. Equally, if we do not possess the tools to be able to decode what we hear and what we read, then communication is again rendered ineffective.

All of our language is based on experience. Communication is about, amongst other things, sharing ideas, experiences and realities with each other. For these to be meaningful we must be able to relate in some way to what we are being told. In other words, we need to have some experience base upon which to build our understanding of the language that we share. Language that communicates common experiences (e.g. my house is made of red bricks; my car is black, etc.) presents no difficulty in being interpreted; the interpretation is rooted in a shared experience. For example, to discuss what it means for water to be wet, it is necessary for us to have experienced water and to understand what the concept 'wet' refers to. Once we have an agreed common understanding of these things, then such statements become both understandable and meaningful. Perhaps, importantly, even if we did not have access to either of these things, we could understand what the meaning was in principle, as we would also understand how we could gain the necessary experience to understand them.

The vast majority of everyday communication is about the physical world – that is, after all, the world we inhabit. However, there are also forms of communication that deal with aspects of our lives that are not to be found in the physical world. Language about emotions, ideas, expressions of artistic preferences, ethical discussions and language about religion all go beyond what is found in our physical realities. Such concepts are sometimes referred to as **metaphysical**. For some, such language is often dismissed, being considered as not having the same level of meaning as language about the physical world because there can be no objective agreement on the experiences being discussed. Indeed, some consider such language to have no value in the empirical world.

David Hume famously stated: 'If we take in our hand any volume; of divinity or school metaphysics, for instance; let us ask, Does it contain any abstract reasoning concerning quantity or number? No. Does it contain any experimental reasoning concerning matter of fact and existence? No. Commit it then to the flames: for it can contain nothing but sophistry and illusion.'

Whilst this is not a direct attack on the use of metaphysical language *per se*, it provided a foundation upon which others would later do precisely that, as we shall see when we look at the work of the logical positivists.

As our language is based upon experience, and our experiences are generally confined to the empirical world and our interactions with it, our language therefore is somewhat limited in its scope to discuss things beyond this. For example, we can describe any object in a three-dimensional physical space but were someone to ask us how we might describe the same object in five-dimensional space, we would struggle. This is because our experiences are rooted in three-dimensional physical spaces. We do not exist in five dimensions.

Therefore, talk about such ideas becomes problematic – unless we are mathematicians. A mathematician might talk about five dimensions with some confidence – albeit in terms of an abstract concept. Other mathematicians might well understand this discussion but, in all likelihood, those who are not mathematicians familiar with fifth-dimensional mathematical constructs, would find such talk beyond their ability to make sense of it.

Different places of worship all use specific and different religious languages!

The same might be said of religious language. Indeed, the language used to express the 'Ultimate' or 'God' within a religious tradition encounters the same problems. For example, God as infinite and timeless appear more like mathematical, abstract claims than they do realities that we see and experience in the world around us. Again God is often seen to be transcendent, a spirit, beyond this world of experience or in the case of Buddhist nirvana, impossible to express.

The main problem, then, remains in that religious language about God is unverifiable in relation to our common base of experiences that give language its meaning.

The challenge to sacred texts and religious pronouncements as unintelligible

If language is the method of communication, then religious language is the method of communicating about religion. In simple terms that might be to describe physical objects with religious connotations such as places of worship, collections of sacred writings or describing the physical action that a religious believer might undertake during a specific religious ritual. In all such cases, the language is understandable and relatable because it deals with the observable and experienced empirical world.

However, once the religious language goes on to describe the divinities that are worshipped in such buildings or the teachings relating to an afterlife that may be

Key term

Logical positivist: describing the philosophers who supported the claim that language could only be meaningful if it could be verified by empirical means

quickfire

4.2 Name two inherent problems of religious language.

Specification content

Challenge to sacred texts and religious pronouncements as unintelligible.

Key quote

If we take in our hand any volume; of divinity or school metaphysics, for instance; let us ask, Does it contain any abstract reasoning concerning quantity or number? No. Does it contain any experimental reasoning concerning matter of fact and existence? No. Commit it then to the flames: for it can contain nothing but sophistry and illusion.

(Hume)

Specification content

Challenge that religious language is not a common shared base and experience.

contained within those sacred writings or even how the ritual actions being performed can purify an individual's soul, then suddenly what is being communicated may not be either understandable or relatable.

For instance, how does a non-believer know what is meant when they are greeted on entering a Pentecostal Church with the question, 'Have you been washed in the blood?' or being told that 'God's presence is here' or even that 'heaven and hell are religious truths'? The same can be said for other religious traditions and their particular descriptions of beliefs and experiences.

How can we talk meaningfully about an infinite God?

The challenge that religious language is not a common shared base and experience

For this reason, there are those philosophers who consider that religious language is inherently problematic; purely on the basis of it not communicating ideas that can be agreed upon by all as possessing an empirically knowable 'truth'. When talking about the traditional conceptions of God, there is no common or shared experience universally applicable to those with a faith commitment and those without. Our language is experience based – and our experiences are time limited (i.e. they are based within the confines of time – in that they have a past, present and future) – thus to talk about things beyond our experience means to move away from that which can be known. To talk about things beyond time – with concepts such as infinity or timelessness, means to talk about ideas that can only ever be expressed in abstract terms – at this point, the empirical understanding of language breaks down.

To reiterate: if I talk about the place of worship that I attend, then I can describe its physical location and features. What I am talking about can be 'known' by others via empirical and experience-based means. There is no problem with my description. Once I begin to talk about my belief of an infinite, timeless, transcendent divinity that loves me and has a specific plan and purpose for my eternal soul, then no empirical or experience-based means could establish the truth of what I have just said.

In a similar way, the experience of darshan for a Hindu performing puja in a Hindu temple, the Buddhist experience of the jhanas, the presence of the Holy Spirit during worship and sacraments for a Christian or the experience of Shekhinah during worship for a Jewish devotee are all beyond the empirical or experience-based means that could establish the truth of what in fact they have all proposed to have 'experienced'. This is because all such language is specific to the individual or community that describe it and it is this fact, for many philosophers, that immediately removes it from the possibility of universal verification.

This, in summary, is the inherent problem of religious language.

The differences between cognitive and non-cognitive language

Philosophers considering how language is used, generally divide it into two main forms. These forms are **cognitive** and **non-cognitive** language. Whilst these terms may appear complex, their meaning is quite straightforward and applying them to the way that we use language is particularly useful when we attempt to consider whether language is meaningful or not. The act of cognition is the act of knowing something; not by intuition but knowledge and understanding that is gained through experiences and the senses. In this sense cognitive language is any form of language that makes an assertion, which is usually factual in nature, in the sense that it can be demonstrated to be true or false by objective means. These means might be through **verification** or **falsification** (see Theme 4 – Section B). Scientific language – in the sense of language used in science to describe the external world, is exclusively cognitive – expressed in terms of what is known or can be known.

Religious language, however, is not as straightforward. When religious language is used in a cognitive sense then it is referring to a statement that is believed to be true – such as in the statements used in the traditional theistic proofs – statements which purport to be able to determine that God exists as an external reality that can be shown to be true via empirically verifiable means – e.g. in the cosmological argument when the series of causes and effects are linked to the concept of there being an initial first cause, that theistic philosophers claim to be God.

In contrast to this, language can also be considered to be non-cognitive. When language is non-cognitive, it is not used to express empirically knowable facts about the external world. It is not something that can be held up to objective scrutiny. This is because non-cognitive language is language that expresses opinions, attitudes, feelings and/or emotions. It is language which relates to a person's view of what reality may mean to them – and this may differ from the view of another, even though they may be experiencing the same reality. Both views are held to be valid – but in a non-cognitive sense. For instance, have you ever woken up in a bad mood? Has it affected the way in which you have viewed the people and world around you? This is because your non-cognitive view of the world has a reality that is 'true' for you – even if it is not an empirically verifiable fact of the actual external reality of the people and world around you! (If you woke up in a really good mood the same world and people would impact on you differently again.)

Non-cognitive language is often used in religious language, according to several religious philosophers, as it is language making claims about a believer's attitude towards the world around them, based on their religiously held beliefs.

Specification content

The differences between cognitive and non-cognitive language.

Key terms

Cognitive: language that is empirically verifiable and makes assertions about objective reality

Falsification: proving something false by using evidence that counts against it

Non-cognitive: language that is not empirically verifiable or falsifiable but instead expresses an attitude towards something

Verification: proving something true by using evidence that counts towards it

Non-cognitive language is not always clear to another because it expresses opinions, attitudes, feelings and emotions.

AO1 Activity

Draw up a table with the following headings and give examples from language for each one: cognitive; non-cognitive; metaphysical; verifiable.

Study tip

To help you remember the meaning of some of the key words for religious language have some clear examples to use in order to help you explain each one.

quickfire

4.3 What is meant by cognitive language?

quickfire

4.4 What was logical positivism?

Key skills Theme 4 ABC

This theme has tasks that deal with the basics of AO1 in terms of prioritising and selecting the key relevant information, presenting this in a personalised way and then using evidence and examples to support and expand upon this.

Key skills

Knowledge involves:

Selection of a range of (thorough) accurate and relevant information that is directly related to the specific demands of the question.

This means:

- Selecting relevant material for the question set
- Being focused in explaining and examining the material selected.

Understanding involves:

Explanation that is extensive, demonstrating depth and/or breadth with excellent use of evidence and examples including (where appropriate) thorough and accurate supporting use of sacred texts, sources of wisdom and specialist language.

This means:

- Effective use of examples and supporting evidence to establish the quality of your understanding
- Ownership of your explanation that expresses personal knowledge and understanding and NOT just reproducing a chunk of text from a book that you have rehearsed and memorised.

AO1 Developing skills

It is now important to consider the information that has been covered in this section; however, the information in its raw form is too extensive and so has to be processed in order to meet the requirements of the examination. This can be achieved by practising more advanced skills associated with AO1. The exercises that run throughout this book will help you to do this and prepare you for the examination. For assessment objective 1 (AO1), which involves demonstrating 'knowledge' and 'understanding' skills, we are going to focus on different ways in which the skills can be demonstrated effectively, and also refer to how the performance of these skills is measured (see generic band descriptors for A2 [WJEC] AO1 or A Level [Eduqas] AO1).

▶ **Your task is this:** Below is a **summary of cognitive and non-cognitive language**. It is 150 words long. There are three points highlighted that are key points to learn from this extract. Discuss which further two points you think are the most important to highlight and write up all five points.

Cognitive language: Language that can be shown to be either true or false; it is empirically verifiable, meaning that any of the five senses (sight, hearing, touch, taste or smell) could be used to determine the truth (or otherwise) of what is being claimed. Cognitive language contains statements that express claims about the world that can be universally accepted (or denied). It is particularly valuable when considering a scientific view of the world.

Non-cognitive language: Language that cannot be shown to be true or false by empirical means, but instead is based on feelings, beliefs or emotions about what is being experienced. Non-cognitive language is not focussed on making empirically verifiable claims about the world but instead expresses an attitude towards the world that may also contain a view of how the world can be understood and which has an impact on how the claimant lives their life in accordance with such a claim.

Now make the five points into your own summary (as in Theme 2 Developing skills) trying to make the summary more personal to your style of writing.

1. ....
2. ....
3. ....
4. ....
5. ....

Cognitive language is about the external and physical world – it relates to objects and facts. Non-cognitive language deals with those things that cannot be empirically proven as easily such as thoughts, feelings and beliefs.

Issues for analysis and evaluation

The solutions presented by religious philosophers for the inherent problems of using religious language

This section covers AO2 content and skills

Specification content

The solutions presented by religious philosophers for the inherent problems of using religious language.

Whilst the challenges to the meaningfulness of religious language have been considerable, there have also been a number of responses that have been made in an attempt to stave off these challenges.

One of the key areas within which this debate has been held has been to do with how we use language and the context within which it is both received and understood.

The challenges from logical positivism (see page 94) rest upon the idea that religious language should be able to be understood in the same way as forms of language that provide information about the external world that can be empirically verified. Indeed, according to Ayer in *Language, Truth and Logic* all language should ultimately be verifiable by empirical means otherwise it is meaningless. This is an assumption that follows the same line of philosophical reasoning established by David Hume who maintained that empiricism was essential for establishing objective truth.

However, these assumptions have been considered by religious philosophers and, even since Aquinas (writing centuries before either Hume or Ayer) the particular function and use of religious language has been regarded as being somewhat specialised and deserving of a different understanding from that attached to non-religious language.

Aquinas considered that meaningful talk about religion, and specifically God, was limited by our experience as human beings. Therefore, ways had to be found within our limited experience to express ideas and truths about the divine. For Aquinas, this was by way of analogy and his two forms of analogical language – that of attribution and that of proportion, were considered to provide meaningful insights into a reality that human beings could only ever hope to glimpse part of. These analogies came from human experience and therefore provided meaning which could be understood. (For example, we know what it is for a person to be good – and as God is considered to be the source of all creation – including creating human beings in his image, then human goodness must, in some way, be a reflection of God's goodness – thus permitting us an insight into what it means to describe God as 'good'.) In this sense, one could argue that Aquinas has successfully met one of the inherent problems of religious language, by recognising the limitations of human language to express ideas about the divine and by linking the use of language to a literary device (i.e. analogy) that provides insights into concepts not yet fully understood.

Of course, the challenge to Aquinas's assertions are that analogy does not give us a full understanding of what it is that is being discussed, nor an objectively agreed idea about what we mean when discussing such ideas. However, Aquinas would say that to try and qualify religious language in such a way is to miss the point of the function of religious language.

Other issues were raised by other philosophers such as Flew, who considered that unless a religious believer would allow something to count against (falsify) their beliefs then those beliefs were meaningless. However, philosophers such as Swinburne said that there exist concepts that we can easily imagine (i.e. toys in a cupboard that dance across the floor when nobody is watching) that we cannot find evidence against but the concept still has meaning for us. Equally Mitchell's Partisan and the Stranger example demonstrates that there may be beliefs that

AO2 Activity

As you read through this section try to do the following:

1. Pick out the different lines of argument that are presented in the text and identify any evidence given in support.

2. For each line of argument try to evaluate whether or not you think this is strong or weak.

3. Think of any questions you may wish to raise in response to the arguments.

This Activity will help you to start thinking critically about what you read and help you to evaluate the effectiveness of different arguments and from this develop your own observations, opinions and points of view that will help with any conclusions that you make in your answers to the AO2 questions that arise.

Is religious language meaningful or simply meaningless?

Key questions

What was the role of the logical positivists with respect to the function of language?

What are the key issues with regards to religious language being considered to be problematic?

How successful do you feel the responses to the inherent problems of religious language are? What are your reasons for thinking this?

AO2 Activity

List some conclusions that could be drawn from the AO2 reasoning from the above text; try to aim for at least three different possible conclusions. Consider each of the conclusions and collect brief evidence to support each conclusion from the AO1 and AO2 material for this topic. Select the conclusion that you think is most convincing and explain why it is so. Try to contrast this with the weakest conclusion in the list, justifying your argument with clear reasoning and evidence.

are held (i.e. that the stranger is helping the partisan's cause) even when there appears to be evidence that counts against these beliefs (perhaps the stranger is seen talking with the enemy in a friendly manner). In such cases, the beliefs are held with the conviction that in the end, the faith in the partisan will be shown to be justified and meaningful, even if it was not possible to say what would have to be the case for it to be falsified. (This bears a striking similarity to the religious believers' faith in God despite the evidence of evil and suffering that exists in the world.) In both case the religious beliefs that are stated are meaningful, even when there is evidence that counts against them.

Key quotes

The Philosopher says that that is perfect, absolutely speaking, in which the perfections of all genera are found. As the Commentator remarks on this passage, such a being is God. But the perfections of other genera could not be said to be found in Him unless there were some resemblance between His perfection and the perfections of other genera. Hence, a creature resembles God in some way. Knowledge, therefore, and whatever else is predicated of God and creatures is not a pure equivocation. Genesis (1:2 6) says: 'Let us make man to our image and likeness'. Therefore, some likeness exists between God and creature. We conclude as before. **(Aquinas)**

As Dionysius says,' God can in no way be said to be similar to creatures, but creatures can be said to be similar to Him in some sense. For what is made in imitation of something, if it imitates it perfectly, can be said to be like it absolutely. The opposite, however, is not true; for a man is not said to be similar to his image but vice versa. However, if the imitation is imperfect, then it is said to be both like and unlike that which it imitates: like, in so far as it resembles it; unlike, in so far as it falls short of a perfect representation. It is for this reason that Holy Scripture denies that creatures are similar to God in every respect. It does, however, sometimes grant that creatures are similar to God, and sometimes deny this. It grants the similarity when it says that man is made in the likeness of God, but denies it when it says: 'O God, who is like to thee?' (Psalms 70:19). **(Aquinas)**

Study tip

It is vital for AO2 that you actually discuss arguments and not just explain what someone may have stated. Try to ask yourself, 'was this a fair point to make?', 'is the evidence sound enough?', 'is there anything to challenge this argument?', 'is this a strong or weak argument?' Such critical analysis will help you develop your evaluation skills

Religious language expresses an attitude towards life, as much as it expresses ideas about external reality. R. M. Hare demonstrated through his idea of the 'blik' that a deeply held belief is meaningful to the individual, even when the language about that belief could not be shown to be empirically verifiable. The way in which the individual lives their life, and how they view the world around them, is deeply meaningful to them because of their religious beliefs, irrespective of what others may be able to understand.

Whilst religious language can be challenged, in terms of it meaningfulness, by those who may have a reductionist view of the function of language, such as logical positivists, it still retains meaning for those that hold religious beliefs. Whether these should have to be shown to be meaningful via empirical means in order to overcome the perceived 'inherent problems' of religious language, is a continued matter for debate.

The exclusive context of religious belief for an understanding of religious language

To claim a belief that 'God loves me'; that 'Allah is The One, The Indivisible'; that 'Vishnu is the Preserver', is to use language that, without context, may appear confusing at best, meaningless at worst. Each of these phrases reflects not just a particular religious tradition, but also a deeply held set of beliefs about the character of the divine being that is being referred to. Such beliefs are often viewed as not being discoverable outside of those religious traditions, as there is no objectively agreed reality, in reference to each of them, that is universally accepted both inside and outside of religious belief.

The question may therefore be asked as to whether this language can have any meaning at all outside of religious belief. Is religious language ultimately an entirely exclusive form of communication, inaccessible to those outside of the tradition?

In his theory of Language Games, Ludwig Wittgenstein considered that the way in which language was to be understood, was by considering how it was used ('ask not for its meaning but for its use'). Wittgenstein considered that each area of human activity could often be recognised by the specialised use of language that it had. He referred to these as 'language games' and suggested that unless you understood the 'rules of the game' then you would not be able to access the meaning of the language. In the same way that you would not play the game of cricket using the rules of backgammon, you would not expect to be able to play the game of 'religious language' using the game of 'secular language'.

Considering the development of Wittgenstein's ideas by D. Z. Phillips, the theory of language games is considered as an anti-realist view of the 'truth'. In other words, as long as the language and associated beliefs are understood and agreed upon by the community that uses them, then they should be held to have the same value as any other similar sets of languages and beliefs in alternative communities. This would reinforce the idea that religious language can only be understood exclusively by those that hold the religious beliefs.

A response from other philosophers, such as Swinburne, is to suggest that this is a misunderstanding of how language functions and that religious language and its meaning are equally valid in the 'realist' theory of truth. By this they mean that when religious believers state their beliefs, the beliefs are not just some community agreed beliefs that do not extend beyond that community, but are instead beliefs which correspond to an objective reality beyond the community. (This is why others, such as the logical positivists, believe that they can legitimately challenge the meaningfulness of religious language as they dispute this belief.)

To further dispute the claim that religious language is exclusive to the context of religious belief, philosophers such as R. B. Braithwaite claimed that religious language is meaningful to those outside of religion, in a similar way to the way that moral claims are meaningful. His view was that religious statements were expressions of a particular attitude or intention of how life was to be lived and, as such was very similar to the way in which moral language is used – i.e. to express an opinion or attitude about the relative ethical value of a belief or action, and to live one's life accordingly. For Braithwaite, religious language was meaningful, whatever the context, as it was a non-cognitive form of language. It was not a form of language that had any empirical significance but was understandable as an attitude towards life.

Specification content

The exclusive context of religious belief for an understanding of religious language.

Can religious language only be understood by religious believers?

AO2 Activity

As you read through this section try to do the following:

1. Pick out the different lines of argument that are presented in the text and identify any evidence given in support.

2. For each line of argument try to evaluate whether or not you think this is strong or weak.

3. Think of any questions you may wish to raise in response to the arguments.

This Activity will help you to start thinking critically about what you read and help you to evaluate the effectiveness of different arguments and from this develop your own observations, opinions and points of view that will help with any conclusions that you make in your answers to the AO2 questions that arise.

Religious language is used to transmit religious beliefs – this is a clearly understandable idea. It is used, most commonly, by people who name themselves as religious – again, an understandable idea. However, what should also be remembered is that, in the vast majority of cases, these people also operate in other spheres of life – beyond just that of their religion. They will therefore engage in other forms of life and language. Is it sensible to suggest that their use of language when discussing religion can only be intelligible to those that share their beliefs? When the Roman Catholic priest speaks of transubstantiation, that the blessed sacrament is the body and blood of the saviour Christ, it is clearly important that the Roman Catholic believers understand what is being said. The communication between these two parties is intimately linked to the beliefs of the religion and it is not important that anyone outside of the tradition actually understands the meaningfulness of these faith claims. Equally, the Islamic believer who speaks of the concept of the Ummah to another Muslim, understands what is meant and how the practices of zakah and salah help to reinforce this belief as an essential part of what it means to be Muslim – again. It is not important whether anyone outside of the tradition understands these things – they are serving a specific purpose – to provide the believers with a context where they can make sense of their faith and understand the contributions of their various actions towards it. In neither of these cases is it being argued that the religious language being used cannot be understood by those outside of the religion, but rather that it is not important for the practice of the religion whether they can or not. If this is so, then how does a religious person 'share their faith' with a non-religious person? Where does this leave the evangelist? How can the theist have a meaningful debate with an atheist? If the view is (seriously) held that religious language is truly exclusive to the context of religious belief, then it would appear that religion is doomed to an insular existence without possibility of conversion, interaction or debate beyond the confines of the seminary, yeshiva or madrassa. The very fact that there is religious debate and discussion between members of different faiths as well as between those of faith of those of no faith, would suggest that this view of exclusivity is quite simply untrue.

Religious language is about the communication of religious beliefs and ideas.

AO2 Developing skills

It is now important to consider the information that has been covered in this section; however, the information in its raw form is too extensive and so has to be processed in order to meet the requirements of the examination. This can be achieved by practising more advanced skills associated with AO2. The exercises that run throughout this book will help you to do this and prepare you for the examination. For assessment objective 2 (AO2), which involves 'critical analysis' and 'evaluation' skills, we are going to focus on different ways in which the skills can be demonstrated effectively, and also refer to how the performance of these skills is measured (see generic band descriptors for A2 [WJEC] AO2 or A Level [Eduqas] AO2).

▶ **Your task is this:** Below is a one-sided view concerning a possible solution to the **inherent problems of religious language**. It is 150 words long. You need to include this view for an evaluation; however, to just present one side of an argument or one line of reasoning is not really evaluation. Using the paragraph below, add a counter-argument or alternative line of reasoning to make the evaluation more balanced. Allow about 150 words for your counter-argument or alternative line of reasoning.

Religious language should not be considered as a statement that can be empirically verified in the way that a scientific statement about the nature of reality can be. To do so is to misunderstand what type of language religious language is. Religious language is not cognitive language – in other words, religious language is not language that expresses empirically verifiable, objectively knowable, facts about the world. That is not its purpose or its function. Instead religious language should be considered to be non-cognitive, in that it is something that expresses an attitude towards something else. For example, a religious believer who states that 'I believe that the world was created by a divine being', is in fact stating their belief that it is a sacred place, and that there exists a being with the power to create it. As non-cognitive language it is not subject to the same criticisms as cognitive language.

Next, think of another line of argument or reasoning that may support either argument or it may even be completely different and add this to your answer.

Then ask yourself:

- Will my work, when developed, contain thorough, sustained and clear views that are supported by extensive, detailed reasoning and/or evidence?

Is the problem of religious language a significant problem for religious believers or not?

Key skills Theme 4 ABC

This theme has tasks that deal with specific aspects of AO2 in terms of identifying key elements of an evaluative style piece of writing, specifically counter-arguments and conclusions (both intermediate and final).

Key skills

Analysis involves:

Identifying issues raised by the materials in the AO1, together with those identified in the AO2 section, and presents sustained and clear views, either of scholars or from a personal perspective ready for evaluation.

This means:

- That your answers are able to identify key areas of debate in relation to a particular issue

- That you can identify, and comment upon, the different lines of argument presented by others

- That your response comments on the overall effectiveness of each of these areas or arguments.

Evaluation involves:

Considering the various implications of the issues raised based upon the evidence gleaned from analysis and provides an extensive detailed argument with a clear conclusion.

This means:

- That your answer weighs up the consequences of accepting or rejecting the various and different lines of argument analysed

- That your answer arrives at a conclusion through a clear process of reasoning.

This section covers AO1
content and skills

Specification content

Logical positivism – Verification by Alfred J. Ayer (A. J. Ayer) – religious ethical language as meaningless; there can be no way in which we could verify the truth or falsehood of the propositions (e.g. God is good, murder is wrong); falsification nothing can counter the belief (Antony Flew).

Key quotes

There is a sharp boundary between two kinds of statements. To one belong statements as they are made by empirical science; their meaning can be determined by logical analysis or, more precisely, through reduction to the simplest statements about the empirically given. The other statements, to which belong those cited above, reveal themselves as empty of meaning if one takes them in the way that metaphysicians intend. **(The Vienna Circle, 1929)**

Logical analysis is the method of clarification of philosophical problems; it makes an extensive use of the symbolic logic and distinguishes the Vienna Circle empiricism from earlier versions. The task of philosophy lies in the clarification – through the method of logical analysis – of problems and assertions. **(Vienna Circle)**

Key terms

Logical analysis: the method of clarification of philosophical problems

Logical positivism: a philosophical movement that grew out of the work of the Vienna Circle, in which the aim was the reduction of all knowledge to basic scientific and logical formulations

Tautological: a self-explanatory statement, i.e. where something is said twice over in different words, for example, 'the evening sunset'

Tenets: key beliefs or principles

B: Religious language as cognitive, but meaningless

Logical positivism

Logical positivism was a philosophical movement that grew out of the work of a group of philosophers known as the Vienna Circle. This highly influential group of philosophers, which included associates such as Wittgenstein, met in the 1920s and 1930s and considered their task to be a philosophically driven systematic reduction of all knowledge to basic scientific and logical formulations.

The Vienna Circle met at the University of Vienna.

Their position can be seen from the following extract:

> It is *the method of logical analysis* that essentially distinguishes recent empiricism and positivism from the earlier version that was more biological-psychological in its orientation. If someone asserts 'there is a God', 'the primary basis of the world is the unconscious', 'there is an entelechy which is the leading principle in the living organism', we do not say to him: 'what you say is false'; but we ask him: 'what do you mean by these statements?' Then it appears that there is a sharp boundary between two kinds of statements. To one belong statements as they are made by empirical science; their meaning can be determined by logical analysis or, more precisely, through reduction to the simplest statements about the empirically given. The other statements, to which belong those cited above, reveal themselves as empty of meaning if one takes them in the way that metaphysicians intend. One can, of course, often re-interpret them as empirical statements; but then they lose the content of feeling which is usually essential to the metaphysician. The metaphysician and the theologian believe, thereby misunderstanding themselves, that their statements say something, or that they denote a state of affairs. Analysis, however, shows that these statements say nothing but merely express a certain mood and spirit. (The Scientific Conception of the World: The Vienna Circle, 1929)

In other words, in considering language as the means by which all human knowledge is transmitted, they applied the same criteria and thus moved to a position that acknowledged two things:

- Anything outside of basic logical and scientific **tenets** is dismissed as meaningless, due to the fact that it is unverifiable.
- What remains are **tautological** (self-explanatory) statements and statements that could be verified by observations from first-person sense experience (this can also be regarded as empirical experience).

The Vienna Circle disbanded when the Nazi Party came to power in Germany in the 1930s. Many of its members subsequently emigrated to America and were able to continue working and developing the ideas associated with the Vienna Circle, in the academic institutions there. However, one of its key founding members, Moritz Schlick, remained and was killed by a Nazi sympathiser in Vienna in 1936. The ideas promoted by the Vienna Circle remained popular until the mid twentieth century.

Verification

To verify something is to show something to be true, to authenticate it, by some form of testimony or evidence. The logical positivists viewed scientific knowledge as the paradigm of knowledge (experiments and observations), since it had proved successful and resulted in agreed knowledge. Therefore, according to logical positivism, the only two forms of knowledge were logical reasoning and statements that were open to empirical evidence. These were considered to be:

- Tautological statements
- Mathematical statements
- Synthetic statements (a statement that could be verified by some form of sense experience or experiment, for example 'my car has four wheels')
- Analytic statements (where the truth of the statement is determined within the statement itself, for example 'all spinsters are unmarried females').

Statements that lay outside of such logical reasoning and empirical evidence were considered to be meaningless.

For Schlick, and the logical positivists, this became known as the 'verification principle': the meaning of a statement is its method of verification. That is, we know the meaning of a statement if we know the logical or empirical conditions that would show that the statement is either true or false.

A J Ayer developed the work of the Vienna Circle's logical positivists (the ideas of Schlick, in particular). The spread of the logical positivist movement in Britain is credited to Ayer, and in 1936 he wrote the influential *Language, Truth and Logic*. In this he set out the criteria for how language could be considered to be meaningful – a synthetic statement is meaningful if and only if it has some relation to observation. Ayer also attacked metaphysics regarding it as being essentially meaningless – being nothing more than a misunderstanding of how reality should be described. He regarded metaphysicians as being 'devoted to the production of nonsense'.

Ayer writes:

'The criterion which we use to test the genuineness of apparent statements of fact is the criterion of verifiability. We say that a sentence is factually significant to any given person, if, and only if, he knows how to verify the proposition which it purports to express – that is, if he knows what observations would lead him, under certain conditions, to accept the proposition as being true, or reject it as being false. If, on the other hand, the putative proposition is of such a character that the assumption of its truth, or falsehood, is consistent, with any assumption whatsoever concerning the nature of his future experience, then, as far as he, is concerned, it is, if not a tautology, a mere pseudo-proposition. The sentence expressing it may be emotionally significant to him; but it is not literally significant.'

quickfire

4.5 What was the main philosophical aim of the Vienna Circle?

Key quote

When are we sure that the meaning of a question is clear? Obviously if and only if we are able to exactly describe the conditions in which it is possible to answer yes, respectively, the conditions in which it is necessary to answer with a no. The meaning of a question is thus defined only through the specification of those conditions. ... The definition of the circumstances under which a statement is true is perfectly *equivalent* to the definition of its meaning. A statement has a meaning if and only if the fact that it is true makes a verifiable difference. **(Schlick)**

The verification principle was an attempt to establish a criterion of meaning for how we use language about the world.

quickfire

4.6 What was the Principle of Verification?

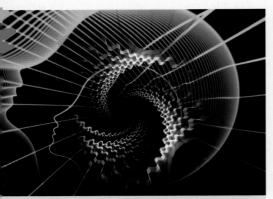

Ayer rejected metaphysical language as meaningless.

Ayer, however, recognised that the principle of verification, as set out by the logical positivists, had a clear limitation. It was not able to take into account those statements that were made about things that were accepted as meaningful even though they were not considered to be immediately verifiable in practice. For example, there is no observation possible now that could verify the truth of historical statements such as' Lord Nelson won the Battle of Trafalgar'. However, clearly most people would argue that this is meaningful (and indeed true). Similarly, scientific statements such as 'water always boils at 100 degrees Celsius (meaningful but actually false). We cannot experience first-hand (and therefore verify) events of the past and it is not possible to observe (and therefore verify) all water boils at 100 degrees Celsius.

It was for these reasons that Ayer made a distinction between verifiability 'in practice' and verifiability 'in principle'.

In the first place, it is necessary to draw a distinction between practical verifiability, and verifiability in principle. Plainly we all understand, in many cases believe, propositions which we have not in fact taken steps to verify. Many of these are propositions which we could verify if we took enough trouble. But there remain a number of significant propositions, concerning matters of fact, which we could not verify even if we chose; simply because we lack the practical means of placing ourselves in the situation where the relevant observations could be made. A simple and familiar example of such a proposition is the proposition that there are mountains on the farther side of the moon! No rocket has yet been invented which would enable me to go and look at the farther side of the moon, so that I am unable to decide the matter by actual observation. But I do know what observations would decide it for me, if, as is theoretically conceivable, I were once in a position to make them. And therefore I say that the proposition is verifiable in principle, if not in practice, and is accordingly significant. On the other hand, such a metaphysical pseudo-proposition as 'the Absolute enters into, but is itself incapable of, evolution and progress,' is not even in principle verifiable. For one cannot conceive of an observation which would enable one to determine whether the Absolute did, or did not, enter into evolution and progress. Of course, it is possible that the author of such a remark is using English words in a way in which they are not commonly used by English-speaking people, and that he does, in fact, intend to assert something which could be empirically verified. But until he makes us understand how the proposition that he wishes to express would be verified, he fails to communicate anything to us. ... A further distinction which we must make is the distinction between the 'strong' and the 'weak' sense of the term 'verifiable'. A proposition is said to be verifiable, in the strong sense of the term, if, and only if, its truth could be conclusively established in experience. But it is verifiable, in the weak sense, if it is possible for experience to render it probable. (*Language, Truth and Logic*)

This criteria of 'in practice' referred to those statements whose truth or falsehood could be determined by some observation or experiment that could be carried out in the present day. In contrast, the criteria of 'in principle' allowed verifiability (and so the statement was meaningful), but only in theory. For instance, historical events could have been verified had you have been present at the time they happened. Likewise, with 'water always boils at 100 degrees Celsius', since we know what it would take to verify it – namely to observe every drop of water. In other words, we establish meaningfulness of a statement by relating it to some set of observation sentences. The observations do not actually have to be made. All that is required is that we could in principle make those observations, i.e. I know under what circumstances it would be verifiable.

However, this still did not allow for religious statements such as 'I saw God last night' as we do not even know in principle what sense experience would count in its favour.

Ayer then introduced another distinction between what he called 'strong verification' and 'weak verification'. He was aware, for instance, that universal claims are not conclusively verifiable. It is in the very nature of these statements that their truth cannot be established with certainty by any finite series of observations. In such cases the verification is said to be 'weak'. Sense experiences merely count towards establishing its truth value. However, it is still meaningful since it is linked to sense experience. In contrast, if the verification is conclusive then Ayer said that it was 'strong' verification. He made this distinction so it would include statements that people regarded as meaningful. In essence, Ayer moved away from focussing on what can be derived from observation claims to focussing on what observation claims might be relevant in order to verify a statement. However, once again religious statements were still not included. For instance, the statement that 'God performs miracles' Ayer would have argued was meaningless since it cannot be verified even in the 'weak' sense.

In 1978 Ayer himself admitted that his earlier work was 'mostly false'.

Falsification

As an alternative view of being able to verify a statement in order to render it meaningful, the concept of falsification took an almost opposite view. Falsification stated that for something to be meaningful, there had to be evidence which could count against the statement (i.e. to empirically refute it). If this was possible, then what was being spoken about clearly had an empirically meaningful basis, otherwise there would not be the possibility to find evidence that counted against it. This idea was championed in the early part of the twentieth century by Karl Popper. His assertion was that if a principle was robustly scientific then it should be inherently disprovable (i.e. you would know 'how' to disprove it; you would know what it would take to find things that count against it). Thus, scientific theories (e.g. gravity) could be tested to see whether any evidence can be found against them (e.g. an object would float away from the earth if gravity were disproven) – in this sense they were falsifiable and, therefore, meaningful. Karl Popper argued that science did not move from observation to theory but rather from theory to observation. Theories are considered true until some evidence shows them false. So for science it was the criterion of falsifiability rather than verifiability.

Some philosophers therefore saw that this criterion could apply to language in general rather than just to science.

If it was known what would have to be the case for a statement to be considered false, then the statement was meaningful. Alternatively, if no observation could ever count against a statement then the statement was considered meaningless. If the statement asserts nothing (since it is consistent with every possible observation), then it cannot mean anything.

So what about religious statements such as 'God exists'? According to the criterion of falsification, there seems no way to disprove it (since God has no empirical attributes).

Anthony Flew developed this and, with reference to Wisdom's Parable of the Gardener set out his view that religious statements could not be falsified and were therefore meaningless. Flew writes:

> Let us begin with a parable. It is a parable developed from a tale told by John Wisdom in his haunting and revelatory article 'Gods'. Once upon a time two explorers came upon a clearing in the jungle. In the clearing were growing many flowers and many weeds. One explorer says, 'Some gardener must tend this plot'. The other disagrees, 'There is no gardener'. So they pitch their tents and set a watch. No gardener is ever seen. 'But perhaps he is an invisible gardener.' So they set up a barbed-wire fence. They electrify it. They patrol with bloodhounds. (For they remember how H. G. Wells' *The Invisible Man* could be both smelled

quickfire

4.7 What did Ayer consider the principle of verification's limitation to be?

Key quote

A further distinction which we must make is the distinction between the 'strong' and the 'weak' sense of the term 'verifiable'. A proposition is said to be verifiable, in the strong sense of the term, if, and only if, its truth could be conclusively established in experience. But it is verifiable, in the weak sense, if it is possible for experience to render it probable. **(Ayer)**

Statue of Karl Popper at the University of Vienna

Key quote

'But there is a gardener, invisible, intangible, insensible to electric shocks, a gardener who has no scent and makes no sound, a gardener who comes secretly to look after the garden which he loves.' At last the Sceptic despairs, 'But what remains of our original assertion? Just how does what you call an invisible, intangible, eternally elusive gardener differ from an imaginary gardener or even from no gardener at all?' **(Flew)**

The parable of the gardener demonstrated the problems in verifying religious language and truths.

and touched though he could not be seen.) But no shrieks ever suggest that some intruder has received a shock. No movements of the wire ever betray an invisible climber. The bloodhounds never give cry. Yet still the Believer is not convinced. 'But there is a gardener, invisible, intangible, insensible to electric shocks, a gardener who has no scent and makes no sound, a gardener who comes secretly to look after the garden which he loves.' At last the Sceptic despairs, 'But what remains of our original assertion? Just how does what you call an invisible, intangible, eternally elusive gardener differ from an imaginary gardener or even from no gardener at all?' (*Theology and Falsification*)

Flew specifically chose the challenge to God's existence with the evidence of the existence of evil and suffering in the world. He asked the question as to why religious believers would not allow such evidence to count against their beliefs in a supposed all-loving, all-powerful God, the characteristics associated with the traditionally held '**God of Classical Theism**'. Flew stated that such believers do not allow such evidence to count against their theistic beliefs and, as a consequence, these beliefs were not falsifiable (and therefore not meaningful) and 'died a death of a thousand qualifications' – in that the believers would always justify such evidence with an 'Oh yes, but ...' response.

Flew comments:

Someone tells us that God loves us as a father loves his children. We are reassured. But then we see a child dying of inoperable cancer of the throat. His earthly father is driven frantic in his efforts to help, but his Heavenly Father reveals no obvious sign of concern. Some qualification is made: God's love is 'not a merely human love' or it is 'an inscrutable love', perhaps – and we realise that such sufferings are quite compatible with the truth of the assertion that 'God loves us as a father (but, of course ...)'. We are reassured again. But then perhaps we ask: what is this assurance of God's (appropriately qualified) love worth, what is this apparent guarantee really a guarantee against? Just what would have to happen not merely (morally and wrongly) to tempt but also (logically and rightly) to entitle us to say 'God does not love us' or even 'God does not exist'? I therefore put to the succeeding **symposiasts** the simple central questions, 'What would have to occur or to have occurred to constitute for you a disproof of the love of, or of the existence of God?' (Flew A. 1950)

Key terms

God of Classical Theism: God as defined in religions such as Christianity, Islam and Judaism – a God who is held to possess certain attributes such as omnipotence, omniscience and omnibenevolence.

Symposiasts: members of a symposium (a conference held to discuss a specific subject or topic)

Specification content

Criticisms of verification: the verification principle cannot itself be verified; neither can historical events; universal scientific statements; the concept of eschatological verification goes against this.

quickfire

4.8 What, in relation to language, was meant by falsification?

Criticisms of verification

Whilst, ostensibly, the standpoint of verification as a means of testing the meaningfulness of language seemed both sensible and, even, laudable, it was not without its problems. Most obvious of which came from the original verification principle itself.

'The meaning of a statement is its method of verification' is neither logically obvious nor is it supported by empirical evidence – thus the statement is not verifiable! A self-defeating principle is not the bedrock upon which to build a criterion for establishing the meaningfulness of language!

As recognised by Ayer, the fact that the initial criteria for the verification principle did not take into account historical statements or even universal scientific statements (all bodies expand when heated, the sun always rises in the east, etc.) as meaningful, further undermines its usefulness. This is why Ayer needed to amend the principle so that a 'weak' form could be established which would allow for such statements to be meaningful.

A further observation was made by religious philosopher John Hick, who argued that in fact the Christian concept of God was verifiable in principle.

Hick writes:

> Two men are travelling together along a road. One of them believes that it leads to a Celestial City, the other that it leads nowhere; but since this is the only road there is, both must travel it. Neither has been this way before, and therefore neither is able to say what they will find around each next corner. During their journey they meet both with moments of refreshment and delight, and with moments of hardship and danger. All the time one of them thinks of his journey as a pilgrimage to the Celestial City and interprets the pleasant parts as encouragements and the obstacles as trials of his purpose and lessons in endurance, prepared by the king of that city and designed to make of him a worthy citizen of the place when at last he arrives there. The other, however, believes none of this and sees their journey as an unavoidable and aimless ramble. Since he has no choice in the matter, he enjoys the good and endures the bad. But for him there is no Celestial City to be reached, no all-encompassing purpose ordaining their journey; only the road itself and the luck of the road in good weather and in bad. ... Their opposed interpretations of the road constituted genuinely rival assertions, though assertions whose assertion-status has the peculiar characteristic of being guaranteed retrospectively by a future crux. (*Theology and Verification*)

Using his parable of the journey to the Celestial City, Hick demonstrates that whilst the knowledge of the existence of the Christian God may not be immediately verifiable in practice, there is the possibility that it can be verified in the future (i.e. after death). This concept is known as **eschatological verification** (quite literally 'to verify in the end times').

Hick's analogy of the road to the Celestial City sees the problems of verifying religious language being answered at the end of the journey.

Criticisms of falsification: Richard Hare

Much like verification, the concept of falsification has been criticised as a philosophical method to establish the meaningfulness of language or concepts. R. M. Hare, in a symposium with Anthony Flew and Basil Mitchell, suggested that the concept of meaningfulness came from the impact that a belief had on an individual – not from the empirically verifiable nor falsifiable nature of the belief. It does not matter if others do not share that belief. As such, he proposed the idea of '**bliks**' – a term coined to describe a way of looking at our lives and our experiences. Hare suggested that a blik had the power to radically affect our behaviour and the relationship that we had with the world (and people) around us. In this sense the 'blik' was meaningful – even if it could not be falsified. To illustrate this, Hare tells the parable of the university dons and the paranoid student who believes that all of the dons are dedicated to causing him harm.

Key quote

All the time one of them thinks of his journey as a pilgrimage to the Celestial City and interprets the pleasant parts as encouragements and the obstacles as trials of his purpose and lessons in endurance, prepared by the king of that city and designed to make of him a worthy citizen of the place when at last he arrives there. The other, however, believes none of this and sees their journey as an unavoidable and aimless ramble. Since he has no choice in the matter, he enjoys the good and endures the bad. (**Hick**)

Key terms

Blik: a term used by R. M. Hare to describe the point of view that someone may hold that will influence the way they live their life

Eschatological verification: John Hick's assertion that certain religious statements may be verifiable at a future point (i.e. after death). In this sense, they are 'verifiable in principle' and should therefore be regarded as meaningful

quickfire

4.9 Why did Flew consider that religious believers' beliefs 'died a death of a thousand qualifications'?

Specification content

Criticisms of falsification: Richard Hare – bliks (the way that a person views the world gives meaning to them even if others do not share the same view)

Hare used the example of a murderous university don to illustrate his idea of a 'blik'.

Specification content

Basil Mitchell – partisan and the stranger (certain things can be meaningful even when they cannot be falsified).

quickfire

4.10 Name two philosophers that put forward objections to falsification as a method for determining meaningfulness in language.

Key term

Partisan: a person who holds a particular political view – usually used in association with those who hold an opposing point of view to the ruling political powers. In Mitchell's case he is most likely referring to the partisans within the resistance movement of the Second World War

I wish to make it clear that I shall not try to defend Christianity in particular, but religion in general – not because I do not believe in Christianity, but because you cannot understand what Christianity is, until you have understood what religion is. I must begin by confessing that, on the ground marked out by Flew, he seems to me to be completely victorious. I therefore shift my ground by relating another parable. A certain lunatic is convinced that all dons want to murder him. His friends introduce him to all the mildest and most respectable dons that they can find, and after each of them has retired, they say, 'You see, he doesn't really want to murder you; he spoke to you in a most cordial manner; surely you are convinced now?' But the lunatic replies, 'Yes, but that was only his diabolical cunning; he's really plotting against me the whole time, like the rest of them; I know it I tell you.' However many kindly dons are produced, the reaction is still the same. Now we say that such a person is deluded. But what is he deluded about? About the truth or falsity of an assertion? Let us apply Flew's test to him. There is no behaviour of dons that can be enacted which he will accept as counting against his theory; and therefore his theory, on this test, asserts nothing. But it does not follow that there is no difference between what he thinks about dons and what most of us think about them – otherwise we should not call him a lunatic and ourselves sane, and dons would have no reason to feel uneasy about his presence in Oxford. Let us call that in which we differ from this lunatic, our respective *bliks*. He has an insane *blik* about dons; we have a sane one. It is important to realise that we have a sane one, not no *blik* at all; for there must be two sides to any argument – if he has a wrong *blik*, then those who are right about dons must have a right one. Flew has shown that a *blik* does not consist in an assertion or system of them; but nevertheless it is very important to have the right *blik*. (Symposium on Theology and Falsification)

Criticisms of falsification: Basil Mitchell

In the same symposium, Basil Mitchell suggested to Flew that he had fundamentally misunderstood the religious believers' perspective when Flew had stated that religious believers allow nothing to count against their beliefs. Mitchell argued that this was simply not true. He stated that religious believers are frequently faced with challenges to their belief and with evidence that seems to be contrary to their beliefs. It was a matter of faith as to how the individual dealt with those challenges but it was not true to say that such evidence had no impact on the religious believer. Mitchell uses another parable, that of 'The **Partisan** and the Stranger' to illustrate his point:

Flew's article is searching and perceptive, but there is, I think, something odd about his conduct of the theologian's case. The theologian surely would not deny that the fact of pain counts against the assertion that God loves men. This very incompatibility generates the most intractable of theological problems – the problem of evil. So the theologian *does* recognise the fact of pain as counting against Christian doctrine. But it is true that he will not allow it – or anything – to count decisively against it; for he is committed by his faith to trust in God. His attitude is not that of the detached observer, but of the believer. Perhaps this can be brought out by yet another parable. In time of war in an occupied country, a member of the resistance meets one night a stranger who deeply impresses him. They spend that night together in conversation. The Stranger tells the partisan that he himself is on the side of the resistance – indeed that he is in command of it, and urges the partisan to have faith in him no matter what happens.

The partisan is utterly convinced at that meeting of the Stranger's sincerity and constancy and undertakes to trust him. They never meet in conditions of intimacy again. But sometimes the Stranger is seen helping members of the resistance, and the partisan is grateful and says to his friends, 'He is on our side'. Sometimes he is seen in the uniform of the police handing over patriots to the occupying power. On these occasions his friends murmur against him; but the partisan still says, 'He is on our side'. He still believes that, in spite of appearances, the Stranger did not deceive him. Sometimes he asks the Stranger for help and receives it. He is then thankful. Sometimes he asks and does not receive it. Then he says, 'The Stranger knows best'. Sometimes his friends, in exasperation, say, 'Well, what *would* he have to do for you to admit that you were wrong and that he is not on our side?' But the partisan refuses to answer. He will not consent to put the Stranger to the test. And sometimes his friends complain, 'Well, if *that's* what you mean by his being on our side, the sooner he goes over to the other side the better.' The partisan of the parable does not allow anything to count decisively against the proposition 'the Stranger is on our side'. This is because he has committed himself to trust the Stranger. But he of course recognises that the Stranger's ambiguous behaviour *does* count against what he believes about him. It is precisely this situation which constitutes the trial of his faith. (Symposium on Theology and Falsification)

Mitchell's point, therefore, was that such beliefs constituted a 'trial of faith' – a test for the religiously held beliefs that an individual had. The evidence against the beliefs was not discounted and the believers did not lose meaningfulness in their beliefs through 'the death of a thousand qualifications'. To believe that was to misunderstand both the purpose and challenge of holding a religious faith. As such, Mitchell stated, religious beliefs, expressed in religious language, should be regarded as being meaningful.

Criticisms of falsification: Richard Swinburne

Furthermore, Richard Swinburne noted that there were plenty of instances where human language was used in ways that were accepted as meaningful by people, even without the empirical evidence to support it. Just because an idea cannot be falsified does not mean, necessarily, that that idea should be automatically discounted as being meaningless. We may not be able to disprove something but that does not mean that such a thing does not actually happen. Indeed there may well be a belief that such things do actually happen, despite the lack of evidence either for or against it – and such ideas and beliefs are held to be meaningful.

As evidence for this, Swinburne gives the example of the 'toys in the cupboard' coming to life – and even though there could be no evidence to support (or deny) this assertion – the idea is meaningful to those who hear it.

AO1 Activity

Using the information regarding the challenges to the meaningfulness of religious language from logical positivism, produce an A3 illustrated information diagram that highlights the key points of both the verification and falsification principles. Your diagram should include pictures and key words to show that you understand both concepts. As a further challenge you may wish to restrict the written information on the diagram to 25 words.

This practises the AO1 skill of being able to demonstrate an accurate understanding of philosophical thought through selecting relevant and accurate material.

Key quote

The trouble is, however, that there are plenty of examples of statements which *some* people judge to be factual which are not apparently confirmable or disconfirmable through observation. For example: some of the toys which to all appearances stay in the toy cupboard while people are asleep and no one is watching, actually get up and dance in the middle of the night and then go back to the cupboard, leaving no traces of their activity. (**Swinburne**)

Specification content

Criticisms of falsification: Richard Swinburne – toys in the cupboard (concept meaningful even though falsifying the statement is not possible).

Key skills

Knowledge involves:

Selection of a range of (thorough) accurate and relevant information that is directly related to the specific demands of the question.

This means:

- Selecting relevant material for the question set
- Being focused in explaining and examining the material selected.

Understanding involves:

Explanation that is extensive, demonstrating depth and/or breadth with excellent use of evidence and examples including (where appropriate) thorough and accurate supporting use of sacred texts, sources of wisdom and specialist language.

This means:

- Effective use of examples and supporting evidence to establish the quality of your understanding
- Ownership of your explanation that expresses personal knowledge and understanding and NOT just reproducing a chunk of text from a book that you have rehearsed and memorised.

AO1 Developing skills

It is now important to consider the information that has been covered in this section; however, the information in its raw form is too extensive and so has to be processed in order to meet the requirements of the examination. This can be achieved by practising more advanced skills associated with AO1. For assessment objective 1 (AO1), which involves demonstrating 'knowledge' and 'understanding' skills, we are going to focus on different ways in which the skills can be demonstrated effectively, and also refer to how the performance of these skills is measured (see generic band descriptors for A2 [WJEC] AO1 or A Level [Eduqas] AO1).

▶ **Your next task is this:** Below is a summary of **Ayer and the verification principle**. It is 150 words long. This time there are no highlighted points to indicate the key points to learn from this extract. Discuss which five points you think are the most important to highlight and write them down in a list.

In rejecting metaphysical statements, Ayer rejected as meaningless any statement that did not fit their criteria of meaning. These statements were rejected as there was no way of being able to determine their 'truth'. What sense experience or logical reasoning could be used to demonstrate the truth of what was being asserted? (This meant a rejection of not only religious language but also language that was related to ethics, and statements relating to any form of abstract thought.) Ayer, however recognised that the principle of verification, as set out by the logical positivists, had a clear limitation. It was not able to take into account those statements that were made about things that were accepted as meaningful even though they were not considered to be immediately verifiable in practice. From this realisation Ayer went on to develop the verification principle by including the concepts of practical verifiability, and verifiability in principle.

Now make the five points into your own summary (as in Theme 1 Developing skills) trying to make the summary more personal to your style of writing. This may also involve re-ordering the points if you wish to do so.

1. ....
2. ....
3. ....
4. ....
5. ....

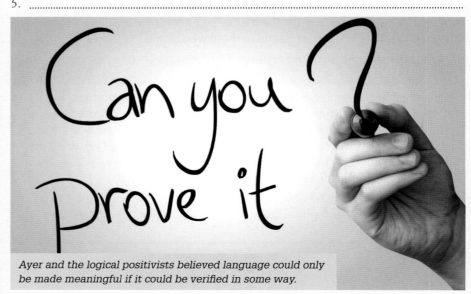

Ayer and the logical positivists believed language could only be made meaningful if it could be verified in some way.

Issues for analysis and evaluation

The persuasiveness of arguments asserting either the meaningfulness or meaninglessness of religious language

It is sometimes suggested that religious language contains ideas that appear to be unusual in relation to our experiences of the everyday, empirical world. Words and phrases such as 'God'; 'Soul', 'Eternal reward' and 'Universal salvation' speak of things which are not easily identifiable or recognisable in the mundane sphere of existence that human beings inhabit. It is little wonder therefore that some philosophers have suggested that such language should be considered as meaningless and that such ideas are nothing more than 'sophistry and illusion'.

Examining these arguments that challenge the meaningfulness of religious language allows us to consider how persuasive they may be in convincing those of both religious belief and none, that what they claim about religious language should be taken seriously.

It can be argued that a statement, or form of language, that relates very clearly to something that can be objectively experienced, should be considered as meaningful. If a person claims that 'the bird has wings' then it is generally understood that the person is referring to an object, present in the world of the animal kingdom and definable, by an agreed set of criteria, as being identifiable as a 'bird'. Furthermore, the physiological structure of this object can be readily identified through visual observation and a basic awareness of the different parts that can constitute a body, as well as how they can be defined in terms of shape and function, would readily lead a person to identify whether or not there was truth to the statement that this 'bird' object did indeed possess the physical characteristic of 'wings'. Such claims, because of our understanding and experiences of the world, mean that language communicated in this way can be readily interpreted – and therefore understood, precisely because it is meaningful. Such is the view of logical positivism – that any language that can be reduced to a set of observable criteria should be understood to be meaningful. Equally, tautological statements such as 'all spinsters are unmarried females' can also, by definition, be understood to be meaningful. In this sense the established criterion for the verification principle, as proposed by the logical positivists, is both meaningful and, as a means for understanding language, persuasive.

The difficulty comes when a person makes a claim such as 'the angel has wings'. Whilst, superficially, this appears to be the same sort of statement as the one made previously, the difficulty comes when one attempts to define the word 'angel'. Unlike the bird, which can clearly be categorised as belonging to the empirical world and readily identifiable through an agreed set of criteria, the same cannot be said for the 'angel'. Whilst we can, as previously noted, understand what is meant by the word 'wings' – how do we know that the wings of an angel are comparable to the wings of a bird? The lack of verifiable information about the angel means that such a statement is therefore meaningless. It has no corresponding reality to the empirical world and can be proven neither by sense experience nor by tautological understanding. Logical positivism makes a powerful case about our understanding of what can be understood to be meaningful and therefore is particularly persuasive, when understood in such a way.

This section covers AO2 content and skills

Specification content

The persuasiveness of arguments asserting either the meaningfulness or meaninglessness of religious language.

Why do we define this object as a bird?

AO2 Activity

As you read through this section try to do the following:

1. Pick out the different lines of argument that are presented in the text and identify any evidence given in support.

2. For each line of argument try to evaluate whether or not you think this is strong or weak.

3. Think of any questions you may wish to raise in response to the arguments.

This Activity will help you to start thinking critically about what you read and help you to evaluate the effectiveness of different arguments and from this develop your own observations, opinions and points of view that will help with any conclusions that you make in your answers to the AO2 questions that arise.

Key questions

What do logical positivists mean when they say that a statement is 'meaningful'?

How does an understanding of language as non-cognitive lead to a rejection of logical positivism?

What are the key issues with Braithwaite's understanding of religious language as purely non-cognitive?

Does everything that we say always have meaning?

AO2 Activity

List some conclusions that could be drawn from the AO2 reasoning from the above text; try to aim for at least three different possible conclusions. Consider each of the conclusions and collect brief evidence to support each conclusion from the AO1 and AO2 material for this topic. Select the conclusion that you think is most convincing and explain why it is so. Try to contrast this with the weakest conclusion in the list, justifying your argument with clear reasoning and evidence.

A counter-claim to the arguments of logical positivism suggests, however, that this category for understanding meaning is not as all-encompassing as at first may appear.

To treat religious language in the way that logical positivists treat it is to understand religious language to be cognitive – that is, it is a form of language which contains information that is objectively knowable about the external, empirically experienced, world. Religious philosophers, such as R. B. Braithwaite, consider this to be a fundamental misunderstanding of both the purpose and function of religious language. They suggest that the logical positivists have 'missed the point' thereby undermining the persuasiveness of their points of view.

Braithwaite, and those that agree religious language has a non-cognitive, rather than cognitive, function point out that to understand religious language, one needs to appreciate that it is expressing an attitude towards a form of life. It is not expressing 'facts' about the world in a scientific sense. The language is meaningful because it affects the way the person chooses to live their life and relate to the world around them, including how they view their relationship with other human beings.

This view is further developed by R. M. Hare who suggested that each person possesses a 'blik' or way of looking at life. Religious belief and by extension, religious language, was such a blik and was meaningful for the individual who held that 'blik' as it influenced everything that they said and did. Such a view is particularly persuasive when it is considered that a person's attitude towards the world can often be considered more 'real' to them than the actual 'facts' of the world around them. Consider how a person's mood can affect the way they interact with others – even though the others may not be behaving in a different way. The prism through which the person sees the others (their 'blik') is what makes things meaningful, not the actual state of affairs.

Study tip

It is vital for AO2 that you present a response that successfully identifies and thoroughly addresses the issues raised by the question set. In order to do this you need to make sure that you have a clear understanding of the statement in question. Take time to read the statement thoroughly a number of times, and note down in your own words what you think it is claiming. This method will help to ensure that you focus on the relevant points.

Whether one accepts that religious language is cognitive or non-cognitive will influence considerably whether the challenges to its meaningfulness are deemed successful. Religious observers may dispute Braithwaite's claim that religious language should be considered to be purely non-cognitive, as they may claim that religious language makes claims about the external world that should be understood cognitively. For example, the statement 'God is the creator of the universe' is intended to be a statement that reveals the circumstances by which the physical universe came into being – not just an attitude that asks religious believers to adopt in understanding that the universe and all that is in it should be considered as a sacred place, worthy of respect and careful treatment. Equally, the logical positivists' claim is so reductionist that it does not take into account the meaningful effects that religious belief has on a believer's life and the impact that has on those around them as well. It also does not take into account the fact that religious believers can make meaningful claims that can persuade others, even from a non-religious background, to their particular point of view (e.g. as in the case of a religious conversion).

How far logical positivism should be accepted as providing a valid criterion for meaning in the use of language

The philosophical movement of logical positivism considered their task to be a philosophically driven systematic reduction of all knowledge to basic scientific and logical formulations. They were heavily influenced by the work of earlier empiricists such as Locke and Hume. The scientific mindset which was increasingly in vogue, as the nineteenth century turned into the twentieth, also had a considerable influence on the thinking of the Vienna Circle – such that it was this mindset that was promoted within their thinking. Thus, the requirement for all language to be subject to a scientific form of 'enquiry' in that it needed to be empirically verifiable, became the focus of their work.

In a consideration of how language was used, the forms of language regarded as analytic and synthetic, were identified. Analytic language – that which was self-explanatory or self-defining (true by definition) was held to be a meaningful form of expression – and it was true *a priori* (independent of experience). Such statements as 'all spinsters are unmarried females' is an example of an analytic statement – and it is easy to see why the logical positivists considered this to be a valid criterion for understanding 'meaning' when language was used. Tautological and mathematical statements were equally accepted under this criterion for meaning.

The other form of language, synthetic language, was regarded as meaningful simply because the language could be understood, *a posteriori*, based as it was on empirically provable first-person observations. Language such as 'the spinster wore a red hat' was deemed to be meaningful as it could be clearly provable, in practice, via sense experience. Synthetic statements corresponded neatly with the sort of observations being made by the scientific community and were thus readily accepted as having valid meaning due to their empirical basis.

It is clearly the case that such a criterion for establishing meaning in the use of language should be readily accepted in the arenas for which it was intended. The difficulty comes when that criterion is applied to areas of knowledge and human activity that lie beyond those readily found in the empirically observable external world.

When considering religious language, logical positivists were dismissive of it as something that could convey meaning. Religious belief, being a form of metaphysical activity, was essentially unverifiable. It did not correspond to the *a priori* form of analytic language as it was not logically obvious nor was it self-explanatory. Equally, it did not correspond to the *a posteriori* synthetic form of language as it was expressing ideas (e.g. God exists) that could be fathomed in the empirical world. At this stage it is worth posing the question as to whether logical positivism should be accepted as providing a valid criterion for meaning in the use of religious language? Opinion is divided!

For logical positivists, the lack of correspondence of religious belief and religious language to their criterion for meaning only served to demonstrate that religious activity was essentially meaningless, to the scientific mindset. It was something that could not be empirically verified and therefore should not be accepted as anything other than meaningless.

However, for those outside of the logical positivist movement, the criterion of meaning established by them was deemed to be flawed and therefore not an adequate way of providing an appropriate criterion for the understanding of the meaning of language. Critics have argued strongly that the insistence on the strict adherence to the principle of verification is clearly problematic as the principle itself cannot be verified.

Specification content

How far logical positivism should be accepted as providing a valid criterion for meaning in the use of language.

Is the scientific method the ultimate arbitrator of truth?

AO2 Activity

As you read through this section try to do the following:

1. Pick out the different lines of argument that are presented in the text and identify any evidence given in support.

2. For each line of argument try to evaluate whether or not you think this is strong or weak.

3. Think of any questions you may wish to raise in response to the arguments.

This Activity will help you to start thinking critically about what you read and help you to evaluate the effectiveness of different arguments and from this develop your own observations, opinions and points of view that will help with any conclusions that you make in your answers to the AO2 questions that arise.

Ayer questioned whether the statement 'The side of the moon that can not be seen by human beings had mountains' was a meaningless statement.

A. J. Ayer attempted to navigate the challenge of the limitations of the verification principle, by proposing an amendment to the criterion and by suggesting that whilst it was entirely laudable to have a situation where something could be verified in practice (what he later referred to as the 'strong' form of the verification principle) it was equally acceptable to appreciate that this was not always possible; however, it was possible to verify something in principle. He later referred to this as the 'weak' form' of the verification principle, in that it was known by which means and according to what criteria it was possible to know what could be used to 'verify' the truth or falsity of a particular statement.

Ayer himself referred to the question of whether the moon had mountains on the side that was 'invisible' to humans on earth – for in Ayer's time, there was no way of ascertaining this truth. However, he recognised that one day it might be possible for a rocket ship to be built that would allow human beings to verify whether there were indeed mountains on this invisible side of the moon and therefore, because the conditions were known by which this assertion could be held to be true it was regarded as being verifiable in principle.

Ayer's moderated form of the verification principle then allowed for both historical statements (e.g. The Battle of Waterloo was fought in 1815) and for universal scientific statements (all metals expand when heated) to be verifiable (in principle) and therefore could be regarded to be meaningful (which the strong form had not allowed for). In this sense Ayer, as a logical positivist, had put forward a criterion of meaning for the use of language that seemed far more acceptable. In fact, using an extension of this reasoning, religious philosopher John Hick, suggested that if there was an afterlife, then the truth of God's existence would be verifiable after death – this became known as 'eschatological verification' and is considered to be a form of verification that establishes the fact that religious language is indeed meaningful.

Key quote

A simple and familiar example of such a proposition is the proposition that there are mountains on the farther side of the moon! No rocket has yet been invented which would enable me to go and look at the farther side of the moon, so that I am unable to decide the matter by actual observation. But I do know what observations would decide it for me, if, as is theoretically conceivable, I were once in a position to make them. And therefore I say that the proposition is verifiable in principle, if not in practice, and is accordingly significant. (Ayer)

AO2 Activity

List some conclusions that could be drawn from the AO2 reasoning from the above text; try to aim for at least three different possible conclusions. Consider each of the conclusions and collect brief evidence to support each conclusion from the AO1 and AO2 material for this topic. Select the conclusion that you think is most convincing and explain why it is so. Try to contrast this with the weakest conclusion in the list, justifying your argument with clear reasoning and evidence

AO2 Developing skills

It is now important to consider the information that has been covered in this section; however, the information in its raw form is too extensive and so has to be processed in order to meet the requirements of the examination. This can be achieved by practising more advanced skills associated with AO2. For assessment objective 2 (AO2), which involves 'critical analysis' and 'evaluation' skills, we are going to focus on different ways in which the skills can be demonstrated effectively, and also refer to how the performance of these skills is measured (see generic band descriptors for A2 [WJEC] AO2 or A Level [Eduqas] AO2).

▶ **Your next task is this:** Below is an evaluation concerning **logical positivism**. It is 150 words long. After the first paragraph there is an intermediate conclusion highlighted for you in yellow. As a group try to identify where you could add more intermediate conclusions to the rest of the passage. Have a go at doing this.

Logical positivism has suggested a simple method for determining the meaningfulness of any given statement. It applies scientific principles in the form of statements that can be considered to be self-explanatory (analytic) practically verifiable via empirical methods (synthetic) as the only criterion for establishing meaning. This criterion was deemed to be too restrictive by some as it did not take into account as meaningful either historic statements or universal scientific statements and that was considered to undermine it as a useful method for establishing meaning. It was therefore modified by Ayer to include a verifiable in practice (strong) and verifiable in principle (weak) form. Religious philosophers point out that something can be considered to be meaning by virtue of the effect it has on a person, rather than just whether it is empirically verifiable. They have pointed out that the logical positivists have misunderstood the purpose of religious language.

When you have done this you will see clearly that in AO2 it is helpful to include a brief summary of the arguments presented as you go through an answer and not just leave it until the end to draw a final conclusion. This way you are demonstrating that you are sustaining evaluation throughout an answer and not just repeating information learned.

Key skills

Analysis involves:

Identifying issues raised by the materials in the AO1, together with those identified in the AO2 section, and presents sustained and clear views, either of scholars or from a personal perspective ready for evaluation.

This means:

- That your answers are able to identify key areas of debate in relation to a particular issue
- That you can identify, and comment upon, the different lines of argument presented by others
- That your response comments on the overall effectiveness of each of these areas or arguments.

Evaluation involves:

Considering the various implications of the issues raised based upon the evidence gleaned from analysis and provides an extensive detailed argument with a clear conclusion.

This means:

- That your answer weighs up the consequences of accepting or rejecting the various and different lines of argument analysed
- That your answer arrives at a conclusion through a clear process of reasoning.

Logical positivists questioned the purpose of religious language.

This section covers AO1 content and skills

Specification content

Proportion and attribution (St Thomas Aquinas) and qualifier and disclosure (Ian Ramsey).

Thomas Aquinas (1225–1274)

Key terms

Equivocally: where there is more than one meaning, usually in relation to a word or phrase

Predicated: stating or asserting something that is the ground or basis of an argument

Univocally: where something has one universal and unambiguous meaning

quickfire

4.11 According to Aquinas, what were the two ways in which language was normally used?

C: Religious language as non-cognitive and analogical

Proportion and attribution (St Thomas Aquinas)

Long before the debates regarding the meaningfulness of religious language from the Vienna Circle, the use of words in the relationship between God and man was being considered by the philosophers of the Middle Ages. One of the most significant of these contributors was St Thomas Aquinas who, in a number of his writings, considered the function of language and how we could further understand the mysteries of the divine nature. God, according to the writings of Aquinas, was essentially unknowable. However, certain properties could be attributed to God and it was the task of the believer to develop increasingly deeper insights into him by reflecting on creation and the teachings of holy scripture and the Church.

Aquinas recognised that language was often used in two main ways – **univocally** and **equivocally**. When language is used univocally, it is used in the sense that there is the same term that means the same thing whatever the context. In other words, there was one term that had exactly one and the same, identical meaning, whenever and wherever it was used. For example, when I use the noun 'carpet' I mean the same thing when I put it in different contexts: 'the bedroom carpet'; 'the carpet in the mosque'; 'the camper van's carpet'; 'the carpet for sale in the carpet shop'. In each and every usage I am referring to a floor covering usually made from a thick woven fabric.

Study tip

Try to come up with a list of how words are used univocally and equivocally to help you explain Aquinas' thoughts.

Aquinas writes:

It is thereby evident that nothing can be **predicated** univocally of God and other things ... Now, the forms of the things God has made do not measure up to a specific likeness of the divine power; for the things that God has made receive in a divided and particular way that which in Him is found in a simple and universal way. It is evident, then, that nothing can be said univocally of God and other things... Again, what is predicated of many things univocally is simpler than both of them, at least in concept. Now, there can be nothing simpler than God either in reality or in concept. Nothing, therefore, is predicated univocally of God and other things... Now nothing is predicated of God and creatures as though they were in the same order, but, rather, according to priority and posteriority. For all things are predicated of God essentially. For God is called being as being entity itself, and He is called good as being goodness itself. But in other beings predications are made by participation, as Socrates is said to be a man, not because he is humanity itself, but because he possesses humanity. It is impossible, therefore, that anything be predicated univocally of God and other things. (Contra Gentiles, 32)

Language being used equivocally was where it was used in the sense that there is the same term that has completely different meanings according to the context in which it is used. For example, when I use the noun 'set', I could be referring to a mathematical device, a television, a place where a play is performed, a hair arrangement, a number of repetitions used in bodybuilding, etc. Here the context changes the meaning of the word – in fact, without understanding the specific context in which it is being used, I would have no insight into what the word 'set' would mean.

The word 'set' can have a different meaning when associated with 'square', 'TV' and 'film'.

Aquinas continues:

> From what we have said it likewise appears that not everything predicated of God and other things is said in a purely equivocal way, in the manner of equivocals by chance … It is not, therefore, in the manner of pure equivocation that something is predicated of God and other things. Furthermore, where there is pure equivocation, there is no likeness in things themselves; there is only the unity of a name. But, as is clear from what we have said, there is a certain mode of likeness of things to God. It remains, then, that names are not said of God in a purely equivocal way. Moreover, when one name is predicated of several things in a purely equivocal way, we cannot from one of them be led to the knowledge of another; for the knowledge of things does not depend on words, but on the meaning of names. Now, from what we find in other things, we do arrive at a knowledge of divine things, as is evident from what we have said. Such names, then, are not said of God and other things in a purely equivocal way. Again, equivocation in a name impedes the process of reasoning. If, then, nothing was said of God and creatures except in a purely equivocal way, no reasoning proceeding from creatures to God could take place. (Contra Gentiles, 33)

Clearly, neither of these uses of language were helpful for the believer in trying to gain a deeper insight into the nature of God. On the one hand, univocal language could not possibly describe God – God is so different from us that any use of a univocal word would be hopelessly inadequate. Equally, using equivocal language would just put us into a place where we knew the word had a different meaning but we would have no knowable terms of reference or understood context to explain what it meant – in which case the word may as well be a nonsense word.

Aquinas therefore settled on the use of **analogy**. Analogy gave a middle ground because, whilst on the one hand it was accepted that part of what was being spoken about was imperfectly understood (and for Aquinas, God could never be fully understood by human beings as human beings were too limited and God was too great). On the other hand, the object being referred to, in making the analogy, was fully understood and this was required in order for the analogy to work. (The example of Paley's Watchmaker is one of the more notable uses of analogy in the history of religious philosophy, and has long been debated as to how effective it is in showing the supposed correlation between a complex mechanism designed by an intelligent human being with the complex universe designed by the intelligent divine being.) One of the key features of a successful analogy was ensuring that there was some link or relationship between the two things being compared.

For Aquinas, God was the source of all existence, the source of all creation. The account in the Judeo-Christian scripture 'Genesis' contains a direct reference to God making humans in his image (Gen 1:26 – 'Let us make man in our image,

Key quotes

For all things are predicated of God essentially. For God is called being as being entity itself, and He is called good as being goodness itself. But in other beings predications are made by participation, as Socrates is said to be a man, not because he is humanity itself, but because he possesses humanity. It is impossible, therefore, that anything be predicated univocally of God and other things. **(Aquinas)**

But, as is clear from what we have said, there is a certain mode of likeness of things to God. It remains, then, that names are not said of God in a purely equivocal way. Moreover, when one name is predicated of several things in a purely equivocal way, we cannot from one of them be led to the knowledge of another; for the knowledge of things does not depend on words, but on the meaning of names. **(Aquinas)**

Analogical language provides insight for the believer according to Aquinas.

Key term

Analogy: where something (that is known) is compared with something else (usually something unknown), in order to explain or clarify

quickfire

4.12 What is meant by the term 'analogy of proportion'?

Key quote

From what we have said, therefore, it remains that the names said of God and creatures are predicated neither univocally nor equivocally but analogically, that is, according to an order or reference to something one ... Thus, therefore, because we come to a knowledge of God from other things, the reality in the names said of God and other things belongs by priority in God according to His mode of being, but the meaning of the name belongs to God by posteriority. And so He is said to be named from His effects. (Aquinas)

The intelligence of foxes and human beings is proportionately different.

Key terms

Attribution: relating to the attribute or characteristic possessed by an object

Proportion: relating to the relative value of something according to its nature

after our likeness'). Thus, for Aquinas, there was a definitive link between human beings and God. Thus, it followed that speaking about God could be understood by reference to our understanding of what it meant to be human – both from human nature and human purpose.

The analogy of proportion

Aquinas considered that the universe was inhabited by different orders of things. These were hierarchical in the sense of status. So, for example, God would be considered to be both above all of creation (as well as its source). Humans were lower than God, but higher than animals. Animals were higher than plants, and so on. Therefore, each order possessed particular characteristics which were appropriate to its hierarchical status, even though the same adjective may be applied.

For instance, we could consider what it means for a human to be intelligent and for an animal, for example a fox, to be intelligent. These both occupy different positions within the created order and therefore, according to Aquinas, we should consider what we mean when we apply the word 'intelligence' to each. Clearly there are common features in the use of the word (relating to ability, judgement, intuition, etc.) but we do not understand the word 'intelligence' to mean exactly the same thing when applied to both a human being and a fox. The intelligence is relative. It is also appropriate. In this sense we can see the link but we understand there is a difference – in **proportion** to the reality that the thing being spoken about possesses. In other words, a human being is intelligent in the appropriate way that it is for a human being to be intelligent; a fox is intelligent in the appropriate way it is for a fox to be intelligent.

To put that yet another way:

- A human being is intelligent in proportion to what it means for a human being to be intelligent.
- A fox is intelligent in proportion to what it means for a fox to be intelligent.

For Aquinas, it was therefore possible to talk analogically about God by making reference to human qualities. So, to talk about God as being 'Good' made sense analogically because we understand what it means for a human being to be good. So:

- A human being is good in proportion to what it means for a human being to be good.
- A God is good in proportion to what it means for God to be good.

The analogy of attribution

The second analogous way that Aquinas believed it was possible to talk about God in a meaningful sense, was through the analogy of **attribution.** An attribute is a characteristic or feature that something possesses. Common positive attributes to describe human beings might be words such as 'good'; 'loving'; 'wise', etc.

However, Aquinas believed that these attributes were entirely divinely inspired. Human beings can only be good because they come from God. God's goodness is the attribute which human beings, who have come from God (as has all creation), are therefore good, in the sense that that goodness comes from God. Human beings are not good independently of God but good because they are dependent on God.

To make this clearer, consider the word 'healthy'. If I talk about an animal having good health, I could attribute my definition of the animal as having good health because I know that its blood is healthy, its diet is healthy, its exercise regime is healthy. None of these three things are 'healthy' in themselves (i.e. blood is not intrinsically 'healthy'; diet is not intrinsically 'healthy' and neither is an exercise regime) but derive their 'healthiness' from the relationship they share with the animal. This is why some philosophers refer to this as the analogy of reference.

Thus, because of this relationship, where the attribute comes from God, to talk of God in any of these ways, (as long as the human equivalent quality is understood) then an insight into what it means, in relation to God, can be gained.

Key quote

Accordingly some hold that the meanings of these terms connote various corresponding divine effects: for they maintain that when we say *God is good*, we indicate God's essence together with a connoted effect, the sense being *God is and causes goodness*, so that the difference in these attributions arises from the difference in his effects. But this does not seem right: because seeing that an effect proceeds in likeness to its cause, we must needs understand a cause to be such before its effects are such. Wherefore God is not called wise because he is the cause of wisdom: but because he is wise, therefore does he cause wisdom. Hence Augustine says (*De Doct. Christ.* ii, 32) that *because God is good, therefore we exist, and inasmuch as we exist we are good.* Moreover according to this view it would follow that these expressions are attributed to the creature before the Creator: just as health is attributed first to a healthy man and afterwards to that which gives health, since the latter is called healthy through being a cause of health. Again if when we say *God is good* we mean nothing more than *God is and is the cause of goodness.* (**Aquinas**)

Qualifier and disclosure (Ian Ramsey)

Ian Ramsey, later to become Bishop of Durham, wrote in 1957 arguably his most famous work *Religious Language*. In this he wanted to examine how we used language and how he felt it should be understood. Ramsey's own beliefs, as can be ascertained from this and other of his theological works, was that all experience is effectively a religious experience because, for him, all experience was essentially a continual encounter between God and his creation. It was through this particular framework that Ramsey developed his distinctive teachings regarding '**disclosure**'.

For Ramsey, the religious language that grew out of religious situations became revelatory in the sense that those religious experiences were variously referred to as disclosures – moments where the person was often able to grasp an understanding of the divine (although not all moments of disclosure were considered to be religious). These were instead moments where not only the superficial moment itself was appreciated but there was also a realisation that there was something else going on, something that could not be easily described in normal language. What was also common of these moments of disclosure was the degree of commitment they provoked from the individual. In order to try and make sense of this, Ramsey developed his idea of 'models'.

Based on philosopher Max Black's argument about insight models and his specific idea of analogue models, Ramsey renames these as disclosure models, which he believed was the characteristic way that religious language functioned. Referring to key terms used for God that were common throughout the Christian Bible such as Father, Shepherd, King and Rock, Ramsey recognised within each of these terms a particular view about a reality that the believer was committing to (i.e. a father protects, as does a shepherd; a king protects and rules – whereas a rock also provides strength and stability – as well as being a firm foundation upon which to build).

However, on their own they were still insufficient ways to properly refer to God, which is why Ramsey believed we needed to make use of **qualifiers** – words, or phrases that could be added to these earlier terms in order to provide them with the quality and sense that they were greater than what their normal reality represented. Thus words and phrases such as 'transcendent', 'almighty',

Aquinas argued that food is only healthy in that it is a cause of good health in humans through attribution; in itself it is just food.

quickfire

4.13 What, for Ramsay, in relation to language, was a qualifier?

Key quote

The central problem of theology is how to use, how to qualify observational language so as to be suitable currency for what in part exceeds it – the situations in which theology is founded. (**Ramsay**)

Key terms

Disclosure: where something is made known where previously it was hidden or unknown

Qualifier: a term used by Ramsay where a word or phrase is used to give a deeper meaning to the model that the qualifier precedes

The idea of God as the Almighty King is a useful example of a qualified disclosure.

Specification content

Challenges including how far analogies can give meaningful insights into religious language.

Key quote

For present purposes, however, we can discern central and recurrent theses of Ramsey's work. First there is his claim that religious language grows from 'religious situations', otherwise described as situations of 'cosmic disclosure', in which a 'characteristic discernment' occurs and a 'characteristic commitment' is made. Since this is intended to account for the origin of religious language, in this discussion we will call it the generative thesis. Second, there is Ramsey's claim that religious language consists of 'models' whose function is to instruct the hearer to proceed imaginatively in a particular way until (it may be) a disclosure occurs for him. Since this is intended to show how the language of religion functions in relation to the disclosures, we will call it the functional thesis. (McClendon and Smith)

'everlasting' and 'all-loving', added another dimension to these terms by 'qualifying' them in relation to God. The father became the 'Almighty Father', the Shepherd the 'all-loving Shepherd', etc. With these qualifications 'the penny drops, the light dawns' (Ramsey) and the believer is brought into a meaningful disclosure through religious language.

Ian Ramsey (1915–1972)

AO1 Activity

After reading the section on Ramsey, note down evidence and examples that could be used to explain his ideas relating to qualifiers and disclosure. This could help you to achieve the best possible AO1 level in an examination answer (B5 AO1 level descriptors).

Challenges

Whilst, in many ways, analogy is a useful way of helping to gain insights into the meaningfulness of religious language, it is not without its limitations.

Firstly, as was recognised by Hume in his *Dialogues concerning Natural Religion*, an analogy is only as good as the point at which the two things being compared are similar. The issue for religious language, which was central to the concerns raised by the Vienna Circle, was do we know what we mean when we use the word 'God'? How do we 'know' (in the sense of being able to empirically quantify what we are talking about) what constitutes 'God' – because unless we are able, in some measure, to do this, then our point of comparison fails. If this fails then so does the analogy, thereby rendering analogical language not only meaningless but, in a very real sense, useless – as far as talking about God is concerned.

Both Aquinas and Ramsey assume God's existence, and, with such an assumption then their assertions regarding analogy have some weight. However, were we to dismiss the assumption then we run into a serious philosophical issue as far as analogous religious language is concerned – without the existence of God there can be no point of comparison!

Even if we accept Aquinas' and Ramsey's assumption in relation to the existence of God, our lack of empirical knowledge of what constitutes God means that the best hope we can have of using language about God is to use it equivocally. In this sense, we know that God is different (even if we can't say precisely how) and therefore the meaning of the words is different – but this takes us back to square one in terms of trying to find a meaningful way to talk about God!

Furthermore, Ramsey's use of qualifiers only serves to underline the fact that we do not fully understand what we mean when referring to God – we can only ever get an insight. Ramsey admitted that this was part of the 'mystery' ('They disclose but do not explain a mystery' – Ramsey, *Models and Mystery*, 1966) of what it meant to have faith, but that does not necessarily satisfy the non-religious believer when considering whether analogy is a suitable way to talk meaningfully about God.

How the views of Aquinas and Ramsey can be used to help understand religious teachings

Regardless of the challenges to the use of analogy to help talk meaningfully about God and other forms of religious language, the work of both Aquinas and Ramsey has been useful for those that profess a religious belief.

Religious teachings, expressed through religious language, can often be seen to be opaque from the perspective of those outside a tradition. (They can also sometimes be considered to be difficult for those within!) However, considering the idea that there is a connection between a creator God and his human creation, means that a suitable point of reference can be drawn between the two – thereby illuminating what would otherwise be virtually impossible to understand.

Understanding that to talk about God is to talk about something that is the source of all human activity, means that insights into religious belief and practice can be gained by considering their root in the realm of human experience. These human experiences, known and understood, form gateways into the realm of the divine. Religious teachings are therefore illuminated, by association. Believers have clear points of reference to begin to try and understand the mysteries of their religious tradition. Analogies of proportion and attribution give clear ways for accessing a meaningful context to begin to come to terms with the spiritual realm – anchored as they are in the physical one.

Ramsey's models that help to disclose divine attributes, and his qualifiers that make a sense of the impossibility of actually describing God, assist religious believers in understanding how it is possible to talk about things which relate to God. At the same time this helped religious believers appreciate that things of this nature are far beyond our actual understanding and that we merely grasp at what these might mean. Far from making religious language meaningless, these actually assist religious believers in providing insights to that which is otherwise without a point of reference.

Thus, the myriad of religious teachings that relate to: God; the revelation of scripture; divine election; angels; salvation; life after death, etc., are well served by the work of both Aquinas and Ramsey who provide a useful means by which to talk about them, to communicate the ideas to others and to reflect on their meanings, whilst retaining a sense of how they relate to the mundanity of the empirical world.

Study tip

When answering a question on analogies, make certain that you know the difference between the two different types described by Aquinas and that you can clearly explain how he considers them to work. Don't confuse the explanations or mix up the examples as this will show you have misunderstood the topic and you will not be able to gain a higher level mark for your response.

AO1 Activity

It is vital that you are able to make thorough and accurate use of specialist language and vocabulary in context. Test your knowledge of the following terms/names/phrases by putting each in a sentence using your own words. Make sure however, that each sentence is relevant to the issues that have been studied in this particular unit: cognitive; non-cognitive; univocal; equivocal; verification; falsification; analytic; synthetic; analogy; attribution; proportion.

Paley used the analogy of a watchmaker to help understand religious teachings that the universe was designed.

Key quotes

Let us always be cautious of talking about God in straightforward language. Let us never talk as if we had privileged access to the diaries of God's private life, or expert insight into his descriptive psychology so that we may say quite cheerfully why God did what, when, and where. (Ramsey)

For the religious man 'God' is a key word, an irreducible posit, an ultimate of explanation expressive of the kind of commitment he professes. It is to be talked about in terms of the object-language over which it presides, but only when this object-language is qualified; in which case this qualified object-language becomes also currency for that odd discernment with which religious commitment, when it is not bigotry or fanaticism, will necessarily he associated. Meanwhile, as a corollary, we can note that to understand religious language or theology we must first evoke the odd kind of situation to which I have given various parallels. (Ramsey)

Key skills

Knowledge involves:

Selection of a range of (thorough) accurate and relevant information that is directly related to the specific demands of the question.

This means:

- Selecting relevant material for the question set

- Being focused in explaining and examining the material selected.

Understanding involves:

Explanation that is extensive, demonstrating depth and/or breadth with excellent use of evidence and examples including (where appropriate) thorough and accurate supporting use of sacred texts, sources of wisdom and specialist language.

This means:

- Effective use of examples and supporting evidence to establish the quality of your understanding

- Ownership of your explanation that expresses personal knowledge and understanding and NOT just reproducing a chunk of text from a book that you have rehearsed and memorised.

What does it mean when it is said: 'God is Good'?

AO1 Developing skills

It is now important to consider the information that has been covered in this section; however, the information in its raw form is too extensive and so has to be processed in order to meet the requirements of the examination. This can be achieved by practising more advanced skills associated with AO1. For assessment objective 1 (AO1), which involves demonstrating 'knowledge' and 'understanding' skills, we are going to focus on different ways in which the skills can be demonstrated effectively, and also refer to how the performance of these skills is measured (see generic band descriptors for A2 [WJEC] AO1 or A Level [Eduqas] AO1).

▶ **Your final task for this theme is:** Below is a summary of **Aquinas' approach to analogy**. It is 150 words long. This time there are no highlighted points to indicate the key points to learn from this extract. Discuss which five points you think are the most important to highlight and write them down in a list.

One of the key features of a successful analogy was ensuring that there was some link or relationship between the two things being compared. For Aquinas, God was the source of all existence, the source of all creation. Thus, for Aquinas, there was a definitive link between human beings and God. Thus, it followed, that speaking about God, could be understood by reference to our understanding of what it meant to be human. For Aquinas, it was therefore possible to talk analogically about God by making reference to human qualities. So, to talk about God as being 'good' made sense analogically because we understand what it means for a human being to be good, just proportionately so. Equally Aquinas believed that human beings can only be good because they come from God. Human beings are not good independently of God but good because they are dependent on God. They derive this attribute from God.

Now make the five points into your own summary (as in Theme 1 Developing skills) trying to make the summary more personal to your style of writing. This may also involve re-ordering the points if you wish to do so. In addition to this, try to add some quotations and references to develop your summary (as in Theme 2 Developing skills).

The result will be a fairly lengthy answer and so you could then check it against the band descriptors for A2 (WJEC) or A Level (Eduqas) and in particular have a look at the demands described in the higher band descriptors towards which you should be aspiring. Ask yourself:

- Does my work demonstrate thorough, accurate and relevant knowledge and understanding of religion and belief?

- Is my work coherent (consistent or make logical sense), clear and well organised?

- Will my work, when developed, be an extensive and relevant response which is specific to the focus of the task?

- Does my work have extensive depth and/or suitable breadth and have excellent use of evidence and examples?

- If appropriate to the task, does my response have thorough and accurate reference to sacred texts and sources of wisdom?

- Are there any insightful connections to be made with other elements of my course?

- Will my answer, when developed and extended to match what is expected in an examination answer, have an extensive range of views of scholars/schools of thought?

- When used, is specialist language and vocabulary both thorough and accurate?

Issues for analysis and evaluation

To what extent do the challenges to logical positivism provide convincing arguments to non-religious believers?

The work of the logical positivists was firmly based upon the scientific principles that had risen to prominence by the beginning of the twentieth century. The use of empirical observation, and a systematic application of what became known as the verification principle, for determining the meaningfulness of any statement, would prove to be a highly influential idea for many years. This approach was entirely free of any influence from non-rational thought and, as such, was highly appealing to those who were not of a religious background. Agnostic and atheistic philosophers such as Russell and Ayer, debated with the religious philosophers of their day regarding matters associated with religious belief and the language that was used to convey those beliefs. As such, it could be argued that the default position towards logical positivism, from the non-religious believers, would be one of firm support.

However, the challenges to logical positivism grew as the twentieth century progressed, and many of its central ideas, particularly in relation to how we establish a criterion for meaningfulness in language, have been largely rejected as we stand at the early part of the twenty-first century. This is because ideas, such as those published by philosophers such as Wittgenstein (ironically himself an early influence on logical positivism through the work of his 'Tractatus') became more widely accepted as being more effective as ways of understanding how we convey meaning through our use of language. Wittgenstein's work on language games being a case in point. It is also fair to say that the majority of philosophers, by the mid-twentieth century, had come to realise that the verification principle was actually self-defeating (there being no way to actually 'verify' the principle itself – thereby rendering it, by its own criteria, essentially 'meaningless'). These criticisms were accepted by those from both the religious and non-religious philosophical communities.

Turning to some of the specific challenges to logical positivism from religious philosophers will allow us to consider further how far challenges to logical positivism have provided convincing arguments to non-religious believers. The logical positivists stated that only those statements which were analytic or synthetic could truly be accepted as meaningful. This was because analytic statements were self-defining – and thereby 'true' by definition (e.g. all bachelors are unmarried males) or because synthetic statements could be rendered meaningful by some sense experience or observation (e.g. the car is black). This led to a conclusion that any form of metaphysical statement, being neither analytic nor synthetic, had to be considered meaningless. Whilst this posed an issue for statements about religion, it also dismissed commonly experienced facets of human existence such as emotions and morality as being ultimately meaningless. This provoked a reaction from philosophers outside of the logical positivist tradition who saw this as a reductionist approach to the 'meaningfulness' of statements beyond the analytic/synthetic scope.

This section covers AO2 content and skills

Specification content

To what extent do the challenges to logical positivism provide convincing arguments to non-religious believers?

Do the ideas of religious philosophers persuade non-believers?

AO2 Activity

As you read through this section try to do the following:

1. Pick out the different lines of argument that are presented in the text and identify any evidence given in support.

2. For each line of argument try to evaluate whether or not you think this is strong or weak.

3. Think of any questions you may wish to raise in response to the arguments.

This Activity will help you to start thinking critically about what you read and help you to evaluate the effectiveness of different arguments and from this develop your own observations, opinions and points of view that will help with any conclusions that you make in your answers to the AO2 questions that arise.

Is the claim that Moses received the 10 Commandments on Mount Sinai an historical claim?

Key questions

What are the criteria for the meaningfulness of language, according to logical positivism?

Why are religious statements considered to be metaphysical statements and are therefore rejected by logical positivists?

How does the work of Hare reflect a non-cognitive approach to understanding language?

AO2 Activity

List some conclusions that could be drawn from the AO2 reasoning from the above text; try to aim for at least three different possible conclusions. Consider each of the conclusions and collect brief evidence to support each conclusion from the AO1 and AO2 material for this topic. Select the conclusion that you think is most convincing and explain why it is so. Try to contrast this with the weakest conclusion in the list, justifying your argument with clear reasoning and evidence.

The religious philosopher R. Braithwaite observed that logical positivism had misunderstood how religious language was used. He noted that language could be used in a cognitive and in a non-cognitive sense. The logical positivists completely disregarded the non-cognitive function of language and therefore, according to Braithwaite, missed the point of what religious language (as well as other forms of metaphysical language) was attempting to do. Religious language was about expressing attitudes towards life that were meaningful by virtue of the impact that they had on the believer's life. To express a religious belief was to also adopt a particular attitude towards the self and those around you. As such, Braithwaite argued, it was highly meaningful.

Another religious philosopher, John Hick, pointed out that Ayer's weak form of verification would actually permit some religious statements to be meaningful, as some sense experience could be identified that would count towards them – particularly historical religious claims (e.g. Moses received the 10 Commandments on Mount Sinai; Jesus was born in Bethlehem, etc.). Hick also pointed out that if there was an existence after death, then faith claims such as 'God exists' would theoretically be verifiable. Hick called this 'eschatological verification' and, if his logic is accepted, this is a convincing argument for both religious and non-religious believers.

Religious philosophers also challenged the logical positivist position of falsification. Richard Swinburne pointed out, in his toys in the cupboard example, that some statements can be considered to be meaningful to us, even when we cannot disprove them. This point can be accepted by non-religious believers, as it depends on understanding concepts which do not depend on an acceptance of any religious belief (i.e. the idea that toys can physically move when not being watched).

R. M. Hare's contribution to the debate with his suggestion of 'bliks' is a powerful way of persuading others to accept the limitations of the logical positivist approach to meaningfulness. Hare argues that the way in which we view life has a greater reality to us, in terms of meaningfulness, than any actual objective reality. Whether our 'bliks' can be substantiated is actually irrelevant to us. As to us, it is how we perceive reality that is important (and therefore meaningful). For instance, if the university student (in Hare's own parable) truly believed that the dons were out to harm him, then it didn't matter what the actual reality was, and what evidence is shown to him, he still lived his life with this point of view intact and it has meaning for him in the way that he interacts with those around him. Thus meaningfulness is as powerfully expressed through a non-cognitive understanding of language as it is through a cognitive understanding. Again, this must surely be considered to be a convincing challenge to logical positivism for non-religious believers.

Study tip

When you are required to draw a comparison between two things or people, i.e. the relative importance of cognitive and non-cognitive forms of language, make sure that you do not give only half an answer by failing to provide a balanced response that considers both.

Whether non-cognitive interpretations are valid responses to the challenges to the meaning of religious language

The challenges to the meaningfulness of religious language have been met over the past century or so with a series of robust philosophical defences, more often than not based on the view that religious language is a form of language that is more properly understood to have a non-cognitive rather than a cognitive function. The responses, in particular, of Braithwaite, demonstrated that religious statements were expressions of a particular attitude or intention of how life was to be lived and, as such, were very similar to the way in which moral language is used – i.e. to express an opinion or attitude about the relative ethical value of a belief or action, and to live one's life accordingly.

However, the challenges to the meaningfulness of religious language were specific, in the sense that they were levelled at the idea that religious language said nothing that could be either verified or falsified. Religious language was not self-evident (analytic) nor could any sense experience or experiment count towards it (synthetic). Both of these assumed that religious language had a similar function to other forms of language. Whether this particular point is accepted or not forms the crux of how far one can consider non-cognitive interpretations of language to be valid responses to the challenges to the meaning of religious language.

The function of any form of language is to communicate. Communication is generally accepted as the exchange of ideas between individuals or groups. Where there is a shared understanding of what is being communicated (and this usually comes from experience) then what is being communicated can generally be regarded as being meaningful. This holds true for both cognitive and non-cognitive forms of language. Therefore, if this point is accepted, then non-cognitive interpretations of language can be considered to be meaningful and they are therefore suitable responses to the challenges to the meaning of religious language.

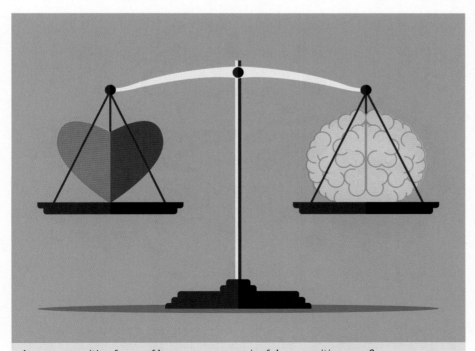

Are non-cognitive forms of language as meaningful as cognitive ones?

Specification content

Whether non-cognitive interpretations are valid responses to the challenges to the meaning of religious language.

Key questions

Is it justified to consider religious language to be purely non-cognitive?

Does the concept of a 'blik' actually mean anything or is it just an excuse to say that anything can be considered meaningful, even if it is entirely irrational?

Does religious language express ideas about the world or merely an attitude towards the world?

AO2 Activity

As you read through this section try to do the following:

1. Pick out the different lines of argument that are presented in the text and identify any evidence given in support.

2. For each line of argument try to evaluate whether or not you think this is strong or weak.

3. Think of any questions you may wish to raise in response to the arguments.

This Activity will help you to start thinking critically about what you read and help you to evaluate the effectiveness of different arguments and from this develop your own observations, opinions and points of view that will help with any conclusions that you make in your answers to the AO2 questions that arise.

However, some philosophers have identified a particular difficulty with the non-cognitive approach. If we accept the idea that religious statements are expressions of a particular attitude or intention of how life was to be lived then, by logical extension, they are not making statements about any kind of reality that could be described as 'objective'. By this, we mean that not only are they not making any 'factual' comments but that, if religious language is purely to be understood as non-cognitive, then it is incapable of making such statements. This poses an issue for the religious believers who might state that 'God exists' or 'sacred writings are the word of God' or 'I believe in a life after death'. These are not just expressions of attitude for the religious believer. They are, in fact, and in the context appropriate to the particular religion, assertions about how reality actually is. In a very real sense, the religious believer considers these to be statements about the external world – in other words, is using them in a cognitive, not non-cognitive, sense. Which brings us back to the original challenge from logical positivism, i.e. that such statements are neither analytic or synthetic – they cannot be verified!

This seems to be conclusive, but again, appearances can be deceptive. Our line of reasoning, which took the view that religious claims are not the same as religious attitudes, does not take into account the context of making such claims in the views expressed by Hare. To make such a claim as part of one's 'blik' could be argued as making a cognitive claim within a non-cognitive framework – in the sense that a person is making statements about what they perceive to be reality – not just their 'attitude' towards it (although the attitude influences the statements being made). If this is held to be true then the concept of a blik, as a non-cognitive concept, provides a context wherein the challenges to the meaningfulness of religious language are successfully met. They are meaningful, and they do successfully meet the specific criticisms levelled at religious language by the likes of logical positivists and any others that may consider religious language to be a meaningless form of communication.

What do religious believers mean when they say that 'God exists'?

AO2 Activity

List some conclusions that could be drawn from the AO2 reasoning from the above text; try to aim for at least three different possible conclusions. Consider each of the conclusions and collect brief evidence to support each conclusion from the AO1 and AO2 material for this topic. Select the conclusion that you think is most convincing and explain why it is so. Try to contrast this with the weakest conclusion in the list, justifying your argument with clear reasoning and evidence.

AO2 Developing skills

It is now important to consider the information that has been covered in this section; however, the information in its raw form is too extensive and so has to be processed in order to meet the requirements of the examination. This can be achieved by practising more advanced skills associated with AO2. For assessment objective 2 (AO2), which involves 'critical analysis' and 'evaluation' skills, we are going to focus on different ways in which the skills can be demonstrated effectively, and also refer to how the performance of these skills is measured (see generic band descriptors for A2 [WJEC] AO2 or A Level [Eduqas] AO2).

▶ **Your final task for this theme is:** Below are listed three basic conclusions drawn from an evaluation of **whether non-cognitive interpretations are valid responses to the challenges to the meaning of religious language**. Your task is to develop each of these conclusions by identifying briefly the strengths (referring briefly to some reasons underlying it) but also an awareness of challenges made to it (these may be weaknesses depending upon your view).

1. Non-cognitive interpretations are insufficient in responding to the direct challenge of logical positivism.

2. The meaningfulness of religious language can be found in the way that it directly affects the way that a person lives their life.

3. Religious language expresses more than just an attitude – it makes actual claims about how the world is, and so should be treated as a cognitive form of language, not non-cognitive.

The result should be three very competent paragraphs that could form a final conclusion of any evaluation.

When you have completed the task, refer to the band descriptors for A2 (WJEC) or A Level (Eduqas) and in particular have a look at the demands described in the higher band descriptors towards which you should be aspiring. Ask yourself:

- Is my answer a confident critical analysis and perceptive evaluation of the issue?
- Is my answer a response that successfully identifies and thoroughly addresses the issues raised by the question set?

Key skills

Analysis involves:

Identifying issues raised by the materials in the AO1, together with those identified in the AO2 section, and presents sustained and clear views, either of scholars or from a personal perspective ready for evaluation.

This means:

- That your answers are able to identify key areas of debate in relation to a particular issue
- That you can identify, and comment upon, the different lines of argument presented by others
- That your response comments on the overall effectiveness of each of these areas or arguments.

Evaluation involves:

Considering the various implications of the issues raised based upon the evidence gleaned from analysis and provides an extensive detailed argument with a clear conclusion.

This means:

- That your answer weighs up the consequences of accepting or rejecting the various and different lines of argument analysed
- That your answer arrives at a conclusion through a clear process of reasoning.

Religious language is an expression of religious belief. Belief affects the way that people live.

T4 Religious language

Specification content
Religious language as non-cognitive and symbolic.

Key terms

Myth: a complex form of writing that contains symbol, metaphor and is highly imaginative. A prevailing view of myths is that they contain truths about the universe and the role of humanity within it

Symbol: something which points beyond itself to a deeper level of reality

Ultimate concern: Tillich's definition of God – that which should concern humans ultimately and be the focus of their lives, providing meaning and motivating behaviours and attitudes

quickfire

4.14 What were the names of the two key thinkers that contributed to our understanding of language as non-cognitive and symbolic?

D: Religious language as non-cognitive and symbolic

Introduction

Having considered previously the function of language when it is considered as non-cognitive, leads us to an alternative consideration of how language conveys meaning. Stepping outside of the confines of cognitive language, such as that employed by empirical disciplines, provides a wider and deeper appreciation of how we convey meaning in our different modes of communication. In the next two sections we shall consider language as non-cognitive and symbolic/mythical. These two latter concepts are necessarily linked, as the **myth** depends on **symbol** to communicate its ideas, whilst the symbol depends on myth to provide the context wherefrom it derives its meaning.

Symbols can be found in all religious traditions.

We shall consider the ideas of two key thinkers who have contributed, firstly, to the understanding of the role of symbol as a form of non-cognitive language: J. H. Randall who, in 1958, wrote the book *The Role of Knowledge in Western Religions*, a volume which attempted to bring together some of the key ideas that had presented themselves to the world of theology over the preceding century from philosophy, psychology and science. Randall recognised that religion and science were both human activities that performed different functions yet both had a vital role to play on the cultural life of human beings. The other thinker, Paul Tillich (described by influential American 20th-century theologian Reinhold Niebuhr as 'A giant among us'), wrote in his book *Dynamics of Faith* (published in 1957) about symbols opening up levels of reality to help people to engage with their '**ultimate concern**'.

Key quote

Both religion and science, we have come to recognise, are things men do: they are human activities. And men do them together with their fellows: they are social activities, organised and institutionalised ways of acting, aspects of group behaviour, traits of the culture of that group. Like all institutions of a society, these religious and scientific ways of acting themselves do something; they perform certain functions. And they incidentally do something to each other, as well as to all the other institutions, especially when they are changing. But the cultural functions of religion and of science our so different that it is difficult to see how, despite their incidental reactions on each other, they can seriously compete. Both functions are clearly indispensable. **(Randall)**

Functions of symbols (John Randall)

When we think of symbols we think of those pictures from everyday life that to us have different meanings according to our own experiences and cultures. These symbols are rich in meaning and therefore can be interpreted in a myriad of different ways. Sometimes the meaning of the symbols can change. These changes occur because society itself changes; our priorities change, our understanding of our own selves changes. Even those things that to us once had prime importance in our lives, because of the passage of time, fade in significance from what they once were.

Understanding the function of these symbols has long been a matter of interest for those individuals and groups who wish to find the deeper meaning to the pictures and words that point to the very heart of what it means to be human. As stated previously, symbols can be found in all walks of life and in all areas of human interest and activity. Therefore, it should be no surprise that religion and particularly religious language share a rich and diverse history of symbol and symbolism.

In the early part of the 20th century, American philosopher John Herman Randall undertook the academic journey which was to explore not only how religious language carries both meaning and knowledge, but also how this form of communication both differed and shared similarities to other disciplines, such as the world of science. In considering what the function of religious language was as a vehicle for conveying knowledge, Randall concentrated specifically on the forms of communication within religion that gave believers the greatest insights into their commonly held beliefs, ideas and cultural identities. Randall's work progressed from looking at the historical issue of the conflict between religion and science, which he saw as having been largely resolved (if not still misunderstood by those outside of academia).

He then looked at the relationship between religion and philosophy particularly those ideas which came from the philosophy of the Ancient Greeks. This led him to realise that the great Christian thinkers of the early church such as Augustine, who were influenced by Greek philosophers, saw philosophy as central in recognising the twin pillars of faith and reason. Turning his attention to natural science, particularly the post-Enlightenment period that developed from the work of Newton, Randall realised that the world of natural science as **natural theology** had a common purpose. That purpose was to reveal the workings of the world and universe within which we lived. Far from seeing these developments of rational thoughts as a threat to religion, Randall realised that the religious ideas of the Middle Ages needed to develop alongside, and along with, the discoveries brought about by science. Recognising the contributions of Hume, Kant and Hegel to this development, Randall identified the central role of religious experience as the key to understanding what it means to be religious. As Randall states in *The Role Of Knowledge In Western Religions*:

'If the function of religious beliefs is not to generate knowledge and truth, what is their function? Very early in every great religious tradition, reflective men came to see that the ordinary ideas entertained and used in worship, prayer and ritual could not be "literally" true. The idea of God, for example, employed by the unreflective in the actual practice of the religious arts, could not be adequate to the true nature of the divine.'

Specification content

Religious language as non-cognitive and symbolic: Functions of symbols (John Randall).

John Randall did not believe that religion and science were in direct competition with each other.

Key term

Natural theology: philosophical reasoning based on information that can be rationally gained about the physical world and which leads to revelation about the divine

quickfire

4.15 According to Randall, what was the key role of religious experience?

Symbols provide us with identity.

Key terms

Anti-realist: the philosophical concept that the truth of something is determined by it fitting in with the views/beliefs of the group who espouse it

Theological propositions: beliefs or ideas put forward in the context of religious doctrines or philosophies

Key quote

'All ideas of God, like all other religious beliefs, are without exception religious symbols. This means that they perform what is primarily a religious function. They are employed in religious experience, and serve to carry on the religious life. They are techniques, instruments, in terms of which ritual and the other religious arts are conducted.' (Randall)

Randall recognised that these things have consequences: they resulted in unifying people together from tribes to city-states, from kingdoms to nations. They gave people an identity: individual, corporate, cultural, national. In doing so, they provided a common vision of the values that held people together – in essence this became the core of what would be recognised as a cultural and religious identity. It provided a common way of communicating, providing a shared set of values. This translated quite literally into a common form of language, at its heart the religious language, a language highly symbolic representing those very things that gave the people their identity. This was the role of religious experience.

Randall went on to observe that religion, as far as he was concerned, was not independent of man's secular knowledge. For Randall, religion was a human activity that demanded: 'careful observation and description, explanation, reflective understanding, and intelligent criticism'. Randall believed that all religious beliefs were mythology, i.e. all religious beliefs are religious symbols. If such symbols were held to contain any kind of truth, Randall believed that this was not the truth of factual statements of the empirical sciences or any other realist-based rational discipline. Randall seems to have held a coherence theory of truth in relation to religious belief. That is to say when it came to belief in God and other such **theological propositions**, Randall can be said to accept **anti-realism**. It is against this background that Randall's identification of the functions of symbolic religious language can be understood. In *The Role Of Knowledge In Western Religions* he writes:

All ideas of God, indeed, like all religious beliefs, are religious symbols. This is as true of the subtle and intellectualised conceptions of the philosophers as of the simple, concrete and familiar images the unreflective man borrows from his experience with his fellows. It is not that the philosopher is right while the average man is wrong, that the former's conceptions are true whilst the latter are false. It is not even that the thinkers of ideas are more adequate than the images of the practical man. The two sets of concepts of God we have been distinguishing both perform necessary and fundamental religious functions. But the two functions are so different that they do not compete. The concrete images of religious practice are in no wise discredited by the refined concepts of the philosophical theologian. For without them men could hardly worship or pray at all while the great majority could and do easily dispense with the concepts which reflective man find necessary in the interests of intellectual consistency. Only for intellectuals are intellectual symbols a religious necessity. But different as their functions are, both sets of ideas serve as religious symbols.

Randall further believed that religion gave humans a valuable insight into what it means to exist as a being within the universe. He did not believe that religion provided additional truths about the world or man or God but instead led to an enhanced view of the experience of existence. Randall stated thus: 'religion gives men more, and how much more only the participant can realise. In this it is like art, which likewise furnishes no supplementary truth, but it does open whole worlds to be explored, whole heavens to be enjoyed.'

According to Randall, religious symbols had a clear primary role, in a non-cognitive sense, to provide a function. This function is sometimes described as a revelation of truth. Randall believed that to articulate this is a complex matter. He acknowledges the work he shared with Tillich in developing this understanding of the function of religious symbols as a form of communication within the religious sphere.

Like Tillich, Randall drew a distinction between signs and symbols. The random sign was something that provoked the same human response as another thing, for which it could stand as a kind of surrogate or substitute. A sign, therefore, according to Randall, 'stands for or represents something other than itself: it is always a sign of something else'.

In contrast, a symbol served an entirely different function, in Randall's view. A symbol was not representative in any sense; it didn't stand for anything other than itself. The function of the symbol was quite unique in that a symbol provokes a response from those that see it or use it. In Randall's words: 'it is important to realise that religious symbols are not signs; they belong rather with the non-representative symbols which function in various ways in both intellectual and the practical life'.

Randall also drew the distinction between symbols that we used in the scientific field and symbols used in the arts and religion. The former, Randall believed, could be identified as cognitive symbols, that is they provided factual knowledge about the empirical world. Such symbols could be found in scientific equations, hypotheses and theorems. Randall believed that they served an entirely different function to the symbols found in the world of the arts and religion: these were exclusively non-cognitive-in that they produced an emotional response, they did not provide **empirical knowledge**.

As a form of communication, religious symbols acted as motivators, they led those who are influenced by them to forms of action. These responses tended to be common or shared because of the nature of the symbol and the identity of the community that shared it. These symbols were also able to communicate qualitative or shared experiences, experiences that were often considered to be difficult to put into words. The power of the symbol was to evoke the feelings of those shared experiences and as such gave a particular power to the symbol itself.

Religious symbols also held a unique characteristic according to Randall, in that unlike the symbols found within art, religious symbols have the ability to reveal or disclose something about the world in which they function. This, for Randall, was particularly important because it was at this juncture that the religious symbol and religious knowledge shared common ground. He writes:
'Religious symbols are commonly said to reveal some truth about experience. If we ask what it is that such symbols do reveal or disclose about the world, it is clear that it is not what we should call in the ordinary sense knowledge, in the sense already defined. This revelation can be styled knowledge or truth only in a sense that it is equivocal or metaphorical. It is more like direct acquaintance than descriptive knowledge: it resembles what we call insight or vision. Such symbols do not tell anything that is verifiably so; they rather make us see something about our experience and our experienced world.'

Randall drew a parallel between religious symbols and **Platonic ideas**. He saw within both that rather than telling us anything was so, the function was instead to make us see something, something which would not otherwise have been apparent. In this way they both engage us in disclosing what the nature of reality truly is. Therefore religious symbols, for Randall, served as instruments of revelation, of visions about the power as possibilities in the world. It was only through symbols that human beings could approach the Divine and only through symbols and symbolic language could we truly live a religious life in any meaningful sense.

A sign is not a symbol!

Key terms

Empirical knowledge: knowledge which is acquired (or acquirable) through the five senses. It is knowledge that provides information about the external, physical world

Platonic ideas: ideas associated with the philosophy of the classical Greek philosopher, Plato, such as his theory of 'forms'

quickfire

4.16 What, in philosophy, did Randall compare religious symbols to?

AO1 Activity

Summarise Randall's ideas into ten bullet points. Learn these bullet points and test yourself on them or ask someone else to test that you can accurately repeat them. This will give you confidence when recalling Randall's ideas when writing your essays and lead to a level of accuracy that is characteristic of a Band 5 AO1 response.

Key quote

… it is not the unconditional demand made by that which is one's ultimate concern, it is also a promise of the ultimate fulfilment which is accepted in the act of faith. The content of this promise is not necessarily defined. It can be expressed in indefinite symbols or in concrete symbols which cannot be taken literally … Faith is the state of being ultimately concerned. The content matters infinitely for the life of the believer, but it does not matter for the formal definition of faith and this is the first step we have to make in order to understand the dynamics of faith. (Tillich)

Symbols have six different characteristics according to Tillich.

Religious Language as non-cognitive and symbolic: God as that which concerns us ultimately (Paul Tillich)

Working as a contemporary to Randall but publishing one year earlier, Paul Tillich in his *Dynamics of Faith*, also contributed to the understanding of symbolic language. In this work, the text describes the contributions of symbols to an understanding of faith. To properly appreciate Tillich's work on symbols we must first give a brief sketch of his work on faith. Tillich saw faith as the state of being ultimately concerned.

Beyond the basic needs such as those recognised in Maslow's hierarchy of needs, i.e. food, shelter, warmth, water, etc., Tillich also saw the need for spiritual concerns – cognitive, aesthetic, social and political. These concerns led to humanity's ultimate concern.

In Tillich's words:

'Man's ultimate concern must be expressed symbolically, because symbolic language alone is able to express the ultimate. This statement demands explanation in several respects. In spite of the manifold research about the meaning and function of symbols which is going on in contemporary philosophy, every writer who uses the term symbol must explain his understanding of it. Symbols have one characteristic in common with signs; they point beyond themselves to something else. The red sign at the street-corner points to the order to stop the movements of cars at certain intervals. Red lights and the stopping of cars have essentially no relation to each other, but conventionally they are united as long as the convention lasts. The same is true of letters and numbers and possibly even words. They point beyond themselves to sounds and meanings …. Sometimes such signs are called symbols; but this is unfortunate because it makes the distinction between signs and symbols more difficult because it is the fact that signs do not participate in the reality of that to which they point, while symbols do. Therefore, signs can be replaced for reasons of expediency or convention, while symbols cannot.'

Tillich identifies six characteristics of symbols. In brief, these are as follows:

1. Symbols point beyond themselves to something else.
2. Symbols participate in the reality of that to which they point.
3. Symbols open up levels of reality that are otherwise closed to us.
4. Symbols unlock dimensions and elements of our soul that correspond to the dimensions and elements of reality.
5. Symbols cannot be produced intentionally. They grow out of the individual or collective unconscious and cannot function without being accepted by the unconscious dimension of our being.
6. Symbols, like living beings, grow and die. They grow when the situation is ripe for them, and they die when the situation changes.

'We have discussed the meaning of symbols generally because, as we said, man's ultimate concern must be expressed symbolically! One may ask: why can it not be expressed directly and properly? If money, success or the nation is someone's ultimate concern, can this not be said in direct way without symbolic language? Is it not only in those cases in which the content of the ultimate concern is called 'God' that we are in the realm of symbols? The answer is that everything which is a matter of unconditional concern is made into a god. If the nation is someone's ultimate concern, the name of the nation becomes a sacred name and the nation receives divine qualities which far surpass the reality of the being and functioning of the nation. The nation then stands for and symbolises the true ultimate, but in an idolatrous way. Success as ultimate concern is not a natural desire of actualising potentialities, but is readiness to sacrifice all other values of life for the sake of a position of power and social predominance. The anxiety about not being a success is an idolatrous form of the anxiety about divine condemnation. Success is Grace; lack of success, ultimate judgement. In this way concepts designating ordinary realities become idolatrous symbols of ultimate concern. The reason for this transformation of concepts into symbols is the character of ultimacy and the nature of faith. That which is the true ultimate transcends the realm of finite reality infinitely. Therefore, no finite reality can express its directly and properly. Religiously speaking, god transcends his own name. This is why the use of his name easily becomes an abuse or a blasphemy. Whatever we say about that which concerns us ultimately, whether or not we call it God, has a symbolic meaning. It points beyond itself while participating in that to which it points. In no other way can faith express itself adequately. The language of faith is the language of symbols.' (Tillich)

For Tillich, Faith in God should be humanity's Ultimate Concern.

For Tillich, therefore, the language of symbols was the language of power. He viewed God as the fundamental symbol of ultimate concern. In this sense the language of symbols was entirely non-cognitive in that it evoked a response at the deepest emotional level of the believer to the symbol, reality and ultimate concern that was God. Tillich also saw the symbols of faith as being closely linked to the idea of myth. Myths, like symbols, participated in human activity. According to Tillich they gave rise to human cultural and religious traditions and like symbols 'were present in every act of faith because the language of faith is the symbol'.

Challenges including whether a symbol is adequate or gives the right insights

The work of Randall and Tillich does much to help us appreciate how symbols and symbolic language can be used to convey deep and powerful meanings for individuals, groups and societies. The symbol is a key component of the religious life, the religious experience and therefore the religious language. The deep-seated emotional responses that some symbols can evoke demonstrate the fact that symbolic language is absolutely meaningful for those that engage with it. However, even with all that said, there have been criticisms.

Firstly, and through his own admission, Randall recognises that the language of the symbol is inherently non-cognitive. As such, symbolic language does not provide information about the empirically knowable, objective world in an objective and empirical way – for to do so would make it cognitive language – which it is not. This immediately puts it at odds with the conclusions of the Vienna Circle and subsequent logical positivists, in that symbolic language – not being verifiable, falsifiable, analytic, synthetic or mathematical, is rendered as essentially meaningless – in a cognitive and empirical sense.

Specification content

Challenges including whether a symbol is adequate or gives the right insights.

How do we know whether symbols provide the right insight?

Study tip

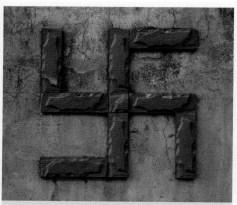

The ichthus and swastika have changed their symbolic meanings over time.

Paul Edwards, the American professor of philosophy, criticised Tillich's work on symbols as 'philosophical confusion'. Edwards noted that Tillich himself recognises, in his *Systematic Theology*, the inability to express in literal terms anything meaningful about God: 'The concession by the author that he is using a certain word metaphorically is tantamount to admitting that, in a very important sense and a sense relevant to the questions at issue between metaphysicians and their critics, he does not mean what he says. It does not automatically tell us what he does mean or whether in fact he means anything at all.' (Tillich)

Edwards recognises that this undermines Tillich's attempt to say anything meaningful by virtue of symbolic language and hearkens back to the logical positivists to support this criticism of Tillich:

'Granting this, it seems to me the logical positivists nevertheless deserve great credit helping to call attention to certain features of many sentences (and systems) commonly called metaphysical. The metaphysicians are sometimes obscurely but never, to my knowledge, clearly aware of these features. On the contrary, they manage by various stratagems to hide these features both from themselves and others.' (Edwards)

Another point at which it can be shown that a symbol may not be adequate, is that symbols change over time. Tillich recognises this himself, yet it did not deter him from believing that symbolic language can still provide meaningful insights into deep and powerful truths. However, if one takes a symbol and changes its meaning, then one is not just altering the symbol but is also altering something even more fundamental – that is, the association of that symbol from and for the culture(s) that it is associated with.

There are a number of examples of such symbols changing over time, for instance the ichthus – a symbol used by early Christians to signify safe place for meeting and to hide their basic creed, arising from the acronym of the word, i.e. Jesus (**I**) Christ (**Ch**), God's (**Th**) Son (**U**), Saviour (**S**), which was originally used in pre-Christian times as a fertility symbol, with the shape being associated with the womb of the Great Mother goddess. Another example, with a more recent historical connotation is the swastika – originally a symbol from the religions originating in the East which is often associated with the universal principle of harmony and peace being perverted into a symbol of hatred for many in the West because of its association with the Nazis in the 20th century.

The changes of meaning are significant. Therefore, what insight can a symbol truly provide, if its meaning can change over time? Equally, how adequate is it at providing that necessary spiritual insight, if the context of the symbol means that the meaning is entirely different? In both of these cases, if symbolic language is being promoted as a form of language that is meaningful, then this undermines that idea. If the meaning changes, how can the symbol be considered to be anything other than ultimately meaningless?

A consideration of how these two views (Randall/Tillich) can be used to help understand religious teachings

Religious teachings can vary from clear instructions on how to conduct oneself to ponderings about the mysteries of the soul. In terms of the former, the views of Randall and Tillich have little to say. However, in relation to the latter, their views can help to illuminate these teachings. A note of caution, however, neither Randall nor Tillich laid claim to having a theological 'Rosetta Stone', in other words, a firm declaration; instead their work was to show how symbols can help us gain insight into the world of religion.

For example, J H Randall's views were that religious beliefs (and the teachings that arose from them) were not to be understood in a literal sense:

'Very early in every great religious tradition, reflective man came to see that the ordinary ideas entertained and used in worship, prayer and ritual could not be literally true. The idea of God, for example, employed by the unreflective in the actual practice of the religious arts, could not be adequate to the true nature of the Divine. God could not be 'really' the animal, or natural force, or carved image, the imaginative picture, in which the average man conceives the Divine. He could not be even the highest human image, the 'Father', or the kind of person who in the present fashion seems appropriately approached in terms of the "I-Thou" experience … They cannot be taken as literal accounts of the divine. They are imaginative and figurative ways of conceiving the relations of men and their ideals to the nature of things and to its religious dimension.'

Randall goes on to explain how these ideas should be understood symbolically instead – for in that non-cognitive structure they make more intellectual sense to the 'reflective man'. As Randall progresses his work, the idea that symbols are able to convey knowledge about the world becomes a central theme. Not knowledge in the cognitive sense, but an almost intuitive knowledge, where insight is gained (even though Randall is not precisely clear about what he means by this) and truths about the world are revealed. Thus, it could be argued, by understanding symbols, we are led to a greater understanding of religious beliefs and their associated teachings.

For Tillich, the key aim of his work was to show how symbols could point beyond themselves and lead the believer to their ultimate concern. By participating in the reality of that to which it pointed, the symbol illuminates the meaning of the object or idea that it represents and provides an insight that would not have been possible through any other means. One such example of this is the reference to God, as expressed by Tillich:

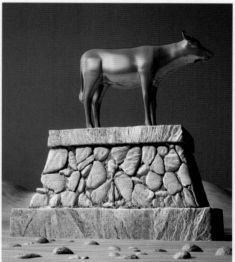

'God is the basic symbol of faith, that's not the only one. All the qualities we attribute to him, power, love, justice, are taken from finite experiences and applied symbolically to that which is beyond finitude and infinity. If faith calls God "almighty", it uses the human experience of power in order to symbolise the content of its infinite concern, but it does not describe the highest being who can do as he pleases. So it is with all the other qualities as with all the actions, past, present and future, which men attribute to God. They are symbols taken from our daily experience, and not information about what God did once upon a time or sometime in the future. Faith is not the belief in such stories, but it is the acceptance of symbols that express our ultimate concern in terms of divine actions.'

Understanding therefore how symbols work in the mundane world, Tillich provides guidance to how religious teachings can be understood – that is, as ideas expressed symbolically, to be interpreted by those that participate in them and therefore accept them for what they are. In this, the believer is led to their ultimate concern.

However, neither Randall's nor Tillich's views are universally accepted. Some find the idea that their religious beliefs and teachings are to be understood purely symbolically, or in a solely non-cognitive way, as potentially offensive as it suggests that they have no basis in objective reality. They argue that religious teachings depict reality as it really is. The view that this is not the actual intention of religious language may cause them concern.

Randall stated that early religious worshippers realised that the objects they worshipped were to be understood symbolically not literally.

127

Key skills Theme 4 DEF

The final sections of Theme 4 have tasks that consolidate your AO1 skills and focus these skills for examination preparation.

Religious symbols can have many functions.

Key skills

Knowledge involves:

Selection of a range of (thorough) accurate and relevant information that is directly related to the specific demands of the question.

This means:

- Selecting relevant material for the question set

- Being focused in explaining and examining the material selected.

Understanding involves:

Explanation that is extensive, demonstrating depth and/or breadth with excellent use of evidence and examples including (where appropriate) thorough and accurate supporting use of sacred texts, sources of wisdom and specialist language.

This means:

- Effective use of examples and supporting evidence to establish the quality of your understanding

- Ownership of your explanation that expresses personal knowledge and understanding and NOT just reproducing a chunk of text from a book that you have rehearsed and memorised.

AO1 Developing skills

It is now important to consider the information that has been covered in this section; however, the information in its raw form is too extensive and so has to be processed in order to meet the requirements of the examination. This can be achieved by practising more advanced skills associated with AO1. The exercises that run throughout this book will help you to do this and prepare you for the examination. For assessment objective 1 (AO1), which involves demonstrating 'knowledge' and 'understanding' skills, we are going to focus on different ways in which the skills can be demonstrated effectively, and also refer to how the performance of these skills is measured (see generic band descriptors for A2 [WJEC] AO1 or A Level [Eduqas] AO1).

▶ **Your new task is this:** you will have to write a response under timed conditions to a question requiring an examination or explanation of **Randall's view of the function of symbols**. This exercise is best done as a small group at first.

1. Begin with a list of indicative content, as you may have done in the previous textbook in the series. It does not need to be in any particular order at first, although as you practise this you will see more order in your lists that reflects your understanding.

2. Develop the list by using one or two relevant quotations. Now add some references to scholars and/or religious writings.

3. Then write out your plan, under timed conditions, remembering the principles of explaining with evidence and/or examples.

When you have completed the task, refer to the band descriptors for A2 (WJEC) or A Level (Eduqas) and in particular have a look at the demands described in the higher band descriptors towards which you should be aspiring. Ask yourself:

- Does my work demonstrate thorough, accurate and relevant knowledge and understanding of religion and belief?

- Is my work coherent (consistent or make logical sense), clear and well organised?

- Will my work, when developed, be an extensive and relevant response which is specific to the focus of the task?

- Does my work have extensive depth and/or suitable breadth and have excellent use of evidence and examples?

- If appropriate to the task, does my response have thorough and accurate reference to sacred texts and sources of wisdom?

- Are there any insightful connections to be made with other elements of my course?

- Will my answer, when developed and extended to match what is expected in an examination answer, have an extensive range of views of scholars/schools of thought?

- When used, is specialist language and vocabulary both thorough and accurate?

Issues for analysis and evaluation

Whether symbolic language can be agreed as having adequate meaning as a form of language

St Paul, in the Christian tradition, said 'If I speak in the tongues of mortals and of angels, but do not have love, I am a noisy gong or a clanging cymbal'. In many ways, his sentiments in his famous 'Hymn to Love' echo what is so important about the use of symbolic terms when employing religious language. In the latter sense, the term 'love' is changed to 'understanding', for if someone makes use of symbols that make no sense to those that hear them then what they are saying is, quite literally, nonsense. The understanding provides the key to unlocking the symbol and prevents the language being no more than 'a noisy gong or clanging cymbal'.

Understanding language in a non-cognitive sense allows us to move beyond a literalistic and empirical interpretation, into one that is more associated with emotions, feelings or the expression of something that relates to some indefinable mental state or image (in many ways similar to Otto's concept of the 'numinous'). Symbols brilliantly evoke these things. In Randall's own work he lists the four functions of symbols as arousing the emotions and bringing about action in direct response to the symbol; they provide a common focal point for a community to centre around; they are able to communicate experiences in a way that normal linguistic functions are unable to and they provide the evocative experience of the world that is often described as 'awe'. Each of these functions provides a more than adequate meaningfulness to how we use and understand language.

Tillich, who worked with Randall on the function of symbols, stated that there were six key aspects, including the ideas that symbols point beyond themselves to something else as well as participating in the reality of that to which they point. From this they were also capable of opening up levels of reality which are otherwise closed to us and unlocking dimensions of our soul which correspond to the dimensions of reality. Symbols then, possess a very real, very meaningful quality that operates on a far deeper level than empirical, scientific language would and, for these reasons the work of both Randall and Tillich very much supports the idea that symbols are capable of providing adequate meanings as a form of language.

It would seem, then, that symbolic language is unassailable in terms of the levels of meaning that it can bring to those that engage with it. The individual and social interactions that occur through engagement with symbolic language is clearly undeniable. The work of sociologists such as Emile Durkheim, and psychologists such as Carl Jung, recognise the significant value that symbols have within human culture as means of providing identity and meaning in an existential sense.

However, not all would agree with the ability of symbols to provide meaning. Indeed one of the key features of symbols that Tillich recognised was that symbols 'grow and die'. In this he meant that there were historically chronological points for the relevance of symbols and, once those times had passed, the symbols' relevance passed too. This would suggest, for all their significance previously stated, that symbols do not provide a constant or consistent meaning that can be interpreted 'at all times and in all places'. Symbols are inextricably linked with cultural norms. As these change, so do the meanings of the symbols. Therefore, is it actually really possible to truly understand symbolic language as it was written three and a half thousand years ago? For instance, can we truly understand the symbolic language that can be referenced in the Jewish Tenakh? Can we truly appreciate what is meant by these terms as it was intended by the original authors? Or, are we doomed to a partial understanding, limited as we are by our own cultural norms and symbolic language as it is relevant to us? Evidence from historians and cultural anthropologists

This section covers AO2 content and skills

Specification content

Whether symbolic language can be agreed as having adequate meaning as a form of language.

St Paul's famous 'Hymn to Love' in 1 Corinthians 13 in the Christian Bible makes use of symbolic language.

AO2 Activity

As you read through this section try to do the following:

1. Pick out the different lines of argument that are presented in the text and identify any evidence given in support.

2. For each line of argument try to evaluate whether or not you think this is strong or weak.

3. Think of any questions you may wish to raise in response to the arguments.

This Activity will help you to start thinking critically about what you read and help you to evaluate the effectiveness of different arguments and from this your answers to the AO2 questions that arise.

advise caution when we try to read meaning into civilisations that have long passed. In this sense, the adequacy of symbolic language to provide meaning can be questioned.

Does the 21st century no longer have need for symbolic language?

Furthermore, in the 21st century, where our unquenchable quest for meaning via the employment of scientific methods is de rigeur, the use of symbolic language seems oddly archaic. It does not seem to fit comfortably with that which can be tested; that which be objectively treated as providing a truth or a falsehood. The very fact that symbols are sensitive to cultural referencing means that different cultures can, quite literally, treat symbols in entirely different ways. Perhaps an obvious example is that of the swastika. Long used in the religions and societies associated with religions of Asia, the swastika represented peace and the universality of the organising principle. Its inclusion in the art of Buddhism, Hinduism and Sikhism is well documented. Its use in Puja as a form to provide inspiration as well as devotion is equally well known. However, in the 20th century, the swastika took on an altogether different meaning. It became linked with a political movement that is historically regarded and associated with fear, hatred, prejudice and some of the worst documented atrocities thus far visited by human beings upon each other. Since then it still has associations with cultural examples of discrimination and ignorant hatred. If such a symbol can have such diverse meanings, how is it that symbols can provide any constant, reliable and, above all, adequate guide to meaning – particularly when used in symbolic language?

In religious terms, if we suggest that the word 'God' should be treated as a symbolic word, does this therefore mean that it should be treated purely as a non-cognitive form of language? In doing so, very significant theological and philosophical questions can then be raised about what is meant by the word 'God'. Does it represent an objective reality that can be spoken about empirically? Or is it merely a representative idea associated with a particular cultural reference that has no specific external reality as such? Is Randall's concept of God nothing more than a human idea? Such a proposal would likely be met with abhorrence by the millions who live their lives in complete contrast to such a suggestion.

Rational thinking should dismiss symbols and symbolic language as being flights of fancy that entertain at best but distract people from the true meaning of life at worst. They promote navel-gazing activities that detract from useful contributions to society and we should therefore dismiss symbolic language as both meaningless and, ultimately, useless.

To draw these arguments together, it seems that the question is not straightforward. Quite simply put, if non-cognitive language is considered as a valid vehicle for language to transmit meaning, then symbolic language does indeed fulfil that role. However, if this idea is rejected, then symbolic language is ultimately meaningless and cannot provide any adequate meaning as a form of language.

AO2 Activity

List some conclusions that could be drawn from the AO2 reasoning from the above text; try to aim for at least three different possible conclusions. Consider each of the conclusions and collect brief evidence to support each conclusion from the AO1 and AO2 material for this topic. Select the conclusion that you think is most convincing and explain why it is so. Try to contrast this with the weakest conclusion in the list, justifying your argument with clear reasoning and evidence.

Study tip

It is vital for AO2 that you actually discuss arguments and not just explain what someone may have stated. Try to ask yourself, 'was this a fair point to make?', 'is the evidence sound enough?', 'is there anything to challenge this argument?', 'is this a strong or weak argument?' Such critical analysis will help you develop your evaluation skills

How far the works of Randall and Tillich provide a suitable counter-challenge to logical positivism

Specification content

How far the works of Randall and Tillich provide a suitable counter-challenge to logical positivism.

The influence of logical positivism at the beginning of the 20th century was significant, as far as philosophy was concerned. Its propositions and philosophies rippled through academia in the West, causing reaction and revolution where such ideas had not been previously countenanced. For the first time, in a systematic way, the empiricism of the scientific world was being rigorously applied to the world of ideas and the challenges to that world were, to say the least, significant. Luminaries such as Schlick and Carnap and associates with the Vienna Circle such as Ayer, Popper and Wittgenstein, were contributing radical ideas that included the fierce rejection of metaphysics due to, in the definition of the empirical thought being proposed, it having nothing meaningful to say about the external world. (Although Popper and Wittgenstein later disagreed with this assertion regarding the outright rejection of metaphysics.)

At its heart, logical positivism was proposing an adoption of a rigid criterion for meaning that was based on the ability to verify a statement. This proposition fit comfortably with the empirical world of the physical sciences and was therefore regarded as a litmus test for meaning. Analytic and synthetic statements, along with mathematical and tautological statements were all regarded as meaningful yet anything that fell outside of these were regarded as ultimately meaningless.

Being exposed to the ideas of logical positivism, both Randall and Tillich took an oppositional view in terms of what constituted meaning. For a start, the logical positivist view of language was that it should be treated in an entirely cognitive sense. In this sense cognitive language is any form of language that makes an assertion, which is usually factual in nature, in the sense that it can be shown to be true or false by objective means. These means might be through verification or falsification. This fits in well with the logical positivist approach. However, it was not how Randall and Tillich viewed language. For them, language was to be viewed non-cognitively. It is not something that can be held up to objective scrutiny. This is because non-cognitive language is language that expresses opinions, attitudes, feelings and/or emotions. It is language which relates to a person's view of what reality may mean to them – and this may differ from the view of another, even though they may be experiencing the same reality. Both views are held to be valid – but in a non-cognitive sense.

Is the Empirical approach of Logical positivism the only valid way of understanding the meaningfulness of language?

Does symbolic language speak directly to the soul?

Randall was interested in the way that religious language, in particular, worked. He believed that religious language carried both meaning and knowledge. He also recognised that this form of communication both differed from and shared similarities with other forms of language – including that of world of the physical sciences. In considering what the function of religious language was as a vehicle for conveying knowledge Randall concentrated specifically on the forms of communication within religion that gave believers the greatest insights into their commonly held beliefs, ideas and cultural identities.

Randall realised that the worlds of natural science and natural theology had a common purpose. That purpose was to reveal the workings of the world and universe within which we lived. Looking at religious beliefs, expressed through religious language as key to this understanding, Randall stated in his *The Role Of Knowledge in Western Religions*: 'If the function of religious beliefs is not to generate knowledge and truth, what is their function?'

Randall recognised that they resulted in unifying people together; they gave people an identity. It provided a common way of communicating, providing a shared set of values. This translated, quite literally, into a common form of language, at its heart the religious language, a language highly symbolic representing those very things that gave the people their identity. This was the role of religious experience. As such, Randall's view of religious language was that it was entirely meaningful – in a powerful, yet non-cognitive way, and his views appear to offer a significant counterpoint to the ideas of the logical positivists.

Similarly, Tillich saw the meaningfulness of religious language through the way it was used. Regarding religious language as having a unique ability to communicate symbolically, he recognised that the meaning came through the function that religious language provided. He believed that symbols not only pointed beyond themselves but were participatory in the reality to which they pointed. For instance, a Christian regarding the symbol of the crucifix, is immediately drawn into the symbolism associated with incarnation, atonement, and sacrifice, as expressed through the Christian tradition. In this the symbols allowed those that encountered them the opportunity to have levels of reality opened to them that may not have been accessible otherwise. Spiritually this is invaluable. Symbolic language, for Tillich, was the language of the soul – and as such was meaningful at the deepest level possible for a human being, albeit not necessarily in the way that the logical positivists may have defined meaningfulness.

In fact, the approaches to language by both Randall and Tillich were, as has already been stated, significantly different from the approach of the logical positivists. As such, it could be argued that their views offer an effective counter-argument to logical positivism even though they are not necessarily approaching the subject from the same philosophical starting point.

Study tip

It is important for AO2 that you include the views of scholars and/or schools of thought when formulating your response to a particular contention. Any discussion of function of religious language would benefit from the views of the classical, medieval as well as from more current philosophers. However, make sure that the views you use are relevant to the point that you are making. Your ability to use such views in an appropriate way would distinguish a high level answer from one that is simply a general response.

AO2 Activity

List some conclusions that could be drawn from the AO2 reasoning from the above text; try to aim for at least three different possible conclusions. Consider each of the conclusions and collect brief evidence to support each conclusion from the AO1 and AO2 material for this topic. Select the conclusion that you think is most convincing and explain why it is so. Try to contrast this with the weakest conclusion in the list, justifying your argument with clear reasoning and evidence.

AO2 Developing skills

It is now important to consider the information that has been covered in this section; however, the information in its raw form is too extensive and so has to be processed in order to meet the requirements of the examination. This can be achieved by practising more advanced skills associated with AO2. The exercises that run throughout this book will help you to do this and prepare you for the examination. For assessment objective 2 (AO2), which involves 'critical analysis' and 'evaluation' skills, we are going to focus on different ways in which the skills can be demonstrated effectively, and also refer to how the performance of these skills is measured (see generic band descriptors for A2 [WJEC] AO2 or A Level [Eduqas] AO2).

▶ **Your new task is this:** you will have to write a response under timed conditions to a question requiring an evaluation of **the effectiveness of the solutions to the problem of symbolic language**. This exercise is best done as a small group at first.

1. Begin with a list of indicative arguments or lines of reasoning, as you may have done in the previous textbook in the series. It does not need to be in any particular order at first, although as you practise this you will see more order in your lists, in particular by way of links and connections between arguments.

2. Develop the list by using one or two relevant quotations. Now add some references to scholars and/or religious writings.

3. Then write out your plan, under timed conditions, remembering the principles of evaluating with support from extensive, detailed reasoning and/or evidence.

When you have completed the task, refer to the band descriptors for A2 (WJEC) or A Level (Eduqas) and in particular have a look at the demands described in the higher band descriptors towards which you should be aspiring. Ask yourself:

- Is my answer a confident critical analysis and perceptive evaluation of the issue?
- Is my answer a response that successfully identifies and thoroughly addresses the issues raised by the question set?
- Does my work show an excellent standard of coherence, clarity and organisation?
- Will my work, when developed, contain thorough, sustained and clear views that are supported by extensive, detailed reasoning and/or evidence?
- Are the views of scholars/schools of thought used extensively, appropriately and in context?
- Does my answer convey a confident and perceptive analysis of the nature of any possible connections with other elements of my course?
- When used, is specialist language and vocabulary both thorough and accurate?

Key skills Theme 4 DEF

The fourth theme has tasks that consolidate your AO2 skills and focus these skills for examination preparation.

Key skills

Analysis involves:

Identifying issues raised by the materials in the AO1, together with those identified in the AO2 section, and presents sustained and clear views, either of scholars or from a personal perspective ready for evaluation.

This means:

- That your answers are able to identify key areas of debate in relation to a particular issue
- That you can identify, and comment upon, the different lines of argument presented by others
- That your response comments on the overall effectiveness of each of these areas or arguments.

Evaluation involves:

Considering the various implications of the issues raised based upon the evidence gleaned from analysis and provides an extensive detailed argument with a clear conclusion.

This means:

- That your answer weighs up the consequences of accepting or rejecting the various and different lines of argument analysed
- That your answer arrives at a conclusion through a clear process of reasoning.

Specification content

Complex form of mythical language that communicates values and insights into purpose of existence. Myths help to overcome fears of the unknown; myths effective way of transmitting religious, social and ethical values.

Key terms

Deconstruct: to analyse a text by taking it apart in order to work out what it means

Ex nihilo: literally 'out of nothing' – a Latin term often associated with creation myths

Sitz im Leben: a German phrase meaning 'Situation in Life' and used as a theological term to refer to the context whereby an account is written, usually influencing the writer because of the particular circumstances of said context

Key quotes

A myth is a story of origin. A myth is a story about how the gods created the world or a part of the world in the beginning, *in illo tempore* or the time before time began, which explains why things are the way they are today. (Peters)

A myth is a story, imagined or true, that helps us make sense of reality .... Without a myth there is no meaning or purpose to life. Myths do more than explain. They guide mental processes, conditioning how we think, even how we perceive. (Matt)

E: Religious language as non-cognitive and mythical

Complex form of mythical language that communicates values and insights into purpose of existence

In the world today, the term 'myth' is often synonymous with 'falsehood'. For many, a myth is another type of story that has fantastical elements to it, but bears no resemblance to the truths found within the empirical world. Myths, according to the view of many in contemporary society, are regarded as 'fairy-stories' – something to entertain children but which have little or no value beyond this particular sphere of life. However, to reduce a myth to these elements is to fundamentally misunderstand the purpose of this form of language.

This is particularly true within the field of religious studies, where myth is actually a highly specialised term that refers to accounts that contain truths which are communicated in the form of picture imagery and symbolic text. To deconstruct a myth purely by empirically based methods is to miss the meaning of these accounts. Such reductionist approaches, as were particularly popular in the 19th and early 20th century, led to the popular view today of myths being little more than fantasies, which provided simplistic views of the complexities surrounding the natural world, and, in particular, events such as the beginning of the universe or the formation of life on earth.

To dismiss myths as simplistic, as previously stated, is factually inaccurate. Myths do require interpretation but to do so requires care. Understanding the original context of the myth is important. German biblical scholars of the 20th century, when looking at the New Testament within the Christian tradition, spoke of the need to understand the '*Sitz im Leben*' (situation in life) of the New Testament writers, so that the meaning of those documents could be properly understood. They also cautioned against applying our own *Sitz im Leben* when interpreting them – because to do so was to add perspectives that would not have been relevant to the time of the writers, and this would lead to a misunderstanding of the original meanings of such documents. This is why a cautionary approach to interpreting myths would bring a more accurate understanding of the original context and purposes of the myth itself.

Myths exist in all human cultures. The very fact that this is so demonstrates the value that they have for all societies. Those myths provide insights into a range of elements that each society holds as significant though not all of these societies and cultures have myths for all of the same elements. There are commonly recurring ones such as the creation of the universe; the roles and persons of the gods; heroic myths; how and why the world operates in the way that it does (including ethical codes); the struggle between good and evil, etc.

Understanding mythical language is essential in helping us to understand those myths. However, studying myths and the language they are written in is a matter of interpretation. Therefore, armed with the best knowledge that we have, it should be remembered that these interpretations are not necessarily always definitive. The myth is a powerful form of literature, it is also, as has already been mentioned, extremely complex. As such, different times and different people may interpret the myth is different ways. As we look at different myths, later in this section, these differences of interpretation will be explored further, as appropriate.

Another issue with the myth is that many myths are remarkably similar to one another – if not in content many are so in structure. An example of this are the ex nihilo creation myths that begin with voids, water and a divine figure or figures.

The ability to appreciate that these represent images and beliefs deeply rooted in the culture from which they arise, allows for the myth to be interpreted accordingly – so whilst the content may have similarities – the interpretations may differ somewhat.

So, myths are a complex form of literature. Mythical language is also complex, being formed of metaphorical, symbolic and analogical terms – having meanings 'hidden' beyond the literal reading of the text. Over the last century, with the work done on mythical language in religious studies, psychology and anthropology, scholars have determined that far from the simplistic and childish fantasies that many in contemporary society erroneously label myths, they serve a far more significant purpose. They talk about events surrounding the natural world and how it came to be, but not purely as simple narratives. Essentially they hold within them deep and lasting truths that are integral to the identity of the culture and society to which they belong. At their very heart, myths explore what it means to be human, what our relationship should be with the world which we inhabit, how we should relate to each other and what our responsibilities are to the powers which, they claim, we owe for our very existence.

Finally it should be understood that the role of myth within religion is integral. Many of the aspects of religion depend on myth to provide a means of expressing those fundamental religious truths that cannot be expressed in any other form of language – for to do so would be to simplify them or devalue them. Myths and mythical language, as has been stated, are highly complex and contain metaphorical, symbolic and analogical aspects within them. Thus attempting to find literal meanings to myths inevitably leads to error – both on behalf of those who may adopt a fundamentalist and literalist approach to their reading of religious texts and of those who may criticise religion as being meaningless in the contemporary scientific world. Meaningful discussion regarding myth needs to take into account the highly specific way in which myths employ language and then to begin to explore and understand the richness of the text as it unveils mythical truths about human existence, the universe we inhabit and, where appropriate, the Divine.

Key quote

The chief difference between the man of the archaic and traditional societies and the man of the modern societies with their strong imprint of Judaeo-Christianity lies in the fact that the former feels himself indissolubly connected with the Cosmos and the cosmic rhythms, whereas the latter insists that he is connected only with History. Of course, for the man of the archaic societies, the Cosmos too has a 'history', if only because it is the creation of the gods and is held to have been organised by supernatural beings or mythical heroes. But this 'history ' of the Cosmos and of human society is a 'sacred history,' preserved and transmitted through myths. More than that, it is a 'history' than can be repeated indefinitely, in the sense that the myths serve as models for ceremonies that periodically reactualise the tremendous events that occurred at the beginning of time. The myths preserve and transmit the paradigms/ the exemplary models, for all the responsible activities in which men engage. By virtue of these paradigmatic models revealed to men in mythical times, the Cosmos and society are periodically regenerated. **(Eliade)**

The word myth is often misunderstood in modern society.

quickfire

4.17 What is the purpose of myth?

Myths can often signpost truths about the human condition.

quickfire

4.18 Why can the word 'myth' be problematic to define?

Specification content

Supportive evidence – different forms
of myths to convey meaning: creation
myths.

Key quote

Myths alone can tell stories about
primordial time because history
relies on knowledge gleaned
from records, preferably records
contemporary with the events
described. No records of the
beginning of time exist, except in
mythology. (Hoffmann)

The mythical language found in the
Genesis creation myth shows how order
was brought out of chaos.

Creation myths

Creation myths have existed for as long as humans have told and recorded their
stories. The account of creation as described in the Judeo-Christian traditions,
is considered by many an account rich in mythical language and one which,
in common with other creation myths from the ancient Near East, proposes a
creation which came about ex nihilo, that is, 'out of nothing'.

The account as recorded in the first chapter of Genesis runs thus:

> 'In the beginning when God created the heavens and the earth, the earth was
> a formless void and darkness covered the face of the deep, while a wind from
> God swept over the face of the waters. Then God said, "Let there be light";
> and there was light. And God saw that the light was good; and God separated
> the light from the darkness. God called the light Day, and the darkness he
> called Night. And there was evening and there was morning, the first day.'
> (Genesis 1:1–5, NRSV)

The mythical language used here is particularly notable. The beginning of the
account describes a vastness of emptiness (void) yet populated by primordial
waters – these would traditionally be signifying chaos. Water, for the ancients,
particularly the waters of the oceans, would have presented a great mystery. The
ability to traverse these oceans was initially not available to ancient societies, who
originally formulated these myths. The seas and oceans were also uncontrollable
and seemingly unpredictable. They were beyond the immediate control of the
ancients and therefore became a natural symbol for chaos. This is what we have
here at the beginning of the Judeo-Christian creation myth; the chaos of primordial
water being brought under the control of the God-figure, signifying that in most
ancient of mythical themes order is brought out of chaos. The God of the myth
is a God who possesses the ability to conquer chaos – to impose his will upon it.
This God then goes on to not only calm the waters but to divide them – bringing
forth land (which would have signified, amongst other things, stability and order).
He further demonstrates his power over the chaotic waters by filling them with
differentiated life, and widens this even further by populating the remaining
spheres – e.g. the skies and the land – with life also – all demonstrating his power
and control over the creation that he wrought. Furthermore, the great theme
of order versus chaos is symbolised again in the light versus darkness. In the
beginning, light (which is universally a symbol for knowledge, understanding and
righteous power) has no place in the chaos. It does not exist. As the creation myth
progresses, light floods creation, initially in the great separation of night and day
and then later by the heavenly bodies of the sun, moon and stars whose function
it is to bring light to the world during these two times. Even the night, the time
of darkness, has not returned to the primordial chaos because this time there are
lights within it. The creator God has exerted influence for all creation, shining a
light in the darkness and causing an order where created life-forms can flourish.

In his 1964 work, *Myths of Creation*, Philip Freund notes the similarity between this
and other myths that start in the waters and, through the actions of an agent of
order, creation is brought about. Myths that belong to Egypt – where the Morning
Sun God, Khepri, lifts himself from the waters in order to bring about creation; in
the Zuni tribe of the America, there is a creation myth that tells how the Sun-Father
brings about creation from the waters through his divine actions, before eventually
creating humankind. The 19th-century Finnish epic poem, based on the myths
of the country, speaks of primordial waters where the virgin daughter of the air
descends in order to become the water-mother. Through her interaction with the
these chaotic waters she ends up giving birth to the first man, Väinämöinen, after
an immaculate conception. The Maoris of New Zealand's creation myth recounts

how the demigod Maui pulled up the islands of New Zealand from the depths of the ocean, beginning the history of life on those islands. Similar stories are told in British Columbia, Japan, South America and Ireland, to name but a few. What is fascinating about all of this is the commonality of order being brought out of chaos – with water being the symbol of chaos and land/life being the symbol of order.

Tillich notes that it is inescapable that the language of myth is found within religion. He states, 'Myths are always present in every act of faith, because the language of faith is the symbol … It puts the stories of the gods into the framework of time and space although it belongs to the nature of the ultimate to be beyond time and space.'

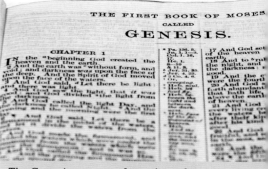

The Genesis account of creation echoes other creation accounts from across different cultures.

AO1 Activity

Research a number of creation myths. Once you have collected information on these, draw up a table that lists the common features of these creation myths. You should then use this information to help you explain in your essays how mythical language can be used to communicate important ideas about religious, social and ethical values. This will then meet the Band 5, AO1 criteria: 'The response demonstrates extensive depth and/or breadth. Excellent use of evidence and examples. Thorough and accurate reference made to sacred texts and sources of wisdom, where appropriate.'

The significance of water as a theme within the creation myths is therefore evident. However, another key feature of most creation myths is to recognise the primacy of human beings within creation and the particular role that they have – usually directly bestowed upon them by the divine being responsible for creation. Again, turning to the Judeo-Christian myth which concludes with the following information:

The mythical image of water is particularly significant in creation myths.

'Then God said, "Let us make humankind in our image, according to our likeness; and let them have dominion over the fish of the sea, and over the birds of the air, and over the cattle, and over all the wild animals of the earth, and over every creeping thing that creeps upon the earth." So God created humankind in his image, in the image of God he created them; male and female he created them. God blessed them, and God said to them, "Be fruitful and multiply, and fill the earth and subdue it; and have dominion over the fish of the sea and over the birds of the air and over every living thing that moves upon the earth."… God saw everything that he had made, and indeed, it was very good. And there was evening and there was morning, the sixth day. Thus the heavens and the earth were finished, and all their multitude. And on the seventh day God finished the work that he had done, and he rested on the seventh day from all the work that he had done. So God blessed the seventh day and hallowed it, because on it God rested from all the work that he had done in creation.' (Genesis 1:26–2:3, NRSV)

The role of human beings, communicated through the mythical language is quite straightforward: To take on the role of stewardship for the creator. To look after the created order, to preserve it – but not just that, here the role is also one with a specific place within the created order. Humankind is given a primacy within creation. It is the only created thing to be made in the image of the creator – to be endowed with the qualities of the uncreated God, even if only initially in potential according to the interpretation of Irenaeus of Lyons, who saw this myth as demonstrating that human beings had the ability to transform into God's likeness, having been created in his image – but only through fulfilling the divine commands and by developing Godlike qualities, would this be possible. It is this complex form of mythical language that communicates directly what the purpose of humankind is to be – and as such provides insight into the purpose of existence.

Humans are often given a specific role with creation myths.

quickfire

4.19 What key feature is common to many creation myths?

Specification content

Supportive evidence – different forms of myths to convey meaning: myths of good against evil; heroic myths.

Key quote

At least with superhero characters, we know … they do fill the gap in a secular culture, because they open up dimensions of the cosmic and transcendent, which is stuff myths usually have to deal with. It's not so much that they are new versions of the gods, because the gods were always just our eternal qualities. Superman possesses the qualities of the very best man we can imagine at any given time. In that sense, he's divine. Batman is representative of our dark subconscious, who nevertheless works for the good of humanity. They embody the same ideals. (G. Morrison, Superhero Myths, Wired.com, 2011)

The meaning that is derived from this mythical account may not be cognitive in nature but it reveals information about the world and the role of human beings in it. This information is meaningful because it provides both context and purpose. The language of myth, albeit a non-cognitive form of language, provides meaning in a deeper way possible than any other form of language could hope to do. As Tillich states: 'Symbols of faith cannot be replaced by other symbols, such as artistic ones, and they cannot be removed by scientific criticism. They have a genuine standing in the human mind, just as science and art have. Their symbolic character is their truth and their power. Nothing less than symbols and myths can express our ultimate concern.'

AO1 Activity

Using the information regarding the purpose/function of myth, produce a presentation that highlights some of the key myths relating to creation. In your presentation you should comment on aspects of mythical language as it occurs and provide a commentary as to its purpose/function within the religious tradition from where it arises

This practises the AO1 skill of being able to demonstrate an accurate understanding of philosophical thought through selecting relevant and accurate material.

Key quote

But religious models can also fulfil many of the non-cognitive functions of myth, particularly in the expression of attitudes; these functions have no parallel in science. Models embodied in myths evoke commitment to ethical norms and policies of action. Like metaphors, religious models elicit emotional and evaluational responses. Like parables, they encourage decision and personal involvement. Like myths, they offer ways of life and patterns of behaviour. (Barbour)

Heroic myths and myths of good against evil

Where creation myths are able to give meaningful insight into the purpose of humanity and its relationship with the rest of the universe (created order), other types of myths can reveal different insights. One such example is the category of myths described as 'heroic'. Inevitably these tend to focus on either one or a small number of individuals and recount stories of how the individual is able to conquer great adversity and be triumphant as a result. Such myths provide insight into the daily struggle of human existence and provide inspiration. These types of myths have existed throughout human history and exist even today in retellings found in the world of cinema, comic book heroes and videogames. Moojen Momen in *The Phenomenon of Religion* notes that there are many ways to interpret myths but a particularly useful method of interpretation:

'… is the mythological approach employed by such scholars as Carl Jung, Mircea Eliade and Joseph Campbell. This is based on the understanding that, if one studies the common themes in the different mythologies of the world, one can find the basic rhythms by which all human beings live. Myth explores the deeper inner questions and problems that have troubled humankind. Among the commonest themes uncovered by such studies are those which relate closely to religion: for example, the themes of creation, transformation, death and resurrection.'

The heroic myth is often retold in cinema, comic book and videogame in the 21st century.

One of the most prevalent forms of the heroic myth is the myth of the Solar Hero. Sun worship was common in many ancient societies. The sun, in purely scientific terms, is the source of all life on earth – being the prime requisite for the process of photosynthesis. However, long before the scientific age, the sun's life-giving properties were well known and their importance became enshrined in the myths of a myriad of different cultures and religions. Perhaps one of the best known 'sun gods' is the Ancient Egyptian sun god Ra. In some creation myths associated with Ra, he rises from the primordial waters and is responsible for creating air and moisture. His role as a life- and light-giver is what he is best known for, travelling across the sky during the day, bringing warmth to the whole world; then, at night, travelling through the underworld to do the same for those that dwelt there. Ra is then both a sun god and a sky god. His heroic deeds are centred around his ability to provide the life-giving properties of the sun and to battle the forces of chaos and darkness that threaten to overrun the ordered world.

This theme is echoed in the ancient Canaanite religion where the God Baal, another key god, is the promoter of life and fertility, and is worshipped for these attributes. The Judeo-Christian literature casts Baal in an unfavourable light, putting his followers in direct opposition with the early Israelites, as Baal and Yahweh battled for supremacy – with Yahweh triumphing each time. Evidence from ancient manuscripts suggests that Yahweh was initially regarded as a sky god, before taking on a role more closely associated with another Canaanite deity, El, who was regarded as the father of the gods. The myths of the Canaanite and Egyptian gods were often rooted in an account which detailed the cycle of the seasons and the associated fertility of the agricultural year. In both cases the key figures give life, are killed by a dark force opposed to life (the agent of chaos) but, usually through the intervention of a female deity, are restored to life to start the cycle of fertility over again. The mythical language here is a clear parallel for the passage of the seasons, as previously stated. However, it is also the precursor for another form of myth – the resurrection myth.

The resurrection myth, most often associated with the notion of the solar hero (a direct evolution of the prominence of the sun god) as an **archetype**, exists in many cultures and details how the agent of order is destroyed by the agents of chaos, only to be brought back to life again in a victory against their enemies:

Ra, the Ancient Egyptian sun god

> **Key term**
>
> Archetype: according to Jung a primitive concept inherited from the earliest human ancestors found in the collective unconscious.

'The myth of the solar hero typically begins with a Golden Age. Then the affairs of the solar hero and his family or nation go into decline; he appears to be defeated and even to die (as does the sun and the fertility of the earth in winter). At this point, the hero is separated from his people. In some versions, he descends into an underworld where he struggles against the forces of darkness. He wins a great victory and acquires the means for saving humanity. And so, just when everything seems hopeless and the world is full of darkness and the earth barren, the hero returns to 'save' the world. He brings a new era of justice and hope, a new order; a new Golden Age dawns (as the sun returns in spring and revives the fertility of the earth).' (Momen)

Rama's victory over the demon-king Ravana symbolises the triumph of good over evil – an important theme in Heroic myths.

quicKpire

4.20 In mythical terms, what is a solar hero?

Specification content

Challenges: problem of competing myths; meanings of myths change over time as they reflect the values of society as societal constructs; demythologisation of myths results in varying interpretations, myths often incompatible with scientific understanding of the world.

Different interpretations of myths can lead to their meaning being considered to be unclear.

Not only does this mythical account exist in the cultures of Ancient Egypt and Canaan, but it is also found in the religions of the present day. The Ramayana in Hinduism, tells how Rama was banished to the forest by his evil stepmother and how his wife Sita is kidnapped by the demon Ravana. The forces of darkness seem to overwhelm Rama until, with the help of his allies, Rama battles the forces of darkness, rescues his wife from the clutches of the evil demon and is restored to his rightful throne. Furthermore, the story in the New Testament of Jesus of Nazareth is seen by some as myth. He is taken prisoner as a result of wicked authorities, has his friends abandon him in his hour of need and is subsequently killed, eventually rises from the dead and heralds the dawn of a new age with the promise of eternal reward for those that follow him. The story of Siddhartha becoming Buddha echoes these themes as he becomes separated from the rest of the world and is accosted by the demon Mara before eventually finding enlightenment and is able to teach his message of hope to his followers. These heroic triumphs, through mythical language, teach not only the ability of the hero to overcome insurmountable odds but also show how good will always triumph over evil – no matter how much it seems that evil has won. These myths provide inspiration for all those exposed to them. The meaningfulness of the message is found within the myth – the archetypal themes exist throughout history, providing a unique insight into the human condition.

Challenges to myths and problems associated with them

For many, mythical language can be a powerful conveyor of meaning, at its deepest level. It invokes a response from the human psyche; for Jung it was an integral part of the collective unconscious and allowed us to gain insights into what it means to be human. However, as with all forms of non-cognitive language, mythical language can be challenged with regards to its meaningfulness.

Firstly, if we consider that any particular myth is meaningful, then that would presume that the integrity of the myth was preserved. By this, we mean that if we are to consider that the myth revealed insights and truths, then we would rightly expect those insights and truths to have a validity worth preserving and even sharing. Such mythical accounts are often the foundation for societies and their key beliefs and values. The importance of their integrity is often paramount.

However, what then happens when another myth stakes a claim to competing truths or competing values? Does this challenge the meaningfulness of the original myth or is it that the competing myth should be disregarded? A particular example of this, it could be argued, is the idea that creation and evolution are competing myths. Since the publication of Darwin's *Origin of the Species* in 1859, a fiercely contested debate has been held as to who has the claim of truth with regards to the question 'Where did humankind come from?' Of course, others would not consider these to be competing myths, assuming that science is based on empirically verifiable data, whilst religion is not. Controversially, that assumption itself may be part of the myth!

Less controversially may be the fact that the Genesis myth of Creation, an event told as a direct action of the Judeo-Christian God is the starting point for his relationship with humankind and a necessary part of the theology for both religions. What happens then, when a very similar account can be found in a culture that predates the Judeo-Christian tradition by several hundred years? If the myth is not unique does that therefore mean that the faith-based truth claims from the myth are likewise not unique? Does this therefore weaken them?

Similarly, the central claim of Christianity that Jesus' resurrection was a unique event in history, if treated as mythical literature, seems to have several parallels in other cultures, suggesting it may not be as unique an event as is claimed within the Christian tradition. Of course, this is based on the assumption that the resurrection of Jesus of Nazareth is a mythical event, which it may not have been.

Much like the value of symbolic language, as addressed earlier in this book, the value of mythical language and therefore its meaning, will inevitably change as the values of societies change. The meaning of a myth may alter to fit the prevailing intellectual mood of the day or it may change as we better understand the ancient cultures from where the myth originated. Either way, this would seem to destabilise the ability of myths to communicate meaningful information, if such information is subject to change over time.

No study of mythical language within religious studies would be complete without reference to the great German theologian Rudolf Bultmann. His work on the text of the New Testament had a significant effect on all biblical scholarship that followed, and on the treatment of the person of Jesus of Nazareth in particular. Bultmann considered that much of the literature in the New Testament, particularly the literature of the four canonical gospels, should be reinterpreted as it was primarily mythical language.

He then set about deconstructing or 'demythologising' these texts in order to make sense of them. Ian Barbour describes Bultmann's approach thus:

> 'He [Bultmann] objects to myth because it tries to represent the divine in the objective categories of the physical world. In the New Testament these misleading categories include space (e.g., Christ as "coming down" and "ascending"), time (eschatology as temporal finality), and causality (miracles and supernatural forces). These first-century thought-forms must be rejected, according to Bultmann, both because they are scientifically untenable in a world of lawful cause-and-effect and because they are theologically inadequate: the transcendent cannot be represented in the categories of the objective world. Moreover, he insists, the true meaning of scriptural myth always did involve man's self-understanding. The gospel was concerned about man's hopes, fears, decisions and commitments in the present, not about miraculous occurrences in the past.' (Barbour)

Key quote

Can Christian preaching expect modern man to accept the mythical view of the world as true? To do so would be both senseless and impossible. It would be senseless, because there is nothing specifically Christian in the mythical view of the world as such. It is simply the cosmology of a pre-scientific age ... Modern thought as we have inherited it brings with it criticism of the New Testament view of the world. **(Bultmann)**

In essence, Bultmann rejected the mythological language of the New Testament as unhelpful to the modern mind. He believed it actually obstructed a modern faith and his work on demythologisation set out to present a gospel message that was free from the unscientific descriptions found in the mythical language of the New Testament.

Key quote

The cosmology of the New Testament is essentially mythical in character. The world is viewed as a three-storied structure, with the earth in the center, the heaven above, and the underworld beneath. Heaven is the abode of God and of celestial beings – the angels. The underworld is hell, the place of torment. Even the earth is more than the scene of natural, everyday events, of the trivial round and common task. It is the scene of the supernatural activity of God and his angels on the one hand, and of Satan and his demons on the other. These supernatural forces intervene in the course of nature and in all that men think and will and do. Miracles are by no means rare. Man is not in control of his own life. Evil spirits may take possession of him. Satan may inspire him with evil thoughts. Alternatively, God may inspire his thought and guide his purposes. He may grant him heavenly visions. He may allow him to hear his word of succor or demand. He may give him the supernatural power of his Spirit. History does not follow a smooth unbroken course; it is set in motion and controlled by these supernatural powers. This **æon** is held in bondage by Satan, sin, and death (for 'powers' is precisely what they are), and hastens towards its end. That end will come very soon, and will take the form of a cosmic catastrophe. It will be inaugurated by the 'woes' of the last time. Then the Judge will come from heaven, the dead will rise, the last judgment will take place, and men will enter into eternal salvation or damnation. (**Bultmann, *Kerygma and Myth*, SPCK, 1953**)

Key skills

Knowledge involves:

Selection of a range of (thorough) accurate and relevant information that is directly related to the specific demands of the question.

This means:

- Selecting relevant material for the question set

- Being focused in explaining and examining the material selected.

Understanding involves:

Explanation that is extensive, demonstrating depth and/or breadth with excellent use of evidence and examples including (where appropriate) thorough and accurate supporting use of sacred texts, sources of wisdom and specialist language.

This means:

- Effective use of examples and supporting evidence to establish the quality of your understanding

- Ownership of your explanation that expresses personal knowledge and understanding and NOT just reproducing a chunk of text from a book that you have rehearsed and memorised.

AO1 Developing skills

It is now important to consider the information that has been covered in this section; however, the information in its raw form is too extensive and so has to be processed in order to meet the requirements of the examination. This can be achieved by practising more advanced skills associated with AO1. For assessment objective 1 (AO1), which involves demonstrating 'knowledge' and 'understanding' skills, we are going to focus on different ways in which the skills can be demonstrated effectively, and also refer to how the performance of these skills is measured (see generic band descriptors for A2 [WJEC] AO1 or A Level [Eduqas] AO1).

▶ **Your new task is this:** you will have to write a response under timed conditions to a question requiring an examination or explanation of **the value of myths in society**. This exercise can either be done as a group or independently.

1. Begin with a list of indicative content, as you may have done in the previous textbook in the series. This may be discussed as a group or done independently. It does not need to be in any particular order at first, although as you practise this you will see more order in your lists that reflects your understanding.

2. Develop the list by using one or two relevant quotations. Now add some references to scholars and/or religious writings.

3. Then write out your plan, under timed conditions, remembering the principles of explaining with evidence and/or examples. Then ask someone else to read your answer and see if they can then help you improve it in any way.

4. Collaborative marking helps a learner appreciate alternative perspectives and possibly things that may have been missed. It also helps highlight the strengths of another that one can learn from. With this in mind, it is good to swap and compare answers in order to improve your own.

When you have completed the task, refer to the band descriptors for A2 (WJEC) or A Level (Eduqas) and in particular have a look at the demands described in the higher band descriptors towards which you should be aspiring. Ask yourself:

- Does my work demonstrate thorough, accurate and relevant knowledge and understanding of religion and belief?

- Is my work coherent (consistent or make logical sense), clear and well organised?

- Will my work, when developed, be an extensive and relevant response which is specific to the focus of the task?

- Does my work have extensive depth and/or suitable breadth and have excellent use of evidence and examples?

- If appropriate to the task, does my response have thorough and accurate reference to sacred texts and sources of wisdom?

- Are there any insightful connections to be made with other elements of my course?

- Will my answer, when developed and extended to match what is expected in an examination answer, have an extensive range of views of scholars/schools of thought?

- When used, is specialist language and vocabulary both thorough and accurate?

Issues for analysis and evaluation

The effectiveness of the terms non-cognitive, analogical and mythical as solutions to the problems of religious language

Religious language is language about beliefs and practices arising from religion. For many who consider themselves to be religious believers there is no issue with the language that they use or apply to their religion. The terms form an integral part of their daily existence and express various aspects of their religious lives from faith commitments to ritual practices. Words ascribed to God by religious believers are meaningful to them in terms of their devotion, worship, prayer or inner thoughts.

However, for those outside of religion, or even those inside who wish to apply a critique to the language used within their particular religious sphere, the language of religion is not necessarily as problem-free as may at first appear. Words may appear abstract, vague or ambiguous. As such they may not readily be easily defined as there is no physical external object to which they relate. This was the issue for the logical positivists who, in recognising that religious language belonged to an essentially metaphysical activity, could neither be verified nor falsified and was therefore considered to be meaningless.

Treating language as if it can be directly provable, verified or falsified, was the domain of those who wished to see language as being open to empirical enquiry. However, whilst certain aspects of language can indeed be open to such things, e.g. statements about the shape of objects, the physical locations of features within the natural world or even the colour of an individual's hair, not all language is used in this way. In fact, to treat language purely cognitively (that is to say, to view language as something that can be empirically tested) is to have a very narrow view of the function of language within the human experience. Statements such as 'I feel happy today' or 'I really miss that person' cannot be objectively verified or falsified yet they reveal information about a person and their relationship to the world they live in, in a way that would make sense to anyone that can speak the language these utterances are made in. Such language is regarded as non-cognitive. When language is non-cognitive, it is not used to express empirically knowable facts about the external world. It is not something that can be held up to objective scrutiny. This is because non-cognitive language is language that expresses opinions, attitudes, feelings and/or emotions. It is language that relates to a person's view of what reality may mean to them – and this may differ from the view of another, even though they may be experiencing the same reality. Both views are held to be valid – but in a non-cognitive sense. The effectiveness of such a way of viewing language is powerful because it is these form of language that give human existence its richness, its depth. The ability to be passionate about beliefs, ideals or relationships can only be expressed in non-cognitive ways – a purely cognitive use of language would remove these things from human existence, an idea almost unimaginable. Why then should religious language be deemed to only have value in a cognitive sense? The reaction to this would be that it is entirely unfair, inappropriate even, to expect of religious language something that would not be fairly expected of human language as a whole. Meaningfulness can come from more than one form of expression and, whilst objective agreement on what is being said may not always be possible, this should not undermine the effectiveness of meaning that can be transmitted in this way.

This section covers AO2 content and skills

Specification content

The effectiveness of the terms non-cognitive, analogical and mythical as solutions to the problems of religious language.

What is the most effective solution for solving the problems of religious language?

AO2 Activity

As you read through this section try to do the following:

1. Pick out the different lines of argument that are presented in the text and identify any evidence given in support.

2. For each line of argument try to evaluate whether or not you think this is strong or weak.

3. Think of any questions you may wish to raise in response to the arguments.

This Activity will help you to start thinking critically about what you read and help you to evaluate the effectiveness of different arguments and from this develop your own observations, opinions and points of view that will help with any conclusions that you make in your answers to the AO2 questions that arise.

However, some philosophers have identified a particular difficulty with the non-cognitive approach. Religious believers are not making statements about any kind of reality that could be described as 'objective'. By this, we mean that not only are they not making any 'factual' comments but that, if religious language is purely to be understood as non-cognitive, then it is incapable of making such statements. This poses an issue for the religious believers who might state that 'God exists' or 'Sacred Writings are the word of God' or 'I believe in a life after death'. These are not just expressions of attitude for the religious believer. They are, in fact, and in the context appropriate to the particular religion, assertions about how reality actually is. In a very real sense, the religious believer considers these to be statements about the external world – in other words, is using them in a cognitive, not non-cognitive, sense. Which brings us back to the original challenge from logical positivism, i.e. that such statements are neither analytic or synthetic – they cannot be verified. As such, perhaps non-cognitive language is not an effective solution to the problems of religious language.

To further look at the use of language in a non-cognitive sense is to consider the value of analogical language. Analogies can be powerful language tools for communicating complex ideas in a far less complex way. They can make the unknowable knowable, albeit in a relational way. Analogies help us to make sense of information that may otherwise be closed to us and therefore are an effective way to use language. When talking about God, analogies – as envisioned by Aquinas – allow us insights into God's character and being which would otherwise be impossible for us. By assuming the relationship between creator and created, it permits the religious believers to have a deeper understanding of the being that they worship that could not be communicated through cognitive means. However, as Hume recognised, an analogy is only as good as the point at which the two things being compared are similar. The issue for religious language is do we know what we mean when we use the word 'God'? How do we 'know' (in the sense of being able to empirically quantify what we are talking about) what constitutes 'God'? – because unless we are able, in some measure, to do this, then our point of comparison fails. If this fails then so does the analogy, thereby rendering analogical language not only meaningless but, in a very real sense, useless – as far as talking about God is concerned. This shows that analogical language is an ineffective solution to the problem of religious language.

The use of mythical language, a further form of non-cognitive language, offers a potentially effective solution to the problem of religious language. By rejecting the claims that religious language must only make empirically verifiable claims, mythical language offers a type of language use which permits insight into universal truths about existence and humankind's relationship with the universe. The myths of creation, the heroic myths and the myths concerning good versus evil do not have to be taken in a literal cognitive sense in order to provide meaning. It is the very fact that they are symbolic, highly imaginable and make extensive use of metaphor that permits myths to convey meaning in a unique way. The particular role of myths, other than providing insight into universal truths about existence, is also to communicate values to its audience. The heroic myths of the Ancient World inspire contemporary readers to place value on positive aspects of behaviour. Linking to Aristotle's Virtue Theory, the hero in myth will often display many of the virtues such as temperance, bravery, justice and fortitude. In this, the meaning of life is revealed – not in an empirical way but rather in an inspirational way. Myths, in this sense, are therefore an effective solution to the problem of religious language.

The counter argument is that myths can be interpreted (demythologised) in a myriad of different ways – and this can result in their meaning being unclear. The issue of competing myths can lead to a undermining of understanding what the

Are myths an effective solution to the problem of religious language?

List some conclusions that could be drawn from the AO2 reasoning from the above text; try to aim for at least three different possible conclusions. Consider each of the conclusions and collect brief evidence to support each conclusion from the AO1 and AO2 material for this topic. Select the conclusion that you think is most convincing and explain why it is so. Try to contrast this with the weakest conclusion in the list, justifying your argument with clear reasoning and evidence.

purpose of human existence is. Is it to worship a creator God who will reconcile us to him after we die or is it to ascend, through our own efforts, to a higher plane of existence or, are we nothing more than the playthings of powerful divinities who, when our lives have ended, move on to other matters as if we had never existed?

From considering the various approaches of non-cognitive language to the problems of religious language, it would seem that it has not provided an effective solution. The challenges of meaningfulness, in the sense of a meaningfulness that can be universally accepted and agreed upon, seem too overwhelming to be easily solved. However, that is not to say that the non-cognitive use of language has no value. There are many things about it that are beneficial in terms of revealing things about the world and humanity's place in it, that should not be readily dismissed. It may not be an effective solution to the problems of religious language but it does provide some partial solutions for these issues and should therefore be treated with a measure of respect.

How can we best determine meaning in religious language?

Study tip

It is vital for AO2 that you present a response that successfully identifies and thoroughly addresses the issues raised by the question set. In order to do this you need to make sure that you have a clear understanding of the statement in question. Take time to read the statement thoroughly a number of times, and note down in your own words what you think it is claiming. This method will help to ensure that you focus on the relevant points.

The relevance of religious language issues in the 21st century

The work of the logical positivists, which came to the fore in the early part of the 20th century, ignited the debate about the meaningfulness of metaphysics, and in our sphere of study, religious language, in particular. The philosophical propositions that affirmed the importance of those tools which gave prominence and support to the field of scientific enquiry, were the same things that were used to undermine the meaningfulness of those things that belonged to the realm of metaphysics. Therefore religious language came under fire – essentially because its propositions and terminology could neither be verified nor falsified, belonged neither to the analytic nor synthetic forms of language that the scientific community were so fond of and, of course religious language was neither tautological nor was it mathematical. It was therefore considered essentially meaningless.

However, those that took a less narrow view of the meaningfulness within the world realised that the logical positivists had missed the point. Even their own verification principle fell foul of its own criteria – somewhat undermining its validity!

Philosophers such as Popper, Randall, Tillich and even later Wittgenstein were able to demonstrate that meaningfulness in language came not from the words themselves but rather from the way in which they were used or the way in which we could interpret the context from where they came. Meaningfulness could be understood in a myriad of ways that logical positivism had not given credit for and therefore, the debates and credibility of logical positivism soon lost their force as the 20th century, and the philosophical movements associated with it, developed. By the beginning of the 21st century, the debate about the meaningfulness of religious language had moved on considerably and the old criticisms just didn't seem to be effective any more.

Specification content

The relevance of religious language issues in the 21st century.

AO2 Activity

As you read through this section try to do the following:

1. Pick out the different lines of argument that are presented in the text and identify any evidence given in support.

2. For each line of argument try to evaluate whether or not you think this is strong or weak.

3. Think of any questions you may wish to raise in response to the arguments.

This Activity will help you to start thinking critically about what you read and help you to evaluate the effectiveness of different arguments and from this develop your own observations, opinions and points of view that will help with any conclusions that you make in your answers to the AO2 questions that arise.

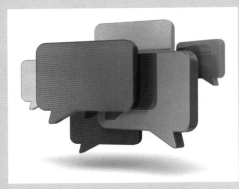

What are the priorities for the 21st century in relation to religious language and communication?

So are these issues no longer relevant in the 21st century? Quite simply, the answer is yes – although the debate has matured somewhat. The issues regarding religious language, when one considers the issue of the inherent problems of religious language, has not disappeared. Religious language can, at its face value, often seem to be saying things that are difficult to understand or difficult to root in any meaningful way, once taken out of the context immediate to religious believers and their dialogue. In some instances, even religious believers can find it difficult to articulate the meaning of some of their own propositions – even though they claim that understanding is a matter of faith not logic and therefore not open to objective verification.

The wider scope of the philosophy of language (as opposed to purely religious language) takes several things into consideration when reflecting on the purpose of language. For instance, what does our language reveal about reality? How does it do this and is it meaningful? What constitutes meaningfulness? Is it related to the ideas of empiricists such as Hume that proposed meanings were nothing more than mental contents brought about by specific signs; or is meaningfulness derived, as Wittgenstein said, through the way in which language is used? Or perhaps the logical positivists had it right when they suggested that meaning came from that which could be proven when linked to our knowledge of the physical world? Each of these can be related back to the debate with how religious language is used and therefore demonstrates the relevance of religious language issues in the 21st century.

In some senses, the debate has also narrowed. For instance, much discussion has been held about specific religious terms, such as the word 'God'. For centuries, the word has been used as either a title, a descriptive noun or a name. In many religions, the word God is used as the respectful proper noun, whereas there is sometimes a more personal utterance that can be used to address the same being – especially in acts of devotion, worship and prayer. Such 'personal' names can be found in the Jewish and Hindu traditions – both of which would also use the word God in its generic sense as well. A similar idea can also be found in the mystical traditions of Christianity (e.g. in the works of Teresa of Avila) and Islam (e.g. In the works of Rumi), where the term 'God' is replaced with a far more intimate form of address. In such cases, do they therefore provide meaningfulness for the word that would otherwise not be available to those outside of the traditions? When the atheists reject the belief in God, they are not dismissing the term as one of nonsense or as something non-verifiable. They reject the term because of its associations of the reality it proposes. In many ways, the New Atheists can be likened to Anselm's Fool, in the way in which they reject the word. Again, the relevance of religious language in the 21st century is evident.

Key quote

A simple and familiar example of such a proposition is the proposition that there are mountains on the farther side of the moon! No rocket has yet been invented which would enable me to go and look at the farther side of the moon, so that I am unable to decide the matter by actual observation. But I do know what observations would decide it for me, if, as is theoretically conceivable, I were once in a position to make them. And therefore I say that the proposition is verifiable in principle, if not in practice, and is accordingly significant. **(Ayer)**

AO2 Developing skills

It is now important to consider the information that has been covered in this section; however, the information in its raw form is too extensive and so has to be processed in order to meet the requirements of the examination. This can be achieved by practising more advanced skills associated with AO2. For assessment objective 2 (AO2), which involves 'critical analysis' and 'evaluation' skills, we are going to focus on different ways in which the skills can be demonstrated effectively, and also refer to how the performance of these skills is measured (see generic band descriptors for A2 [WJEC] AO2 or A Level [Eduqas] AO2).

▶ **Your new task is this:** you will have to write a response under timed conditions to a question requiring an evaluation of **whether religious language still has meaning today**. This exercise can either be done as a group or independently.

1. Begin with a list of indicative arguments or lines of reasoning, as you may have done in the previous textbook in the series. It does not need to be in any particular order at first, although as you practise this you will see more order in your lists, in particular by way of links and connections between arguments.

2. Develop the list by using one or two relevant quotations. Now add some references to scholars and/or religious writings.

3. Then write out your plan, under timed conditions, remembering the principles of explaining with evidence and/or examples. Then ask someone else to read your answer and see if they can then help you improve it in any way.

4. Collaborative marking helps a learner appreciate alternative perspectives and possibly things that may have been missed. It also helps highlight the strengths of another that one can learn from. With this in mind, it is good to swap and compare answers in order to improve your own.

When you have completed the task, refer to the band descriptors for A2 (WJEC) or A Level (Eduqas) and in particular have a look at the demands described in the higher band descriptors towards which you should be aspiring. Ask yourself:

- Is my answer a confident critical analysis and perceptive evaluation of the issue?
- Is my answer a response that successfully identifies and thoroughly addresses the issues raised by the question set?
- Does my work show an excellent standard of coherence, clarity and organisation?
- Will my work, when developed, contain thorough, sustained and clear views that are supported by extensive, detailed reasoning and/or evidence?
- Are the views of scholars/schools of thought used extensively, appropriately and in context?
- Does my answer convey a confident and perceptive analysis of the nature of any possible connections with other elements of my course?
- When used, is specialist language and vocabulary both thorough and accurate?

Key skills

Analysis involves:

Identifying issues raised by the materials in the AO1, together with those identified in the AO2 section, and presents sustained and clear views, either of scholars or from a personal perspective ready for evaluation.

This means:

- That your answers are able to identify key areas of debate in relation to a particular issue
- That you can identify, and comment upon, the different lines of argument presented by others
- That your response comments on the overall effectiveness of each of these areas or arguments.

Evaluation involves:

Considering the various implications of the issues raised based upon the evidence gleaned from analysis and provides an extensive detailed argument with a clear conclusion.

This means:

- That your answer weighs up the consequences of accepting or rejecting the various and different lines of argument analysed
- That your answer arrives at a conclusion through a clear process of reasoning.

Specification content

Meaningful to people who participate in same language game (Ludwig Wittgenstein); Supportive evidence – Non-cognitive form of language provides meaning to participants within language game; consider use of language not meaning; language games fit with coherence theory of truth; religious language as expressions of belief.

Key quotes

One can mistrust one's own senses, but not one's own belief. (Wittgenstein)

Every word has a meaning. This meaning is correlated with the word. It is the object for which the word stands. (Wittgenstein)

quickfire

4.21 What is meant by the term 'the vernacular'?

Key terms

Language games: Wittgenstein's analogy which stated that language was meaningful to those that used it within their own form of life/language game

Realist: the philosophical position that adopts the correspondence theory of truth

F: Religious language as a language game

Ludwig Wittgenstein's contribution to the debate about religious language

Ludwig Wittgenstein

Imagine that a person comes to your home. They are there with the express purpose of helping to make some kind of home improvements. They talk about two by fours, noggins, risers, renders, second fixes and stocks. These words are interspersed by other words that you would understand from a standard conversation in the vernacular. You may feel justifiably confused by their conversation with you. However, you may find yourself agreeing with what they are asking of you just because you don't want to seem ignorant of words that, for all intents and purposes, are part of a standard English language conversation but the words themselves seem as if they form part of a different language.

In many ways, this is precisely what they are and it is understanding how language is used in this way (and, more significantly, how language is understood by using it in this way) that led Wittgenstein to develop his earlier philosophy of language (where he discussed language as a kind of picture-based system of communication) to a philosophy of language which described language, and its use, in terms of 'language games'.

Before explaining Wittgenstein's ideas further, it is useful to put forward two philosophical concepts related to the understanding of 'truth'. In the sense of understanding language, we understand language because we understand its meaning. In other words, the words that we hear, or articulate, bear some resemblance to something within our experience that relates to some kind of reality which we can define. In simpler terms, the meaning of something is its 'truth'.

In philosophical terms, there are two main understandings of the concept of truth. These are correspondence and coherence.

The correspondence understanding of truth, is often referred to by certain philosophers, as the 'realist' position. In this understanding of truth, something is held to be true (or 'meaningful') by virtue of its relationship to the external and knowable world. It is very much an empiricist position and would have been a view of truth that is sympathetic to the philosophical position of the logical positivists. For instance, if I assert that 'the grass is green' then the truth of that statement can be verified by determining what is meant by the noun 'grass' and then identifying whether that noun was 'green' in the sense of the colour green as agreed by the standard interpretation of the light spectrum. If the colour of the grass corresponds to the statement (i.e. the grass is green) then the truth of that statement is established. If the grass is any other colour then the statement is considered to be 'false' in the sense that it is not meaningful to say that the grass is green because it is some other colour.

Another way to appreciate the **correspondence theory of truth** is to cite an example from history. For instance, the belief that the planet that we live on is spherical in shape. This belief is true because we know that it corresponds to the actual reality of the shape of the planet – as verified by photographic, geophysical and mathematical evidence.

The **coherence theory of truth** is somewhat different. In this instance (sometimes referred to as the '**anti-realist**' position) the truth of a matter is determined, not by its correspondence to an external reality but rather by its interpretation within a specific group of people. For instance, with reference to the previous example of the colour of the grass, if, for whatever reason, a group of people decided that the use of the adjective 'red' was the correct adjective for the colour of the grass, then the statement 'the grass is green' would not, in their view, be true. That is because the 'grass is green' does not 'cohere' (or fit with) their understanding of what it means for the grass to be a specific colour. For them, the statement 'the grass is red' would be meaningful and therefore true, in their view of the world. Truth is not determined by an external reality but rather by an interpretation of that reality that may (or may not) be true.

Again, an example from history is useful here. Prior to the seventeenth century, the shape of the earth was not widely accepted as spherical. Many people believed that the Earth was flat and their world-view was determined as 'true' because it fit with how they believed reality actually was. The fact that this was scientifically inaccurate did not matter – for them it was 'true' because it helped them make sense of the world in which they lived. It 'cohered' with their understanding of the physical world and therefore represented a truth of what the shape of the world was.

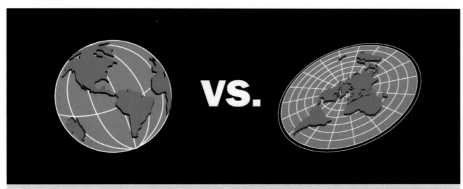

Flat vs round Earth – Coherence vs correspondence theories of truth

These two views of truth are particularly useful when it comes to looking at the meaningfulness of language.

In simple terms, the use of language games to determine how language is meaningful to the people that participate in that particular language game, is an anti-realist or coherence theory of truth position.

For Wittgenstein, it was imperative that we understand which game we are playing when we use particular forms of language. If we are unable to do this, then it would be inevitable that we could be led to misunderstand how that particular language game is being played.

Language was a facility used by people to communicate ideas that were specific to their particular form of life – their 'game'. Language is a social and public activity – it is through this that language is understood and its meaning is established. There are many ways to use language, in the same way that there are many different ways to play games. This 'family resemblance' was an idea that permeated Wittgenstein's language games philosophy.

Key terms

Anti-realist: a philosophical position that adopts the coherence theory of truth

Coherence theory of truth: belief that something is true when it fits in (coheres) with the views of those within the community

Correspondence theory of truth: belief that something is true because it relates to (corresponds) an objective external reality

Key quotes

Augustine, we might say, does describe a system of communication; only not everything that we call language is this system. And one has to say this in many cases where the question arises 'Is this an appropriate description or not?' The answer is: 'Yes, it is appropriate, but only for this narrowly circumscribed region, not for the whole of what you were claiming to describe.' It is as if someone were to say: 'A game consists in moving objects about on a surface according to certain rules . . .' – and we replied: 'You seem to be thinking of board games, but there are others. You can make your definition correct by expressly restricting it to those games.' **(Wittgenstein)**

Here the term '*language-game*' is meant to bring into prominence the fact that the *speaking* of language is part of an activity, or of a form of life. **(Wittgenstein)**

quickpire

4.22 What is an anti-realist?

Key quote

For a *large* class of cases – though not for all – in which we employ the word 'meaning' it can be defined thus: the meaning of a word is its use in the language. (**Wittgenstein**)

The concept of different ways to play games allows us to understand how we can use language in different ways, too.

As such, language in this context, is understood to be non-cognitive, rather than cognitive. The meaningfulness comes from the context within which the form of language is used. It therefore provides meaning to those who participate in the game, even if it is not always clear what the meaning is to those outside of the game. Wittgenstein does not conclude that each language game is entirely exclusive as each game can be 'learned', as long as the rules can be explained and understood. This is because, in common with games, language use has common features – a 'family resemblance', as already stated. As language is always a public activity – Wittgenstein strongly denied that language could ever be considered as a private activity – it was an activity that was potentially open to all. To restate what was previously said: Each language game could be learned.

Once the individual understands the rules of the language game they will understand the meaning of the language. Or, to put it in the way that Wittgenstein did – the meaningfulness of the language comes not from the words themselves but rather from the way in which those words are used: 'For a *large* class of cases – though not for all – in which we employ the word "meaning" it can be defined thus: the meaning of a word is its use in the language.'

AO1 Activity

Wittgenstein's ideas are complex and it can be easy to get confused. To support your learning of his language games analogy, construct an information diagram or mind-map that breaks his ideas down into key areas for focus.

Once you have completed this task, compare your work with someone else in the class. Have you both chosen the same ideas? Is there anything absent in your work that is accurately present in the other person's? You should then adapt your work so that it is as detailed and accurate as possible. Repeat this checking process up to five times, this will help you gain a good understanding of Wittgenstein's key ideas and meets the following Band 5, AO1 criteria:

- Thorough, accurate and relevant knowledge and understanding
- An excellent standard of coherence, clarity and organisation.

Extract taken from *Philosophical Investigations*

Here we come up against the great question that lies behind all these considerations. – For someone might object against me: 'You take the easy way out! You talk about all sorts of language-games, but have nowhere said what the essence of a language-game, and hence of language, is: what is common to all these activities, and what makes them into language or parts of language. So you let yourself off the very part of the investigation that once gave you yourself most headache, the part about the *general form of propositions* and of language.'

And this is true. – Instead of producing something common to all that we call language, I am saying that these phenomena have no one thing in common which makes us use the same word for all, – but that they are *related* to one another in many different ways. And it is because of this relationship, or these relationships, that we call them all 'language'. I will try to explain this.

Consider, for example, the proceedings that we call 'games'. I mean board-games, card-games, ball-games, Olympic games, and so on. What is common to them all? – Don't say: 'There *must* be something common, or they would not be called "games" ' – but *look and see* whether there is anything common to all. – For if you look at them you will not see something that is common to *all*, but similarities, relationships, and a whole series of them at that.

To repeat: don't think, but look! – Look for example at board-games, with their multifarious relationships. Now pass to card-games; here you find many correspondences with the first group, but many common features drop out, and others appear. When we pass next to ball-games, much that is common is retained, but much is lost. – Are they all "amusing"? Compare chess with noughts and crosses. Or is there always winning and losing, or competition between players? Think of patience. In ball-games there is winning and losing; but when a child throws his ball at the wall and catches it again, this feature has disappeared. Look at the parts played by skill and luck; and at the difference between skill in chess and skill in tennis. Think now of games like ring-a-ring-a-roses; here is the element of amusement, but how many other characteristic features have disappeared! And we can go through the many, many other groups of games in the same way; can see how similarities crop up and disappear. And the result of this examination is: we see a complicated network of similarities overlapping and criss-crossing: sometimes overall similarities, sometimes similarities of detail.

In his examination of the different types of games that people may have experienced, Wittgenstein points out that the games have many elements that they share in common with each other. He also notes that these elements will change according to the types of game being played. He notes similarities in certain sorts of games that do not exist when those games are compared with other types of games, even though all are regarded as games. For Wittgenstein this ebb and flow of shared characteristics seemed to be particularly pertinent when the analogy between games and the use of language was made. Language, in the way that it was used by the empiricists and logical positivists shared a very close relationship. The relationship between these two uses of language and the use of religious language could also be drawn – as both uses of language use words, phrases, speech patterns and serve to communicate particular information to their particular audiences. In this sense they bore the same sort of resemblance as the games of chess and cricket. Both are games, yet both have significant differences.

These family resemblances 'overlap and criss-cross' which is what gives them their resemblances. Yet they are not the same. It would be a mistake to treat them in the same way as they are clearly different – even though they share commonalities. The same can be said for the way in which language is used.

Wittgenstein further noted that understanding language was not always a straightforward task. He drew a parallel with what it meant to understand a picture. When we listen to words and sounds, ultimately they mean nothing unless placed into context. Wittgenstein said the same was true of a picture or painting. A painting is actually nothing more than the arrangement of colours, 'patches of colour on the canvas', and should not make any sense at all but because we appreciate what the picture is related to, we are able to make sense of it. The arrangement of colours takes on relatable shapes, images and means something to use – so that the picture becomes a picture of something. The same is true with language – the random sounds become sounds that mean something because they are relatable, we understand them because we have learned to understand them – we associate them with their respective meanings according to the way in which we have learned them. To put it another way, in learning the rules of the particular language game that we are involved in, we are able to understand the sounds that we hear or the words that we read because we are able to understand the rules of the language game.

Key quote

What does it mean to know what a game is? What does it mean, to know it and not be able to say it? Is this knowledge somehow equivalent to an unformulated definition? So that if it were formulated I should be able to recognise it as the expression of my knowledge? Isn't my knowledge, my concept of a game, completely expressed in the explanations that I could give? That is, in my describing examples of various kinds of game; showing how all sorts of other games can be constructed on the analogy of these; saying that I should scarcely include this or this among games; and so on. If someone were to draw a sharp boundary I could not acknowledge it as the one that I too always wanted to draw, or had drawn in my mind. For I did not want to draw one at all. His concept can then be said to be not the same as mine, but akin to it. The kinship is that of two pictures, one of which consists of colour patches with vague contours, and the other of patches similarly shaped and distributed, but with clear contours. The kinship is just as undeniable as the difference. **(Wittgenstein)**

When we understand what the colours and shapes represent, we can understand the picture. In the same way, when we understand the sounds that are being made or the shapes on the page, we can understand the language.

Key quote

What does it mean to understand a picture, a drawing? Here too there is understanding and failure to understand. And here too these expressions may mean various kinds of thing. A picture is perhaps a still-life; but I don't understand one part of it: I cannot see solid objects there, but only patches of colour on the canvas. Or I see everything as solid but there are objects that I am not acquainted with (they look like implements, but I don't know their use). Perhaps, however, I am acquainted with the objects, but in another sense do not understand the way they are arranged. (Wittgenstein)

quickfire

4.23 Why did Wittgenstein view religious language as meaningful?

Specification content

Challenges, including rejection of any true propositions in religion that can be empirically verified; does not allow for meaningful conversations between different groups of language users; does not provide adequate meaning for the word 'God'.

Ultimately, Wittgenstein recognised that the scope of his investigations into the use of language was to present a philosophical view of how language was used – not to influence its use or to change how we use language, purely to recognise, through the tools of the philosopher, what the function of language in the human sphere of existence was: 'Philosophy may in no way interfere with the actual use of language; it can in the end only describe it. For it cannot give it any foundation either. It leaves everything as it is.'

> Extract taken from *Philosophical Investigations*
>
> But now it may come to look as if there were something like a final analysis of our forms of language, and so a *single* completely resolved form of every expression. That is, as if our usual forms of expression were, essentially, unanalysed; as if there were something hidden in them that had to be brought to light. When this is done the expression is completely clarified and our problem solved. It can also be put like this: we eliminate misunderstandings by making our expressions more exact; but now it may look as if we were moving towards a particular state, a state of complete exactness; and as if this were the real goal of our investigation. This finds expression in questions as to the *essence* of language, of propositions, of thought. – For if we too in these investigations are trying to understand the essence of language – its function, its structure, – yet *this* is not what those questions have in view. For they see in the essence, not something that already lies open to view and that becomes surveyable by a rearrangement, but something that lies *beneath* the surface. Something that lies within, which we see when we look *into* the thing, and which an analysis digs out.

> **AO1 Activity**
>
> After reading the section on Wittgenstein, note down evidence and examples that could be used explain his ideas relating to language games. This could help you to achieve the best possible AO1 level in an examination answer (B5 AO1 level descriptors).

Challenges to Wittgenstein's theory of language games

First and foremost, Wittgenstein's theory of language games is a theory that treats language in a non-cognitive rather than a cognitive way. As such, many of the criticisms or challenges that can be levelled against non-cognitivism, also apply to language games. So, for example, where a statement is regarded as cognitive, we know that it is providing us information about the external world that we can verify, by applying empirical methods. This means that some things that we speak about can be objectively verified or proven as true. In this instance, the statement 'God exists', which many theists contend as being a statement that is knowable through experience, is true. However, as soon as we treat language as being non-cognitive, we are – by the very fact that we are recognising that language is not being used in the way that can be held up to objective scrutiny, we are denying, through implication, that any religious language statement cannot be held up to be objectively true – or at least, we cannot prove it as such. Many theists would find this position at best distasteful and at worst abhorrent. The statement 'God exists' for them is objectively true. Similarly any faith claim, used cognitively, is open to empirical verification whereas when it is treated as being non-cognitive is not open to such verification.

One of the key challenges to Wittgenstein's theory of language games came from one of his close friends, philosopher Rush Rhees, who, in his 1959 article: *Wittgenstein's Builders*, noted that the strength of Wittgenstein's theory rested upon the assumption that the link between 'games' and 'language' was a strong one, in analogical terms.

As you may remember from your studies of Paley's teleological argument, the strength of the watchmaker analogy is essential if it is to succeed as a method of persuasion that the argument is valid. Most of the attacks on Paley's teleological argument begin by dismantling the effectiveness of the analogy between the designer of the watch and the designer of the universe. David Hume, when examining Paley's argument noted that analogies normally work on the following basis: (i) X and Y are similar (ii) X has the characteristic Z (iii) Therefore Y has the characteristic Z. However, to claim what is true of Y based purely on a similarity to X is only as strong as the point at which X and Y are similar. If the similarity between them is weak, then, likewise, the conclusion drawn by the analogy is likewise weak. Hume concluded, in the case of the watchmaker analogy, that, as the universe is unique, no analogy is sufficient to explain its origins. Rhees presented his argument along the lines of making three challenges to Wittgenstein's analogy:

1. He noted that the language was about making sense to other people, not just following a set of protocols that were agreed upon, like following the rules of a game.

2. Whilst it is possible to explain a game to someone who has never experienced a game before, it is not possible to explain the concept of language to someone who has never spoken language, or heard language before. This is because an explanation of language has to be given in language, whereas this does not apply to an explanation of games.

3. In order to know what it means to play a game, you need to know what people are doing when they play games (you do not necessarily need to understand the game in order to recognise that they are playing a game). However, when a person uses language it is not enough to just know what they are doing – you also need to be able understand it.

One of the other general critiques of Wittgenstein's theory is that each language game has its own rules which are pertinent to it and which do not extend, in their entirety, to any other game (although other language games may share similarities with it). If so, then it would suggest that it would not be possible to communicate in an entirely meaningful way between two users of different language games – for each would be using language in a way that was unique to them. The anti-realist position, whilst defending the 'truth' within each group, is unable to objectify that truth between groups and so could lead to both misunderstanding and confusion. If neither group can lay claim to an objective truth (as would be the case with the realist position) then how can they find a middle ground where they are able to communicate meaningfully with each other? The inclusivity of meaningfulness within each language game would seem to inevitably lead to an exclusivity of meaningfulness when the two (or more) groups attempt to communicate with each other.

Finally, if the word 'God' has no objective meaning, then how can we talk meaningfully about God? An anti-realist approach to the word God would undermine attempts to define God, such as those offered by Anselm (God is that than which nothing greater can be conceived); Descartes (God is the supremely perfect Being); or Malcolm (God as unlimited being). If the word God becomes subject to a language game then that would imply that there is no definitive, objective, cognitive way to use the word and it could therefore lead to uncertainty about what is meant when the word is used in any given context. For instance, would the word God mean the same to the theist and atheist? Wittgenstein would regard them as playing different language games, so how therefore can we know what the atheist is denying is actually the same thing that the theist is affirming? Many religious believers would assert that the word God has a definitive, cognitive, meaning and would struggle to accept anything else. This suggests that perhaps Wittgenstein's language games seem not to allow for an adequate meaning for the word 'God'.

Analogies can be useful ways to describe those things we don't know much about – but what are the drawbacks?

Is there a cognitive way to talk about God?

AO1 Activity

It is vital that you are able to make thorough and accurate use of specialist language and vocabulary in context. Test your knowledge of key terms/names/phrases that you have studied by putting each in a sentence using your own words. Make sure however, that each sentence is relevant to the issues that have been studied in this particular unit.

Key skills

Knowledge involves:

Selection of a range of (thorough) accurate and relevant information that is directly related to the specific demands of the question.

This means:

- Selecting relevant material for the question set

- Being focused in explaining and examining the material selected.

Understanding involves:

Explanation that is extensive, demonstrating depth and/or breadth with excellent use of evidence and examples including (where appropriate) thorough and accurate supporting use of sacred texts, sources of wisdom and specialist language.

This means:

- Effective use of examples and supporting evidence to establish the quality of your understanding

- Ownership of your explanation that expresses personal knowledge and understanding and NOT just reproducing a chunk of text from a book that you have rehearsed and memorised.

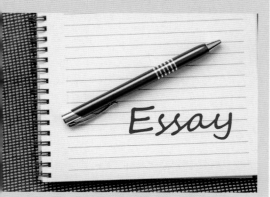

Planning your essays is a great way to boost your confidence with exam technique.

AO1 Developing skills

It is now important to consider the information that has been covered in this section; however, the information in its raw form is too extensive and so has to be processed in order to meet the requirements of the examination. This can be achieved by practising more advanced skills associated with AO1. For assessment objective 1 (AO1), which involves demonstrating 'knowledge' and 'understanding' skills, we are going to focus on different ways in which the skills can be demonstrated effectively, and also refer to how the performance of these skills is measured (see generic band descriptors for A2 [WJEC] AO1 or A Level [Eduqas] AO1).

▶ **Your new task is this:** It is impossible to cover all essays in the time allowed by the course; however, it is a good exercise to **develop detailed plans that can be utilised under timed conditions**. As a last exercise:

1. Create some ideal plans by using what we have done so far in the Theme 4 Developing skills sections.

2. This time stop at the planning stage and exchange plans with a study partner.

3. Check each other's plans carefully. Talk through any omissions or extras that could be included, not forgetting to challenge any irrelevant materials.

4. Remember, collaborative learning is very important for revision. It not only helps to consolidate understanding of the work and appreciation of the skills involved, it is also motivational and a means of providing more confidence in one's learning. Although the examination is sat alone, revising as a pair or small group is invaluable.

When you have completed each plan, as a pair or small group refer to the band descriptors for A2 (WJEC) or A Level (Eduqas) and in particular have a look at the demands described in the higher band descriptors towards which you should be aspiring. Ask yourself:

- Does my work demonstrate thorough, accurate and relevant knowledge and understanding of religion and belief?

- Is my work coherent (consistent or make logical sense), clear and well organised?

- Will my work, when developed, be an extensive and relevant response which is specific to the focus of the task?

- Does my work have extensive depth and/or suitable breadth and have excellent use of evidence and examples?

- If appropriate to the task, does my response have thorough and accurate reference to sacred texts and sources of wisdom?

- Are there any insightful connections to be made with other elements of my course?

- Will my answer, when developed and extended to match what is expected in an examination answer, have an extensive range of views of scholars/schools of thought?

- When used, is specialist language and vocabulary both thorough and accurate?

Issues for analysis and evaluation

The extent to which language games provide a suitable way of resolving the problems of religious language

Language is the vehicle that we use for most of our communication. It allows us to articulate our wishes, our feelings, our knowledge, our beliefs. As language functions in this way for us to articulate, it also functions in a way where all those things are potentially decipherable for the receivers of these communications. Language then is a two-way process involving both transmitters and receivers – relying on the assumption that what is being transmitted can be received and understood. When a person learns a language for the first time, it is something that is done in infancy and is intimately bound to the cultural and societal conventions wherein the language is being learnt.

As such, the words, phrases, and idioms that belong to each language are acquired in such a way that (in the vast majority of cases where such acquisition is not impeded by any physical or intellectual barriers) understanding occurs. This means that at any future date, where such language is used, the nuances and subtleties associated with the language, as well as the straightforward meanings, can be accessed.

However, whenever a second, third or further language is learned, these tend to be acquired at a later stage in life – even if that means later infancy in those cultures where multilingualism is the norm. As such, the same depth of language appreciation may take longer to be developed than would be the case with the primary learned language.

When it comes to the use of specialised, technical language, this is true to an even greater extent. Religious language is one such form of specialised language. Whatever vernacular is employed, religious language functions in such a way to transmit information about religion and religious beliefs and practices. Theological and philosophical concepts relating to the religion are transmitted through the same medium.

The problems of religious language arise when someone from outside the tradition (comparable to someone attempting to understand a language that they have not been taught) attempts to try to understand what is being said. If a person is not schooled in the form of language being used then it is highly unlikely that they will be able to appreciate what the religious person is trying to communicate. To explain religious concepts to a person with no appreciation of the religion being discussed is akin to attempting to communicate between two individuals using two different languages.

Communication can be problematic when you don't understand what the other person is saying.

This section covers AO2 content and skills

Specification content

The extent to which language games provide a suitable way of resolving the problems of religious language.

Language learning usually happens at a very young age.

AO2 Activity

As you read through this section try to do the following:

1. Pick out the different lines of argument that are presented in the text and identify any evidence given in support.

2. For each line of argument try to evaluate whether or not you think this is strong or weak.

3. Think of any questions you may wish to raise in response to the arguments.

This Activity will help you to start thinking critically about what you read and help you to evaluate the effectiveness of different arguments and from this develop your own observations, opinions and points of view that will help with any conclusions that you make in your answers to the AO2 questions that arise.

Is religious language nonsense?

This has inevitably led to some regarding religious language as a 'nonsense', suggesting that the propositions within it have no place in the 'real' world. In many of these cases the language of religion is interpreted through an empirically focused lens. The words and phrases of the religious person are held up to the scrutiny of objects relating to the external physical world and, again inevitably, are unable to be understood in such a way. The empirical world deals in the here and now, the things that can be tested through the use of the five senses. Religious statements, particularly relating to belief, are most commonly relating to the transcendent world, the metaphysical reality that cannot be determined via empirical means. Meaningful dialogue can therefore not be established and the task of the non-religious believers in understanding the religious believer is doomed to failure. This then leads to a dismissal of religious beliefs and the language that expresses them, as being ultimately meaningless – but is this fair?

The work of Wittgenstein with language games leads to a resounding denial of the last claim. Wittgenstein's assertion that we should not be looking for the meaning of words but how they are used is an essential gateway into understanding the world of religious language. Equally the idea that language can be categorised into a series of 'games' according to the form of life that they are representing (in this case the religious form of life) is particularly useful in helping us to realise that it is inappropriate to try and understand the rules of the religious language game by applying the rules of another language game (in the case of the logical positivists, the empirical game).

Therefore, recognising religious language as a specific game, means that there is an appreciation that it has certain rules which apply to it. By engaging with those rules and coming to an understanding of them, one is able to at least appreciate what is being communicated within the 'game'. Of course, if there is no willingness to engage learning the rules, then the game may remain 'closed' to the observer – but this is not the fault of those that 'play' and live the game. The challenges to religious language that come from the logical positivists can therefore be largely resolved.

Finally, the problems of religious language can be resolved by the use of Wittgenstein's language games because understanding that something has validity for those within the game – even if it doesn't for those external to it – is to adopt a coherence theory of truth. Meaningfulness is established through participation. What is meaningful for those within the group may be nonsense to those outside, but that view should not detract from the point that there is a very real sense of meaning attached to the use of that particular language within the group. I may not understand the language employed by those working within the building trades but I recognise that it has meaning for them and the structure and integrity of the house that I live in depends on their language having a very real meaning for all those associated in the work that they do. My understanding of their language should not detract from the meaningfulness that it has for them. The same can be applied to the logical positivists and those others that claim that religious language is problematic and ultimately meaningless. Religious language may not be meaningful to them or to others outside of the sphere of religious activity but as long as it serves the purpose to bring meaning and cohesion to the community that uses it, then religious language is a valid and meaningful form of language. Adopting such a view shoes that the problems of religious language are therefore resolved by using Wittgenstein's language games.

AO2 Activity

List some conclusions that could be drawn from the AO2 reasoning from the above text; try to aim for at least three different possible conclusions. Consider each of the conclusions and collect brief evidence to support each conclusion from the AO1 and AO2 material for this topic. Select the conclusion that you think is most convincing and explain why it is so. Try to contrast this with the weakest conclusion in the list, justifying your argument with clear reasoning and evidence.

Study tip

Ensuring that you know the key information about each philosopher and their views is essential if you want to access the higher bands in both AO1 and AO2. You may therefore want to write a series of flashcards that summarises the key points of each philosopher and regularly revisit and re-read these so that you are able to readily recall this information in an assessment.

Whether the strengths of language games outweigh the weaknesses

Wittgenstein's contribution to the religious language debate is significant. The initial challenge from the logical positivists, in asserting that religious language, as essentially metaphysical was meaningless, was a particularly bold assertion. Nevertheless, it caused reaction from those who wished to defend the integrity of language use in religion and the language debate widened. The logical positivists had treated language as entirely cognitive – something that could be held up to objective scrutiny. This meant that it could be proven either true or false and, consequently meaningful or meaningless. As religious language, understood in this sense, could not be verified or falsified, it was condemned as meaningless and consigned to Hume's flames as being little more than sophistry.

Wittgenstein, who was initially associated with the logical positivists, developed his earlier philosophy and ended up refuting much of his early work. He recognised that language use was the means by which it was made meaningful, not purely by its definition and application to empirical testing. In this interpretation, Wittgenstein saw language as non-cognitive – it held meaning for those that used it: deep meaning, meaning associated with passionate statements, significant emotional attachments and life changing commitments. This then was one of language game theory's initial strengths, namely that it was able to recognise that religious language was made meaningful through its use by the religious believer. The way the religious believer accessed and utilised the language gave the words meaning. Those words had clear transformational effects on the lives of religious believers, how then could they not be regarded as meaningful? In establishing religious language as a particular language game, Wittgenstein recognised that it related to a form of life that was unique; a way of living that defined itself through religious activity. As such, adopting Wittgenstein's analogy as being accurate, the meaningfulness of religious language was unquestioned.

Religious language, as a language game, had its own rules, in common with all other language games. It was therefore possible for religious believers to teach other believers about these rules, to share them and thereby demonstrate the meaningfulness of the language. The strength of language games was evident as it showed how the meaningfulness of religious language could not only be shared amongst the community but that the rules could be taught to those that wished to learn and thereby permitted religious language to be a self-sustaining system.

All games have their own rules which may appear very confusing to those that don't play them. In order to understand the game it is important that you learn the rules.

Specification content

Whether the strengths of language games outweigh the weaknesses.

Key questions

Are language games a valid response to the challenges raised by logical positivism?

Do Wittgenstein's ideas make sense?

Does religious language express ideas about the world or merely an attitude towards the world?

AO2 Activity

As you read through this section try to do the following:

1. Pick out the different lines of argument that are presented in the text and identify any evidence given in support.

2. For each line of argument try to evaluate whether or not you think this is strong or weak.

3. Think of any questions you may wish to raise in response to the arguments.

This Activity will help you to start thinking critically about what you read and help you to evaluate the effectiveness of different arguments and from this develop your own observations, opinions and points of view that will help with any conclusions that you make in your answers to the AO2 questions that arise.

*Can language used in religion be
compared to the rules of a game?*

One of the criticisms sometimes levelled against language games is that they do not permit those outside the game to understand the way in which language is true. This would suggest that the language game analogy was weak. However, this critique is only partially accurate. If there is willingness to learn, and a willingness to participate in the activity, then it is possible to learn the rules of the language game and thereby gain an understanding of the meaning of the language. Whilst Wittgenstein recognised that those outside of particular games, with no experience of them, may find them strange in terms of understanding what was going on. He never claimed that such games were entirely exclusive, only that those who had not had the experience or opportunity to learn the rules of the game, would not be able to understand them.

Whilst there are several strengths to the language games analogy, it is not without its weaknesses. The first weakness is within the analogy itself. If one rejects the similarities between games and language then Wittgenstein's language games analogy is severely weakened. As with any analogy, the strength of it is entirely determined by how far the two things being compared are similar. Whilst there may be a passing resemblance between the two, it could also be argued that Wittgenstein stretches the similarity too far. It is possible to explain a game to someone who has never experienced a game before; however, it is not possible to explain the concept of language to someone who has never accessed language before. This is because an explanation of language has to be given in language, whereas this does not apply to an explanation of games. A further weakness in the analogy is in order to know what it means to play a game, you need to know what people are doing when they play games. However, when a person uses language it is not enough to just know what they are doing, you also need to be able understand it.

Another weakness in the language game theory comes from its non-cognitive stance. If language in religion cannot be treated cognitively then does that mean that statements such as: 'God exists' are not an expression of an external reality but are instead nothing more than an opinion or expression of emotion? This would significantly undermine any rational basis that religion may lay claim to if this were the case. Following this, how would a religious believer know what they meant by using the word 'God' if it meant something different in every religious language game that was played? It is also possible to suggest that, whilst the religious language game could be learned, the fact that it would be initially unclear could be seen as something that would alienate rather than attract those from outside the game. Such an attitude would certainly seem contrary to the mission of some of the world religions that seek to spread their faith beyond their existing membership.

It would seem that the weaknesses of language games are significant and cannot be easily dismissed. Whether they present a fatal flaw in Wittgenstein's analogy may well be a matter of personal opinion, rather than considered academic debate. This is because Wittgenstein's work is based on certain assumptions (that language is non-cognitive and that the rules of a game and the use of language are similar) that can either be accepted or rejected and this, depending which view is chosen, will affect whether one will accept that the strengths of his language games analogy outweigh the weaknesses.

AO2 Activity

List some conclusions that could be drawn from the AO2 reasoning from the above text; try to aim for at least three different possible conclusions. Consider each of the conclusions and collect brief evidence to support each conclusion from the AO1 and AO2 material for this topic. Select the conclusion that you think is most convincing and explain why it is so. Try to contrast this with the weakest conclusion in the list, justifying your argument with clear reasoning and evidence.

AO2 Developing skills

It is now important to consider the information that has been covered in this section; however, the information in its raw form is too extensive and so has to be processed in order to meet the requirements of the examination. This can be achieved by practising more advanced skills associated with AO2. For assessment objective 2 (AO2), which involves 'critical analysis' and 'evaluation' skills, we are going to focus on different ways in which the skills can be demonstrated effectively, and also refer to how the performance of these skills is measured (see generic band descriptors for A2 [WJEC] AO2 or A Level [Eduqas] AO2).

▶ **Your new task is this:** It is impossible to cover all essays in the time allowed by the course; however, it is a good exercise to **develop detailed plans that can be utilised under timed conditions**. As a last exercise:

1. Create some ideal plans by using what we have done so far in the Theme 4 Developing skills sections.

2. This time stop at the planning stage and exchange plans with a study partner.

3. Check each other's plans carefully. Talk through any omissions or extras that could be included, not forgetting to challenge any irrelevant materials.

4. Remember, collaborative learning is very important for revision. It not only helps to consolidate understanding of the work and appreciation of the skills involved, it is also motivational and a means of providing more confidence in one's learning. Although the examination is sat alone, revising as a pair or small group is invaluable.

When you have completed the task, refer to the band descriptors for A2 (WJEC) or A Level (Eduqas) and in particular have a look at the demands described in the higher band descriptors towards which you should be aspiring. Ask yourself:

- Is my answer a confident critical analysis and perceptive evaluation of the issue?
- Is my answer a response that successfully identifies and thoroughly addresses the issues raised by the question set?
- Does my work show an excellent standard of coherence, clarity and organisation?
- Will my work, when developed, contain thorough, sustained and clear views that are supported by extensive, detailed reasoning and/or evidence?
- Are the views of scholars/schools of thought used extensively, appropriately and in context?
- Does my answer convey a confident and perceptive analysis of the nature of any possible connections with other elements of my course?
- When used, is specialist language and vocabulary both thorough and accurate?

Key skills

Analysis involves:

Identifying issues raised by the materials in the AO1, together with those identified in the AO2 section, and presents sustained and clear views, either of scholars or from a personal perspective ready for evaluation.

This means:

- That your answers are able to identify key areas of debate in relation to a particular issue
- That you can identify, and comment upon, the different lines of argument presented by others
- That your response comments on the overall effectiveness of each of these areas or arguments.

Evaluation involves:

Considering the various implications of the issues raised based upon the evidence gleaned from analysis and provides an extensive detailed argument with a clear conclusion.

This means:

- That your answer weighs up the consequences of accepting or rejecting the various and different lines of argument analysed
- That your answer arrives at a conclusion through a clear process of reasoning.

Questions and answers

Theme 2 Challenges to Religious Belief

AO1 question area

A strong answer examining Freud's view that religion was a form of neurosis.

Freud defined neurosis as being manifestations of anxiety producing unconscious material that is too difficult to think about consciously, but must still find a means of expression. The expression was the neurotic behaviour. Hence, he focussed on a patient's past, seeing the cause of the neurosis in repressed events or traumas. He also saw parallels between neurosis and religion. People who suffered from an obsessional neurosis repeated actions compulsively. Freud argued that religious people showed similar patterns of behaviour such as saying the rosary or the prescribed washing ritual and prayer in Islam. Both the religious and those suffering neurosis were also meticulous about the detail of the way actions had to be carried out. Hence Freud saw religion, with its repetitive rituals which are found universally, as a universal obsessional neurosis. His conclusion was that religion therefore was the result of repressed traumas that originated in the past. **1**

Freud's saw the explanation of the origin of the traumas in the theories of Darwin – in particular Darwin's theory of the primal horde. Darwin conjectured that human beings had originally lived in small 'hordes'. Freud speculated that over many generations the horde had been dominated by single dominant males who had seized the women for themselves and had driven off or killed all rivals, including their sons. At some stage a group of those expelled returned to kill their father whom they both feared and respected. They then became the dominant ones but also rivals amongst themselves. Filled with guilt and realising the imminent collapse of their social order, they united, and a totem took the place of their father. The totem became worshipped and became the god. For Freud, this explained the inherited sense of guilt that we all have. It also explained the Christian ritual of Holy Communion. **2**

Freud maintained that the source of the traumas that led to neurosis were usually sexual. Hence, in addition to the primal horde explanation for religion he also developed the Oedipus complex. Again it involved the son seeing his father as a rival for his mother's love, but fearing the repercussions if he tried to replace his father. The repression results in neurotic behaviour and is another possible explanation for the guilt and anguish that is repressed but expressed

through the belief and practices of religion. In his book *The Future of an Illusion*, Freud wrote 'Religion is comparable to a childhood neurosis'. **3**

Therefore, Freud concluded that religion was something negative – an illness that people needed curing from. In *Civilisation and its Discontents* Freud commented that '[Religion] is so patently infantile, so foreign to reality... It is still more humiliating to discover how a large number of people living today, who cannot see that this religion is not tenable, nevertheless try to defend it piece by piece in a series of pitiful rearguard actions.' **4**

Examiner commentary

1 A good opening paragraph that immediately centred on the focus of the question. It made a clear connection between neurosis and religion. A pity that opportunity was not taken to link with Freud's theory of the psyche. Helpful illustrations given but perhaps needed to be explained more fully. Reached a neat stepping stone at end of paragraph to move to Freud's theories about the origins of religion

2 A clear development from previous paragraph showing good logical structure. Again, a concise summary of primal horde theory. Lacks explanation of totem. The illustration of Holy Communion needs further explanation to draw out the link with inherited guilt.

3 The reference to Oedipus Complex is introduced without clear explanation. The expression of the Oedipus Complex neurosis needed closer linking to the belief and practices of religion. However, the essence of Freud's theory is accurately stated.

4 A helpful quote but the thrust of the conclusion concerning religion as something negative is slightly away from the focus of the essay title.

Summative comment

For this answer, its weaknesses are that some areas are not explained fully such as totems, the link with Holy Communion and the Oedipus complex. Neither is there any discussion of the psyche especially the id, which is the primitive and impulsive part of our psyche. However there are some examples given from religion and the two main areas (Primal Horde and Oedipus Complex) that link with neurosis are identified and mostly explained. There are some quotes but no reference to scholars other than Darwin.

AO2 question area

A weaker answer evaluating whether Freud's view of religion is persuasive.

Freud concluded that religion is an illness – a neurosis, caused by repressed events or an inability to face the reality of the world so expressed wish fulfillments and a reaction against helplessness. Whether neurosis or wish fulfillment, religion was false and needed to be replaced by scientific thinking and a proper world-view. But was Freud correct? Certainly there do seem to be similarities with aspects of neurotic behaviour and rituals in religion. It must also be acknowledged that sex is a base and impulsive instinct that is linked to the id. **1**

Others question his conclusions, accusing him of a lack of evidence. A key aspect is Darwin's Primal horde theory. However most scholars would reject the theory and it is not even clear that Darwin himself believed it. Although Freud regarded himself as a scientist and viewed psychoanalysis as a science, many regard his methodology as anything but science. It is unverifiable since they appeal to causes that cannot be verified. It is all subjective. Even the Oedipus Complex theory is questioned as a result of the work of Malinowski. **2**

Perhaps the strongest attack on Freud is his understanding of religion. He saw it merely in terms of ritual acts rather than a set of beliefs that could be debated around evidence. So is Freud persuasive? No, he definitely is not. **3**

Examiner commentary

1 Although an argument is put forward to support Freud's view, it consists of just a very basic summary, without any real explanation. It lacks any evidence, discussion or debate.

2 This is more a list of points than any clear attempt at evaluation. They are not developed. There is no weighing up of the arguments or any attempt to discuss whether Freud's views are persuasive.

3 It is very one sided in that arguments are just stated. There is no analysis. The arguments are not really explained. There is a conclusion reached that is consistent with what has been written.

Summative comment

This answer is brief, has a tendency to be one sided and also lacks explanation and discussion. It has some key points but they are not developed or analysed or debated in depth at all. There is no real discussion about the extent of persuasiveness which is, after all, the main focus of the question.

Theme 3 Religious Experience

AO1 question area

A weaker answer examining Hume's definition of a miracle.

In his book '*On Miracles*', Hume defined a miracle as a transgression of a law of nature by a particular violation of the Deity. Therefore miracles are happenings that break the laws of nature and have a divine cause. An example would be the healing of the leper.

However it is not clear if Hume considered miracles possible. If laws are fixed then miracles can't happen. If laws can be broken, how can we know if the supposed law is actually a correct law? Perhaps another description of the law would include the happening that seems contrary to it. Certainly Hume seems to think miracles can't happen. When he reported the events at Abbé Paris he just dismissed them as impossible regardless of the evidence. **1**

Most philosophers think it is a contradiction to talk about laws of nature being broken. God doesn't break his own laws. Surely if he was God then he would make laws that would fit all happenings. If he had to break his own laws it suggests God does not have omniscience. **2**

Better definitions are given by Holland and Swinburne. Holland argued for contingency miracles that required an observer to recognise an event as miraculous. The observer sees it as a religious sign. He used the example of the boy in a toy car caught in train tracks. A train is approaching that he can't see and the driver cannot see the boy. However, his mother can see both. The train stopped before it hit the boy and the mother saw that as a miracle even though the train stopped because the driver had a heart attack and the train automatically stopped. Laws of nature were not broken but that did not stop the mother still seeing it as a miracle. In this case deciding whether a happening is a miracle is subjective. If the person sees it as a miracle then it is a miracle. In contrast Swinburne still goes for the objective but includes purpose. Overall, Hume's definition is flawed and unhelpful. **3**

Examiner commentary

1 The paragraph contains a number of errors such as the title of Hume's book and the use of violation instead of volition. In addition the actual definition by Hume is only partly quoted. The example is not explained and the examples need widening in type.

2 This paragraph is more a critique of Hume's definition and is not the focus of the question.

3 The question is about Hume but this paragraph discusses alternative definitions by Holland and Swinburne. As it stands the material is not relevant.

Summative comment

The essay lacks depth and breadth when discussing Hume's definition. It has the basic statements and shows awareness of the element involving breaking of the laws of nature. There is a brief reference to examples to illustrate but these are not explained or developed. There is little evidence of a study of Hume's definition. No reference is made to the hard and soft understandings of the definition. No reference is made to other relevant scholars who have commented on Hume's definition. A significant part of the essay is irrelevant to the question asked.

AO2 question area

A strong answer evaluating whether miracles are impossible.

The understanding of what exactly is meant by 'a miracle' has been much debated. The conclusion, as to whether miracles can happen or not, will depend on which of the meanings is being referred to. Perhaps the most straightforward definition in this respect is the one by Holland. He argued for 'contingency miracles'. By this, he meant that an unexpected beneficial happening can be considered a miracle even though no law of nature has been broken. On this interpretation, miracles are subjective and are clearly not impossible. However, many may feel that such a definition of 'miracle' is far from satisfactory and that the essence of a miracle must involve some intervention by a supernatural agent. It is true that it is still possible to see God at work in the timing of events that make up a contingency miracle. Perhaps God intervenes to bring those timings about – if so then it is unverifiable and though not impossible, it does seem it would be impossible to know. [1]

If there is no God or supernatural, then miracles by definition would be impossible. However, proving a negative (i.e. that there is no supernatural) is rather problematic. So it would be difficult to say that miracles were impossible. It would be more accurate to say they were unlikely or there was no evidence. But that is far from saying they are impossible. Indeed, many would offer arguments and evidence to support the existence of a God, such as the traditional arguments for God or the evidence for the resurrection of Jesus. [2]

One approach when considering miracles as understood by Hume and Swinburne, would be to focus on the idea of laws of nature being violated. Science might challenge such a concept, so making miracles (defined in this way) impossible. Similarly, Alastair McKinnon rejects the idea of miracles when he argues that laws of nature are merely generalised shorthand descriptions of how things do in fact happen. Perhaps a better understanding of the term 'law of nature' is 'the actual course of events'. Hence, whatever happens must be included in the understanding of natural laws. However, many would reject such an approach and support Swinburne's view of rephrasing 'a violation of a law of nature' to 'a non-repeatable counter-instance to a law of nature'. This would preserve the idea of a supernatural intervention to normal happenings. Others would still take issue with this and point out that modern science seems to favour some degree of unpredictability with the findings of quantum physics. Although this does not make miracles impossible, it does question how one can ever know that there has been a supernatural intervention rather than just the unpredictable nature of the universe. Swinburne would argue that if it is consistent with the nature of God, has a religious significance and in answer to prayer, then it seems likely it is the workings of God. [3]

It seems clear that the claim that a miracle is impossible is hard to support. The lesser claim that a miracle is unlikely seems a better position to adopt. However, showing that a miracle has happened is very problematic and will depend very much on a person's prior world-view – whether it is naturalistic or supernatural. [4]

Examiner commentary

[1] A promising start to the essay as awareness is shown about the implications of different definitions of miracles. The focus concerning 'possibility' is immediately addressed. It is succinct and contains evaluative elements that contain a logical thread.

[2] This paragraph picks up the 'impossible' aspect in the question. Why proving a negative is problematic needs explaining.

[3] The essay develops logically by moving on from the subjective understanding of miracles to the objective illustrated by Hume and Swinburne. Good use of a scholar and a clear statement about their contribution to the debate.

Again the evaluative skills are present with arguments being weighed up and counter arguments considered.

[4] A conclusion is reached that is supported by the preceding paragraphs. Alternative views have been considered and counter arguments assessed.

Summative comment

Good evaluative skills are displayed. The essay has a logical thread that concludes with a reasoned and supported judgement. However there is only limited reference to other scholars and very few quotes are given.

Theme 4 Religious Language

AO1 question area

A strong answer examining the inherent
philosophical problems with religious language.

Some philosophers believe that religious language is inherently problematic for many reasons. The first reason is that our communication depends on language. If we are either reading or speaking, we make many assumptions about the nature of the communication. The main assumption is that we can be understood and if we cannot be understood then our communication is ineffective. Our communication is solely based on random sounds and shapes that our intended audience can interpret. If we do not possess the ability to understand what we hear or read, then our communication is again ineffective. [1]

Another problem is that our language is based on experience. For our language and communication to be meaningful then we must be able to relate in some way to what we are saying or being told. In other words, in order for a statement to be meaningful, we must have some form of experience to show our understanding of the language. When we communicate about common experiences (e.g. my car is blue), there is no difficulty in our understanding as the interpretation is in a shared experience. On the other hand, to discuss the means of whether or not water is wet is different as we have to be able to understand the concept of what 'wet' is. Once a general understanding is established then the statement is then meaningful and understandable. If we did not have the ability or knowledge of what 'wet' is then the statement would be meaningless and we would then need to work out how we would gain experience for the situation. [2]

Another problem with religious language is that the majority of our communication is about the physical world. We can communicate easily about things around us in the physical world but there are some things that we experience that are harder to communicate through language. Any language about emotions, ideas, ethical discussions and language about religion are dismissed as it is not considered to be on the same level of meaning as language about the physical world. This means that any language that is about emotions or religion is considered meaningless. This is the inherent problem with religious language. In an era dominated by factual and scientific knowledge, statements that can be proven and verified are far more plausible and meaningful than a statement displaying an abstract aspect of one's faith. The issue here is that of the difference between cognitive and non-cognitive language. Cognition is the act of knowing something, through experience and understanding. These statements are usually factual in nature, empirically based and thus verifiable and considered meaningful. Religious language is generally non-cognitive, addressing individual opinions, feelings and attitudes. Consequently, often there is no shared experience of what is being discussed, and the recipient has no understanding of what is being discussed. Saying that 'God exists' is problematic on a number of levels: we cannot prove that he exists, we do not know if our understanding of God is the same as the person we are talking to, and how do we know what we are saying is accurate at all? These clear limitations of religious language are what has prompted its many critics and doubters. [3]

One such group were the logical positivists, a movement which grew out of the work of the Vienna Circle during the 20th century. In essence, the logical positivists aimed to reduce all forms of language to basic scientific, empirical formulations. To them, only certain statements could be accepted as true, if they complied with the criteria set out. Statements must be tautological, mathematical, analytic and synthetic. Anything outside of this was considered meaningless and void. Naturally, religious language fell outside of these limited criteria. In fact, anything that wasn't immediately verifiable in person at the time was considered meaningless. This became known as 'the principle of verification': the meaning of a statement, for the logical positivists, was in its method of verification. We can comprehend the meaning of a statement if we can understand and verify the conditions in which it is true or false. Religious statements, dealing with abstract concepts, could not be verified, and thus were futile. Arguing an element of one's faith is not itself explanatory, nor is it backed up by experience or evidence. It is not mathematical, and the definition is not contained within the statement. [4]

Our language is experienced based but also time-limited which means that our experiences are confined within time. Language that is confined in time has to be either from the past, present or future. So to talk about anything beyond our experience of time, means we have to move away from what is known to us. To talk about a divine being that has a specific plan for us, is meaningless as we have no form of empirical evidence and language to talk about it. [5]

When discussing God there is no common or shared experience, universally applicable to those with a faith commitment and those without. If a place of worship was described with factors such as its physical location and features then this topic can be known by others by empirical and experience-based meanings, On the other hand, if someone was to describe an infinite, transcendent God that is omnibenevolent and has a specific plan for everyone on Earth but had no empirical evidence to support this claim or no experience shared with others to establish the truth of this statement. This is the inherent problem of religious language. [6]

Examiner commentary

1. The response opens by acknowledging the issue and then suggesting reasons why communication could be rendered ineffective (and therefore result in problematic issues with language use). This qualifies as both accurate and relevant material and demonstrates that the candidate has at least a good understanding of the topic.

2. A further exploration of how language is based on experience is then undertaken. Whilst the candidate could be clearer in their response, the general theme is that the value of language and its meaningfulness is entirely dependent on those that share it having some form of common experience which makes the language relatable and therefore meaningful.

3. The response refers indirectly to the cognitive/non-cognitive debate at first, but then develops their response to refer directly to it. The response makes informed reference to the debate and draws upon appropriate evidence and reasoning to support the point being made.

4. A consideration of the logical positivist movement provides a particular focus to this response's consideration of why religious language is often considered to be problematic. The information contained is accurate and articulate, and shows an excellent standard of coherence, clarity and organisation.

5. The response then returns to a specific issue relating to the alleged inherent problems of religious language and explains why this presents a particular problem. The answer would have benefitted from further exemplification to meet the criteria of good use of evidence/examples.

6. The response finishes with a brief summary of information being presented and a consideration of precisely why the issue is considered as such. The candidate has clearly demonstrated a relevant response which answers the specific demands of the question set.

Summative comment

This is a well written response that clearly demonstrates a good understanding of the topic. The response is articulate in the main and develops each point well, with well-selected evidence and a good level of depth in the response. Clarity and coherence are evident, along with accurately represented views from philosophical schools of thought. Not all of the traditional areas for consideration addressed. However, those that are addressed are in sufficient depth to gain merit.

AO2 question area

A weaker answer evaluating whether religious philosophers have successfully solved the inherent problems of religious language.

The problems of religious language are many and seem to suggest that religious language is ultimately meaningless. Philosophers such as the logical positivists have proven that religious language cannot be verified or falsified and so it means that it cannot be considered to be meaningful. This is because they treat language in a cognitive sense. **1**

However, other philosophers, such as Richard Swinburne, a well-known religious philosopher, have proven that there are sometimes things which we consider to be meaningful even when we cannot directly prove them; he used the example of the toys in the cupboard where the toys come alive when no one is watching them and move around the room. They do this and when someone comes in the room they magically go back to where they were. Swinburne said that because we understand what this would mean then it is meaningful to us even if we can't prove that they were moving. **2**

Aquinas stated that talking about God through analogy was a good way to solve the problems put forward by the logical positivists as he stated that because God is our creator when we talk about us and say things like 'we are powerful' or 'Sioned is a good person' then it means we can understand what it means to say God is powerful or God is good because there is a link between the two. This shows how Aquinas has successfully solved the inherent problems of religious language. **3**

Finally, we can say that they haven't solved the problems because you still can't verify statements like 'God exists' because we don't know what we mean by God – and neither can we say there is life after death because no one has ever proved it true or false for definite. **4**

Examiner commentary

1. The opening paragraph demonstrates a limited understanding of the issue. The candidate appears to understand that the debate is linked partly to the issues raised by logical positivism but does not give any consideration for the issues raised beyond this. Reasoning is simplistic.

2. The issue of the toys in the cupboard parable is an accurately selected, if poorly expressed, piece of evidence to support the argument that religious philosophers have presented a solution to the problems of religious language.

3 The information about Aquinas demonstrates a level of misunderstanding regarding the relative timelines of philosophical debate. The erroneous linking of Aquinas and logical positivism highlights evidence of limited accuracy in the response. However, the concept of analogy as a way of talking meaningfully about God is accurate.

4 The final paragraph shows an attempt to put forward an opposing view but it is under-developed and poorly expressed. There is no evidence of a final conclusion in the candidate's response.

Summative comment

This response demonstrates a basic level of understanding from the candidate. Whilst the information selected is generally relevant, it is almost entirely underdeveloped and almost always poorly expressed. Lack of coherence reduces the effectiveness of the evaluation, and the lack of a final conclusion is a significant omission for an AO2 response.

Theme 4 Religious Language

AO1 question area

A reasonable answer explaining Randall and Tillich's understanding of religious language as symbolic.

J H Randall was an American philosopher that wanted to bring ideas from theology, philosophy and psychology together with science. He recognised that science and religion had different functions but both had a vital role to play in the life of human beings. He wanted to explore how religious language compared to the knowledge and meaning of science before looking into the relationship between religion and philosophy. He discovered how Greek philosophers influenced Christian thinkers of the time and how philosophy connected to religious language. 1

Randall found that natural theology and natural science both sought to gain understanding of the natural world which humans lived in. He began to recognise that religious ideas and scientific discoveries developed alongside each other. Both unified groups of people within the ways that they thought and gave people a sense of identity, in the sense that it formed their values and the language they used for communication. 2

Randall identified religious beliefs as mythology and religious language as symbols, as he saw the function of them was to communicate religious experiences and convey the identity of religious believers. He believed that religious language provided humans with an understanding of their existence and that it gave them a wider perspective of the world, though he did not believe that it revealed any truths about the world itself. 3

His understanding of symbols was that they were not to represent anything other than itself and to serve a function. This function was meant to provoke a response from those who saw the symbol, due to the nature and identity surrounding it. Symbols are able to communicate experiences, and religious symbols are able to reveal one's experience of the world from a religious perspective. 4

On the other hand, Tillich saw religious belief as a state of being ultimately concerned. Alongside the basic needs which humans need to survive, Tillich identified that there was a need for spiritual concern, which led to an ultimate concern. He understood that spiritual concern can be expressed through the symbols of religious belief and they give the believer their spiritual identity. 5

Tillich explained that there were six characteristics of symbols. These include the idea that symbols point beyond themselves to something else, which means that they hold a deeper meaning than what is literally shown through the symbol itself. Symbols open up levels of reality that are otherwise closed to us, which describes the levels of meaning within the symbols and human interpretation of that meaning. Symbols are able to unlock dimensions and elements of our soul which correspond with reality, which provides a greater understanding of the human experience and the world. Symbols can also not be produced intentionally, as they grey out of consciousness and cannot function without relevance, showing that some symbols are more powerful than others and maintain their meaning within the lives of humans. 6

Tillich viewed symbols as the language of power. The language of symbols in non-cognitive due to the emotional response that it gains from believers, due to a person's attitudes and feelings. Tillich recognised that symbols were also concerned with myths, because they both participated in human life and culture, maintaining their presence within cultural traditions and beliefs. 7

Examiner commentary

1 A clear opening paragraph that is well written, stating the initial parameters of Randall's work.

2 Again, this is well written and clearly shows how Randall started to develop his ideas and the basis from which these ideas came. The information is highly accurate and relevant to the question.

3 This continues to develop the theme of the essay effectively and links clearly to how Randall viewed religious language as symbolic.

4 A point well made but needs considerable expansion if it is to meet the trigger word 'explain'.

5 An accurate point but could have been developed to demonstrate that Tillich recognised this as having faith in God.

6 Missed two of the six explanations, i.e.: the second is that symbols participate in the reality to which they point, meaning that symbols contribute within the culture that they are associated with and lastly, symbols grow and die as situations change, developing along with society and the cultures which they depend on.

7 Misses the opportunity to note that, for Tillich, the fundamental symbol for ultimate concern was God itself.

Summative comment

The student clearly understands the subject and has written an essay demonstrating this. Some parts are explained well but this is not always balanced. Better explanation of Randall's view on symbols and their function within society and culture would have allowed the answer to access additional marks and raise the overall standard of the response. The work on Tillich would also have benefitted from further development of his ideas.

AO2 question area

A strong answer evaluating whether symbolic religious language is entirely meaningful.

How do we establish what is meaningful? Are we going to categorise meaning through a series of empirical (sense-based) experiences or should we take a different approach? If I argue, as did David Hume, that things which can't be proven should be 'consigned to the flames for containing nothing but sophistry and illusion' then am I not in fact guilty of reducing meaning down to nothing more than physical events? If this is so then what does that say about my emotions? Are they meaningless? In which case why then is it my emotions that fuel my drive and passions in life? Surely such an approach is too reductionist? [1]

Considering our approach to language is significant here: do we treat language as having an entirely cognitive function – in that it transmits facts and objectively verifiable knowledge about the world in which we live. It is certainly true that language provides this function – but is it restricted merely to this? The logical positivists would have us say that it was so – but their own criteria can be readily undermined as they failed to establish a criterion for meaning that could itself be verified! [2]

What about non-cognitive functions? Language that finds its meaning established through the expression of thoughts, feelings, emotions and belief. This certainly seems to resonate more closely with the function of symbols. In this sense, were we to consider that language should be treated purely non-cognitively then we could also be accused of being reductionist in our approach. If we are to make empirical sense of our world then there is a place for objective knowledge and the language that transmits it. It would seem that both approaches to language have a significant role to play in establishing a criterion of meaning that is reflective of the totality of human experience. [3]

Having established those perspectives, how then can we establish the meaningfulness of symbolic language? On one hand, Tillich's assertion that symbols have clearly definable characteristics implies that they have meaning that can be understood. The fact that symbols and signs can be differentiated is also significant. If symbols alone have the ability to unlock dimensions and elements of our soul which correspond to the dimensions and elements of reality, then their value is likewise significant. Religious language, which deals with the dimensions of religious belief and practice, expresses ideas and concepts which have direct impact on both individuals and groups alike. If I subscribe to a belief that derived from symbolic language that being charitable to one's neighbour will culminate in an eternal reward in paradise, then I am strongly motivated to behave in such a manner. The language which motivates me is not cognitive – it describes things beyond my immediate physical existence, yet it causes me to live my life in such a way that may only be described as meaningful. In this sense symbolic religious language is entirely meaningful. [4]

By the same token, however, it has to be recognised that symbolic language relies upon interpretation. Both Randall and Tillich noted that the interpretation of symbols can change over time – particularly in relation to the values and ideas of culture and society. If this is held true, then establishing a constant sense of meaning through symbolic language becomes difficult, if not impossible. If I take the position that meaningfulness is objective or purely cognitive, then symbolic language is far from meaningful and in fact could even be described as misleading and meaningless. Tillich also recognised this – yet it did not deter him from believing that symbolic language can still provide meaningful insights into deep and powerful truths. However, if one takes a symbol and changes its meaning, then one is not just altering the symbol but is also altering something even more fundamental – that is, the association of that symbol from and for the cultures that it is associated with. [5]

The original assertion that symbolic language is entirely meaningful is therefore problematic. It can be described both positively and negatively in respect to the assertion. It will largely depend on one's own predisposition towards how language is treated – cognitively or non-cognitively, as well as the natural disposition towards the validity and meaningfulness of forms of symbolic language such as those expressed within religion. For the religious believer, the assertion may be agreed with as it affirms a deliberate lifestyle and belief set; for the empirically minded atheist, it may well be considered to be nothing more than an idle distraction from describing reality as it actually is. [6]

Examiner commentary

1. The essay response starts by taking a view on the concept of meaningfulness. This sets the parameters for the response as a whole and is focussed on the subject of the question, which is asking for an evaluation of this concept in relation to symbolic language. The language is engaging and the use of the paraphrased Hume quotation demonstrates a synoptic application of knowledge, as well as using the view of a scholar in an appropriate context.

2. The response then further develops by drawing on the relevance to the cognitive vs non-cognitive debate alongside the assertions of logical positivism in determining what constitutes meaningful language. Again, this is applying knowledge from outside the direct focus on symbolic language in order to support an evaluation of the assertion made in the question. This could be considered as a perceptive approach to the issue, as the issue of meaningfulness extends beyond the consideration of whether religious language can be considered meaningful if it is viewed as symbolic language.

3. An alternative view is presented and challenged in a counter response to the previous paragraph. This demonstrates a confident approach to critical analysis.

4. Accurate reference to Tillich, as well as a consideration of why symbolic language can be considered to be meaningful is carefully evaluated here. An appropriate conclusion is drawn after making reference to suitable evidence – thus demonstrating sophisticated and detailed reasoning.

5. Again, an alternative view is presented and challenged in a counter response to the previous paragraph. This provides a layered approach to the evaluation that takes a piece of evidence, from either side of the debate, and gives consideration to it, before challenging the assumptions within it and drawing a conclusion based upon the reasoning used.

6. The final paragraph makes no final conclusion as such but takes a middle ground. It provides summative statements for both sides of the debate and invites the reader to adopt a position based on personal predisposition. Whilst not providing a definitive response, in terms of entirely agreeing or dismissing the assertion in the initial question, this approach supports the overall theme of the evaluation and can therefore be considered to be effective.

Summative Comment

A balanced and interesting response. Whilst it does not draw solely on information from the specification section on symbolic language, it does make intelligent and informed use of other areas of the religious language debate that supports a mature consideration of the debate.

Quickfire answers

T2 DEF

2.1 The id, ego and superego

2.2 They both exhibited repeated actions that caused concern if they neglected them

2.3 Those suffering from obsessional neurosis did not understand the meaning of their actions whilst the religious believers did

2.4 A totem is a symbol of the family or tribe, usually an animal or plant

2.5 A character in the play *Oedipus Rex* by Sophocles

2.6 The natural forces of nature and the internal forces of nature

2.7 Daniel Schreber, Little Hans, The Wolf Man

2.8 Bronislaw Malinowski

2.9 Primordial images derived from early human history

2.10 The ego (consciousness), the personal unconscious, the collective unconscious

2.11 Original pattern

2.12 The Persona, the Shadow, the Anima or Animus, the Self

2.13 Individuation

2.14 Christ, the Eucharist, the trinity

2.15 Because it is achieved through religious images

2.16 Freud saw it as a mental illness; Jung saw it as helpful to mental health

2.17 Western searched for outer reality, Asian searched for the psyche

2.18 He was accused of corrupting Athenian's youth by encouraging them not to believe in the city's gods

2.19 Renaissance and Reformation

2.20 Bishop John Robinson

2.21 New Atheism

2.22 Thomas Huxley

2.23 Sam Harris, Richard Dawkins, Christopher Hitchens, Daniel Dennett

2.24 Non-thinking, infantile worldview, impeded scientific progress

2.25 John Polkinghorne, Alister McGrath

T3 DEF

3.1 Alister Hardy

3.2 Belief-that is about objective facts whilst belief-in is about an attitude of trust or commitment

3.3 Guru Nanak

3.4 His conversion on Road to Damascus, seeing the resurrected Jesus

3.5 Buddhism

3.6 A pilgrimage in Islam

3.7 Rosh Hashanah ending in Yom Kippur

3.8 The definition, the grounds for deciding whether a miracle has taken place

3.9 The hidden potentials in nature that make miracles possible have been placed there by God

3.10 Hume saw behaviour of things in terms of natural law rather than the power residing in the object's nature

3.11 *Enquiry Concerning Human Understanding*

3.12 A transgression of a law of nature by a particular volition of the Deity, or by the interposition of some invisible agent

3.13 Laws of nature can have exceptions, such as when God intervenes

3.14 Contingency miracle

3.15 Rephrased 'violation of a law of nature'; religious significance of the miracle

3.16 Believe God exists so any strong evidence for miracles believable; authenticates a revelation; consistent with nature of God; an answer to prayer (any 3)

3.17 It is seen as confirming the authority and truth claims of a particular faith tradition

3.18 Only testimony so strong that its falsehood would itself be more miraculous than the alleged miracle

3.19 Lack of sufficient number of witnesses; people prone to look for marvels and wonders; stories originate from ignorant people

3.20 Evidence for one faith because of a miracle is evidence against another faith that also claims a miracle, therefore they counteract each other

3.21 Historical evidence is often appealing to a singular past event that is no longer possible to examine directly

3.22 The miraculous nature of the event was sufficient to reject it

3.23 Evidence of different kinds ought to be given different weights; different pieces of evidence ought to be given different weights in accordance with their past reliability; multiple similar testimonies from different witnesses ought to be given more weight against lesser number of contrary testimonies (any 1)

T4 ABC

4.1 Communication is about, amongst other things, sharing ideas, experiences and realities with each other. For these to be meaningful we must be able to relate in some way to what we are being told. In other words, we need to have some experience base upon which to build our understanding of the language that we share.

4.2 To talk about things beyond time – with concepts such as infinity or timelessness, means to talk about ideas that can only ever be expressed in abstract terms – at this point, the empirical understanding of language breaks down. Our language is experience based and religious language deals with things beyond our experience.

4.3 Any form of language that makes an assertion, which is usually factual in nature, in the sense that it can be proved to be true or false by objective means.

4.4 A philosophical movement that grew out of the work of the Vienna Circle.

4.5 To systematically reduce all knowledge to basic scientific and logical formulations.

4.6 'The meaning of a statement is its method of verification.'

4.7 It was not able to take into account those statements that were made about things that were accepted as meaningful even though they were not considered to be immediately verifiable in practice.

4.8 Falsification stated that for something to be meaningful, there had to be evidence which could count against the statement (ie to empirically refute it).

4.9 He believed that religious believers would not allow any evidence to count against their beliefs.

4.10 Mitchell and Hare

4.11 Univocally and equivocally

4.12 The analogy of proportion is where a statement is meaningful because we can see the link between the two things being compared but we understand there is a difference – in proportion to the reality that the thing being spoken about possesses.

4.13 Words, or phrases that could be added to these earlier terms in order to provide them with the quality and sense that they were greater than what their normal reality represented.

T4 DEF

4.14 John Randall & Paul Tillich

4.15 It provided a common way of communicating, providing a shared set of values

4.16 Platonic ideas

4.17 To provide insights into a range of elements that each society holds as significant

4.18 It is a very complex form of language that can be interpreted in many different ways, making it difficult to categorise at times.

4.19 Water

4.20 A hero that represents the Sun god in some way

4.21 The way of speaking that is commonly understood by a particular community or society

4.22 Someone that subscribes to the coherence theory of truth

4.23 It was an activity that belonged to a particular form of life – and was therefore a 'language game' that could be understood by those that participated in it.

Glossary

Alpha-male: the dominant male in a community or group

Amrit: the name of the holy water that is drunk in the baptism ceremony into the Khalsa in Sikhism – the word 'amrit' literally means 'immortality'

Analogy: where something (that is known) is compared with something else (usually something unknown), in order to explain or clarify

Anti-realism: the philosophical concept that the truth of something is determined by it fitting in with the views/beliefs of the group who espouse it

Anti-realist: a philosophical position that adopts the coherence theory of truth

Archetype: according to Jung a primitive concept inherited from the earliest human ancestors found in the collective unconscious

Archetypes: literally meaning 'original pattern' –they refer to symbolic forms which all people share in their collective unconscious. The archetypes give rise to images in the conscious mind and account for the reoccurring themes. These mould and influence human behaviour

Atonement: making up for wrongdoing; the reconciliation of human beings with God through life, suffering and the sacrificial death of Christ

Attribution: relating to the attribute or characteristic possessed by an object

Belief-in: a belief that conveys an attitude of trust or commitment

Belief-that: a belief that claims to be an objective fact

Blik: a term used by R. M. Hare to describe the point of view that someone may hold that will influence the way they live their life

Charismatic worship: exuberant and expressive forms of worship often involving ecstatic religious experiences such as speaking in 'tongues' and healing miracles

Cognitive: language that is empirically verifiable and makes assertions about objective reality

Coherence theory of truth: belief that something is true when it fits in (coheres) with the views of those within the community

Collective neurosis: a neurotic illness that afflicts all people

Collective unconscious: elements of unconsciousness that are shared with all other people

Contingency miracle: a remarkable and beneficial coincidence that is interpreted in a religious fashion

Correspondence theory of truth: belief that something is true because it is related to (corresponds) an objective external reality

Deconstruct: to analyse a text by taking it apart in order to work out what it means

Disclosure: where something is made known where previously it was hidden or unknown

Ego: the part of the psyche that is residing largely in the conscious and is reality-orientated. It mediates between the desires of the id and the superego

Empirical: observation, experience or experiment based on the five physical senses

Empirical evidence: knowledge received by means of the senses, particularly by observation and experimentation

Empirical knowledge: knowledge which is acquired (or acquirable) through the five senses. It is knowledge that provides information about the external, physical world

Empiricist: a person who believes that all knowledge is based on sense experience

Enlightenment: in Buddhism, experience of awakening to insight into the true nature of things

Equivocally: where there is more than one meaning, usually in relation to a word or phrase

Eschatological verification: John Hick's assertion that certain religious statements may be verifiable at a future point (i.e. after death). In this sense they are 'verifiable in principle' and should therefore be regarded as meaningful

Eucharist: the Christian ceremony based on Jesus Christ's last meal with his disciples, and is also known as Mass or Holy Communion

Ex nihilo: literally 'out of nothing' – a Latin term often associated with creation myths

Falsification: proving something false by using evidence that counts against it

God of Classical Theism: God as defined in religions such as Christianity, Islam and Judaism – a God who is held to possess certain attributes such as omnipotence, omniscience and omnibenevolence

Id: the part of the psyche that is residing in the unconscious and relates to basic needs and desires

Incarnation: the embodiment of God the Son in human flesh as Jesus Christ

Individuation: the process of attaining wholeness and balance

Instinctual impulses: an instinct that is in the unconscious but active in the psyche

Khalsa: the name for those who have undergone the Amrit ceremony – the word 'khalsa' literally means 'pure'

Language games: Wittgenstein's analogy which stated that language was meaningful to those that used it within their own form of life/language game

Lent: in Christianity, it is a season of forty days before Easter of prayer and fasting

Logical analysis: the method of clarification of philosophical problems

Logical positivism: a philosophical movement that grew out of the work of the Vienna Circle, in which the aim was the reduction of all knowledge to basic scientific and logical formulations

Logical positivist: describing the philosophers who supported the claim that language could only be meaningful if it could be verified by empirical means

Mandala: geometric designs symbolic of the universe, often used in Buddhism as an aid to meditation; they are usually circular in form with one identifiable centre point

Metaphysical: that which is beyond, or not found in, the physical world

Myth: a complex form of writing that contains symbol, metaphor and is highly imaginative. A prevailing view of myths is that they contain truths about the universe and the role of humanity within it

Natural theology: philosophical reasoning based on information that can be rationally gained about the physical world and which leads to revelation about the divine

Naturalist: a person who believes that only *natural* (as opposed to supernatural or spiritual) laws and forces operate in the world

Negative (weak) atheism: where the atheist does not make the positive claim that God does not exist

New Atheism: also known as antitheism, it is the belief that religion is a threat to the survival of the human race

Nirvana: Buddhist enlightenment

Non-cognitive language: When language is not used to express empirically knowable facts about the external world. It is not something that can be held up to objective scrutiny. This is because non-cognitive language is language that expresses opinions, attitudes, feelings and/or emotions

Obsessional neurosis: sometimes called compulsive neurosis; uncontrollable obsessions that can create certain daily rituals

Oedipus complex: the theory that young boys are sexually attracted to their mothers but resent their fathers. The feelings are repressed as they fear the father. Oedipus refers to a character in a Greek legend that unwittingly killed his father and married his own mother

Partisan: a person who holds a particular political view – usually used in association with those who hold an opposing point of view to the ruling political powers. In Mitchell's case he is most likely referring to the partisans within the resistance movement of the Second World War

Personal unconscious: memories that have been forgotten or repressed

Platonic ideas: Ideas associated with the philosophy of the classical Greek philosopher, Plato , such as his theory of 'forms'

Positive (strong) atheism: believes that both the atheist and the theist have to give reasons to defend their belief

Predicate: stating or asserting something that is the ground or basis of an argument

Primordial: existing from the beginning

Proportion: relating to the relative value of something according to its nature

Protest atheism: a revolt against God on moral grounds

Psyche: the mental or psychological structure of a person

Psychoanalysis: a method of studying the mind and treating mental and emotional disorders based on revealing and investigating the role of the unconscious mind

Psychology: the study of the mind and behaviour

Psychotherapy: treatment of mental or emotional illness by talking about problems rather than by using medicine or drugs

Qualifier: a term used by Ramsey to where a word or phrase is used to give a deeper meaning to the model that the qualifier precedes

Realist: the philosophical position that adopts the correspondence theory of truth

Reformation: the religious movement in Europe in 16th century which led to the creation and rise of Protestantism

Renaissance: period of European history between 14th and 17th century which was a time of great revival of art, literature and learning

Revelation: a supernatural disclosure to human beings

Rosh Hashanah: the Jewish New Year

Sacrament: one of the Christian rites considered to have been instituted by Christ to confer or symbolize grace

Sitz im Leben: a German phrase meaning 'Situation in Life' and used as a theological term to refer to the context whereby an account is written, usually influencing the writer because of the particular circumstances of said context.

Sophists: Greek teachers and writers particularly skilled in reasoning

Sraddha: the closest term to 'faith' in Buddhism sometimes translated from the Sanskrit as 'trust' or 'confidence'

Strong agnosticism: the assertion that it is impossible to know whether or not God exists

Superego: part of the unconscious mind

Symbol: something which points beyond itself to a deeper level of reality

Symposiasts: members of a symposium (a conference held to discuss a specific subject or topic)

Tabernacle: box-like vessel for the exclusive reservation of the consecrated Eucharist

Tautological: a self-explanatory statement, i.e. where something is said twice over in different words, for example, 'the evening sunset'

Tenets: key beliefs or principles

The Age of Enlightenment: an intellectual and philosophical movement in Europe in the 18th century

Theological propositions: beliefs or ideas put forward in the context of religious doctrines or philosophies

Theravada Buddhism: a school of Buddhism that draws its scriptural inspiration from the Pali canon

Totem: something (such as an animal or plant) that is the symbol for the family or tribe

Totemism: a system of belief in which human beings are said to have some kinship or mystical relationship with a spirit-being, such as an animal or plant

Transubstantiation: the Roman Catholic doctrine that in the Eucharist, the whole substance of the bread and wine changes into the substance of the body and blood of Christ

Ultimate concern: Tillich's definition of God – that which should concern humans ultimately and be the focus of their lives, providing meaning and motivating behaviours and attitudes

Univocally: where something has one universal and unambiguous meaning

Verification: proving something true by using evidence that counts towards it

Weak agnosticism: the belief that the existence of God is currently unknown, but it is not necessarily unknowable

Yom Kippur: in Judaism, it refers to the day of Atonement and is the holiest day of the year

Index